single state
of mind

single state

of mind

ANDI DORFMAN

GALLERY BOOKS

New York   London   Toronto   Sydney   New Delhi

G

Gallery Books
An Imprint of Simon & Schuster, Inc.
1230 Avenue of the Americas
New York, NY 10020

First Gallery Books trade paperback edition October 2018

GALLERY BOOKS and colophon are registered trademarks of Simon & Schuster, Inc.

For information about special discounts for bulk purchases, please contact Simon & Schuster Special Sales at 1-866-506-1949 or business@simonandschuster.com.

The Simon & Schuster Speakers Bureau can bring authors to your live event. For more information or to book an event, contact the Simon & Schuster Speakers Bureau at 1-866-248-3049 or visit our website at www.simonspeakers.com.

Manufactured in the United States of America

10 9 8 7 6 5 4 3 2 1

Library of Congress Cataloging-in-Publication Data

Names: Dorfman, Andi.
Title: Single state of mind / Andi Dorfman.
Description: New York : Gallery Books, 2018.
Identifiers: LCCN 2017036968 (print) | LCCN 2017043889 (ebook) |
   ISBN 9781501174230 (ebook) | ISBN 9781501174223 (hardback) |
   ISBN 9781501189661 (trade paperback)
Subjects: LCSH: Dorfman, Andi. | Television personalities—United States—
   Biography. | BISAC: BIOGRAPHY & AUTOBIOGRAPHY / Personal
   Memoirs. | PERFORMING ARTS / Television / General. | BIOGRAPHY &
   AUTOBIOGRAPHY / Entertainment & Performing Arts.
Classification: LCC PN1992.4.D57 (ebook) | LCC PN1992.4.D57 A3 2018
   (print) | DDC 791.4502/8092 [B] —dc23
LC record available at https://lccn.loc.gov/2017036968

ISBN 978-1-5011-7422-3
ISBN 978-1-5011-8966-1 (pbk)
ISBN 978-1-5011-7423-0 (ebook)

To all those doing it alone . . . life is tough, but so are you.

disclaimer

I am a total overanalyzer. I often think way beyond the present moment and worry about all the little hiccups I encounter in life. I am emotional at times, irrational at others. But I also suspect I'm not the only woman in the world like this. I'm pretty much your everyday, average, run-of-the-mill woman. Only instead of internalizing it all, I purge it onto paper—sometimes contributing to my own embarrassment*—all for the enjoyment of every other woman out there just like me.

I don't live a worry-free life. I don't overplay the good times or sugarcoat the bad. I need to work on being less cynical. But for better or worse, what I think, feel, and do is what makes me me. So you are about to embark on one woman's tale of what life looks like beyond the smiling face, filtered photos, and canned politically correct answers of a reality television "star." This is the raw story of a woman in her late twenties who, with a broken heart, two suitcases, and a one-way ticket, moved to New York City in an attempt to figure out who she was and what she stood for. This is the story of a woman living in . . . a *Single State of Mind*.

---

*   Certain names and identifying characteristics have been changed.

my life has officially begun—again

It's been a mere two hours since I boarded this plane, said farewell to life as I knew it in Atlanta, and took the terrifying first step toward my new life. All my goodbyes have been said, my tears have been shed, and now only a few thousand feet stand between me and the world of a single woman living in New York City.

The pilot comes over the loudspeaker to announce that we are making our final descent into the New York area. I return my seat and tray to the upright and locked position so the flight attendant doesn't yell at me, lift the window shade up, and look out at the sheet of white clouds below. As the plane gets lower and lower, the sheet becomes thinner and thinner, until finally all the clouds have disappeared. And there it is. New York City.

Dozens of mammoth skyscrapers are grouped in a large cluster, with the newly built Freedom Tower reigning supreme. They sit strikingly along the water beside picturesque bridges. It's marvelous; majestic, even, like a kingdom right out of the pages of a fairy tale. And though I've seen this kingdom a dozen times before, it feels as if I'm laying eyes on it for the very first time. My vantage point, both physically and mentally, has me seeing this glorious city so differently from how I ever have; it's bigger, bolder, and more mysterious than ever. It's as if this city is speaking to me; it's as if it's begging me to come and play with it.

"Ladies and gentlemen, welcome to LaGuardia Airport, where the local time is three forty-five and the current temperature is thirty-three degrees . . ." *Damn, thirty-three degrees!* I think to myself. "On behalf of our entire Atlanta-based crew, we'd like to thank you for joining us and look forward to seeing you in the near future. For those of you who are visiting, we hope you enjoy your stay. For those of you whose final destination is New York, let us be the first to say welcome home." A grin washes over my face. I realize *I* am one of those passengers in the latter category. This is my final destination. *I am home.*

It's not long before I've deplaned and am nearly skipping with eagerness through the terminal and to the baggage claim, where the first of my two suitcases, bearing the embarrassing neon orange HEAVY tag, is coming around on the conveyor belt. As I struggle to lug it off, a middle-aged man helps me. I thank him and wonder if this is the first of many more damsel-in-distress moments I'll play in the future. I haul my two suitcases behind me as I make my way toward the giant yellow sign that reads TAXIS. The instant I walk through the double doors, a gust of bitter cold New York air greets me. I take a whiff. It smells a tad like garbage, with a hint of urine and maybe a note or two of sewage. But it also smells like freedom. I close my eyes for a moment and smile. Somehow this putrid, bone-chillingly cold air is the best I've ever felt.

I make my way through a zigzag of steel barricades and wait in the taxi line behind a handful of other passengers. I look around, noticing how similar everyone looks: phones out, headphones in, all-black ensembles. Meanwhile, I'm wearing the Sorel snow boots that I borrowed from my best friend, Kelly, a marshmallow-looking puffer coat I found on sale at Forever 21 just yesterday, mittens, and, to top it all off, a flamboyant faux-fur-lined trapper hat. My entire outfit instantly brands me as a Southerner who can't handle a measly thirty-three degrees. I make a mental note of how to fit in here: black on black on black . . . on black.

It doesn't take long until I reach the front of the line and am greeted by a man directing the long line of waiting taxis. "Where to?" he asks.

"New York City," I say proudly.

"*Where* in New York City?" His bored tone had suddenly acquired a hint of irritation.

"Oh, sorry, of course—the West Village, please." I've said it in such an excessively overconfident and slightly pompous tone that there's no doubt he knows I'm just a typical tourist pretending to be a local. He scribbles on a pink slip of paper that he hands to me before pointing to the second cab in line. The driver gets out, hoists one of my suitcases into the trunk of the yellow sedan, looks at the second one before telling me it's not going to fit and puts it in the backseat. As I'm buckling my seat belt, the driver without so much as a flinch of his head back toward the plexiglass that separates him from my oversized suitcase and me shouts, "Where to?"

"The West Village," I reply.

"*Where* in the West Village?"

"Umm . . . Grove Street, please."

"Grove and *what?*"

Shit, I can't remember. I pull up the confirmation email and shout out the number.

"Lady, I don't need the number, I need the cross street."

He rolls his eyes as I scramble to plug the address into my phone's map. I haven't even left the airport, and already I've managed to annoy both the man directing the taxi and the man driving the taxi. Finally, the map loads, and I shout victoriously, "Bleecker and Grove. Between"—I zoom in—"between Seventh Avenue and Hudson Avenue." Though on closer look, it's actually Hudson

Street, not Hudson Avenue, and Seventh Avenue isn't that close to Bleecker.

"Which way do you want me to take?" he asks.

"Excuse me?"

He gives a second eye roll accompanied by his first audible moan. "Lady, which way? The FDR, Midtown Tunnel, or the bridge?"

Rather than succumb to being outed as a tourist, I channel what I think a New Yorker would do and pretend not to have heard him the first time, before rolling my own eyes and telling him to pick the fastest route as if that should have been obvious.

He starts the meter. I slump back and rest my head on the greasy leather seat, knowing it's only a matter of time before I'll be home. I guess that's not entirely true, since where I'm going isn't my real home, but just a three-week rental. Long story short, I tried to find an apartment back when I was still living in the land of Depressionville, also known as Atlanta, but with thousands of options in dozens of different neighborhoods, it was more than my broken heart could handle. I couldn't commit to something sight unseen again, considering the last time I did that, I ended up on a reality television show where I got engaged, which didn't work out and left me so devastated that I bought a one-way ticket to a city I knew nearly nothing about. So to avoid being the village idiot yet again, I decided to take baby steps and go with a short-term rental while I searched for a more permanent pad. I settled on a cute place that was only slightly out of my budget in a neighborhood called the West Village.

As the meter hits eleven dollars, we emerge from a dark four-lane hole and out into the light. With my face pressed up against the smudged window, I find myself transfixed by my surroundings. The gray buildings are so high that their tops are invisible. Mounds of brown slushy snow are piled up along the streets next to sidewalks crowded with people moving quickly in their black peacoats and headphones. They weave past one another with an aggressive sort of ease. Backed by an occasional siren, horns blare from every direction, including from my own taxi. It's everything I imagined New York to be and more. There is an aura, a vibe, an energy that's impossible to describe. It's permeating so deeply that I can feel it from within the cab.

Finally, we arrive at Grove Street. The owner, whom I recognize from his Airbnb profile picture, is standing outside a nondescript brownstone nestled between what appears to be a German beer garden and a small grocery store. I pay the fare, a whopping forty-eight dollars not including tip, before getting out and meeting Jay, who introduces himself with a flimsy handshake. He's much slimmer and shorter than he appears in his profile photo. He generously offers to help me carry my suitcases up the two flights of stairs.

"Well, this is it," he says as he opens a red door.

There's a glass side table immediately to the left of the door, on which I place my purse. Instantly, I realize that not only is Jay smaller in person, but so is the apartment. He begins giving me the tour, starting off with the alcove kitchen to the right, which is very . . . how shall I put this . . . it's very . . . vintage. There's a rusted stovetop above an oven that looks like it's from the seventies, next to a matching microwave. A makeshift butcher's block has mismatched coffee mugs, plates, and glasses stacked on it. It's a far cry from Kelly's ostentatious kitchen equipped with a Viking stove and a Sub-Zero fridge that I'd grown accustomed to while living there for the past two months.

The alcove kitchen opens up to the living room, which is much more chic. A large L-shaped light gray couch, adorned with a plush cream-colored blanket and coordinating colorful throw pillows, is positioned in front of the fireplace. A white shaggy rug lies below the lacquered white coffee table, where a vase of fresh peonies sits, along with a Diptyque candle and a stack of GQ magazines. Jay must be gay. That, or he has a stylish girlfriend who's too busy being fabulous to have time to slave away in a kitchen. Next, he shows me the coat closet, which is jam-packed with wool trenches, a few furs, and one eye-catching silver-sequined jacket that could only belong to a fabulous gay man.

"Sorry there's not a lot of room. My partner and I, well, what can I say, we love our clothes." He raises both hands and wiggles his fingers. *Gay. Knew it!*

Next, Jay leads me to the bedroom, which barely fits a queen-size bed, but which is equally as chic as the living room. The bathroom is small; white subway tiles line the walls of the bathtub, and there's a ceramic pedestal sink next to the toilet. It takes all of forty-five seconds for the tour to wrap, and Jay and I find ourselves back in the alcove kitchen.

"So, a few things to go over. There's no garbage disposal; food goes in the trash. And no dishwasher, but there's a sponge and soap." He points to a bottle of Mrs. Meyer's dish soap and a blue sponge. "So . . . I've cleaned out the fridge for you. The stove and oven work fine, though I won't lie, we don't really use either. And by don't really, I mean, like, never." He laughs in a please-don't-judge-me kind of way. I laugh back in an I-don't-plan-on-cooking-much-anyway kind of way.

"Hmm, what else?" He taps his Gucci loafer on the hardwood floor as he thinks silently. "Oh, the trash gets picked up on Tuesdays and Fridays, so you can just take it downstairs and outside to the bins. There are tons of amazing restaurants around the area, and the neighborhood is great. Super safe."

"Awesome. One question, where's the washer and dryer?"

"Oh, *girl*." He tucks his chin into his neck and curls his lip. "There is no washer and dryer. I wish! But there's a wash-and-fold place just on the corner. That's where we go, and they'll pick up and deliver for free."

"Oh, perfect. Yeah, that's what I usually do, too." I lie so Jay won't know that I don't come from the land of Gucci loafer sophistication where it's customary to send your laundry out and have it delivered.

He hands me the keys and tells me to call him if anything goes wrong. I thank him and hug him goodbye. I'm not sure why I hug him, considering he's a complete stranger. Maybe it has to do with the Southerner in me or the sequined jacket that I will undoubtedly throw on the second he leaves. He's taken aback but out of courtesy follows my lead and, unbeknownst to him, gives me my very first New York hug.

I lock the door behind him, and just like that, I am alone in New York City, for the first time ever. I collapse on the couch, taking a moment to look around and process the small but charming apartment. I look at the kitchen, or lack thereof, and figure I can manage without a dishwasher or a garbage disposal for now, because, let's be honest, I'm not planning to cook. Nothing reeks of depression like a single girl, alone in New York City, burning something in the oven. Though on second thought, it would be a good way to check out the local firefighters. I decide that for my real apartment I'll definitely be needing a bigger kitchen, as well as a washer and dryer. I can't afford to send my dirty clothes out every week, nor can I afford to gain a reputation as the Southern single girl who smells. I'll also need more square footage, along with more closet space and an updated kitchen. Additionally, I'll need a dishwasher and a bathtub and a garbage disposal. Though this place may not be perfect, it's a roof over my head, a bed to sleep in, and, most important, it's miles away from the shit memories of Atlanta. Plus, I am living in fucking NEW YORK CITY!

Speaking of living here, I can't forget that I have some apartment showings tomorrow. As I'm setting reminders on my phone, my mom calls. Shit, I forgot to tell her I made it here safely. Come to think of it, I'm shocked that she hasn't called me a dozen times by now, considering the last time we talked was more than three hours ago.

"Hi, Pookie! How was the flight?" she squeals.

"Hi, Mom!" I tell her that the flight was fine and I've made it to the apartment.

"Ahhhh, yay! How is it? Faaaaaabulous?" She sounds like a white-mom version of Oprah.

"It's really cute. Really small but cute."

"Have you heard any sirens yet? Is it freezing?" The rapid-fire questions continue, and I'm beginning to wonder who is more excited about this move, Mom or me. Not only is she the quintessential type of mom who calls every day, usually at the worst moment possible, but she's also the kind of mom who loves asking impertinent questions when she gets excited about something. It's funny, because my mom was actually born in upstate New York, but she moved to Georgia to go to college and never left, so she's this rare mix of Yankee-meets-Dixie. She's super-friendly and talkative but avoids confrontation like the plague.

"Well, I told you everything is small in New York. I remember when Nanny used to live there. She just had a tiny little studio. It was on Bleecker and—"

"Christopher. I know, I know, you've told me a million times, Mom." In addition to being a Chatty Cathy, my mother also has a habit of repeating stories, not just once but dozens of times. It must be a parental thing, because my dad does it, too. Only every time *he* repeats a story, his exaggerations grow. The first time he tells the tale, he caught a fish that was a foot long, and by the tenth time, I swear, the fish has somehow morphed into a great white shark.

"You have to go see her place. It's right near where you're staying. I can't remember the apartment number."

"Mom, I don't think I can just walk into a building and randomly ask to see a place."

"True." She's in the middle of asking me what my plans are for tonight when she abruptly cuts off the entire conversation so she can be on time for her daily mah-jongg game at the country club.

I hang up the phone and stare at my suitcases, which are still zipped with stuffed clothes inside begging for air. I know I should unpack, but I'm too excited. Instead, I grab my puffer coat, slip on Kelly's snow boots, and take my very first voyage out into the neighborhood. As I'm walking, the air feels colder than it was a mere hour ago, but it's crisper. With no scent of garbage or urine, it's chilly but refreshing. The neighborhood is far less crowded than the streets I passed on my way here. It's antiquated yet enchanting at the same time, and the sight of the bare trees lining the streets have me imagining just how beautiful it must look in springtime. I envision myself twirling around these same streets one day, only in a ruffled dress and heels instead of these snow boots. As I turn the corner onto Hudson Street, an overwhelming aroma of pizza pervades the air. A generic white and red sign that simply reads PIZZA has my mouth watering. I walk in and approach the counter, which displays a dozen different types of pizza.

"What'll ya have?" a man in a white apron shouts at me.

"Two slices of cheese, please."

"For here or to go?"

I look around at the dingy interior with its few dirty tables and a metal countertop. "To go, please." I make my way down to the register.

"Four seventy-five."

I hand him a five, leave a quarter in the tip jar, and within minutes, I'm *that* chick. The one walking around the West Village in a trapper hat with a pizza box in hand. I'm tempted to devour it while walking, but the pleasant sight of a small wine shop distracts me. I pop in. Forty dollars later, and I find myself headed for home. My first day in my new home has come to an end. And with nightfall looming, it's time for me, my two slices of pizza, and my two bottles of wine to have our very first date in New York City.

i'm going to be homeless

It's only been one day and two apartment showings, but I'm pretty sure I'm going to be homeless. I'll be living in a cardboard box here on the side of Grove Street and praying every Tuesday and Friday that the garbagemen don't throw me into the back of the truck, or I'll have three roommates in a two-bedroom apartment above a dim sum restaurant in Queens and hoping they offer a resident's discount. Yeah, turns out that the city that never sleeps is also the city that ain't cheap.

It's not like I wasn't prepared for the astronomical costs this move would involve. Before recklessly buying my one-way ticket, I did actually do some research. I talked to every person I knew who had ever lived in the city, sifted through Craigslist and an app called "Street Easy," and even dove into some online forums. The summation of all these outlets made it clear that when it comes to living in New York, the most important thing is location, location, and did I mention location. Evidently, I want to be in a safe neighborhood, preferably one with tree-lined streets that has access to a good train line and hip restaurants. The precise neighborhood I want to live in depends on what type of person I am and how much money I'm willing to shell out. In essence, finding the right neighborhood in New York City requires a Myers-Briggs test and a thorough credit check.

There's the borough of Brooklyn, which isn't technically in "the city," at least not in the opinion of an out-of-towner like myself. According to Brooklyners, including two of my cousins, it's very "up and coming," offers more bang for your buck in regard to square footage, and boasts incredible views of the Manhattan skyline. While I could use as much space as possible, I have to be honest, spoiled, and an utter brat for a moment and admit that if I'm moving to New York City, I'm *not* moving to Brooklyn. I wouldn't be able to bear looking out my window and seeing the glorious sight of downtown Manhattan, all the while wondering why the hell I didn't move *there*. Not yet, at least.

With Brooklyn out, then the question became "what kind of *Manhattan* girl shall I be?" Within Manhattan are three main geographical regions: uptown, midtown, and downtown. They have different zip codes and different vibes. Uptown is home to Central Park and families. It's quieter and more spacious, and the easy access to the park makes up for the nonexistent plots of land known to everyone not from New York as "backyards." It was clear to me even before my feet touched the New York concrete that I was not going to be an uptown girl, because I don't have the required accessory to live there: a child. Not only do I not have a child, but with no man in sight, I'm at least nine months away from that. And I can't spend nine months having everyone looking at me and scowling as they think to themselves, *What a waste of real estate*. Plus, there are probably rules about grown adults being at playgrounds. I can just see it now, there I am sitting alone on a bench eating a slice of pizza as I depressingly watch the cute kids play, when suddenly a suspicious mother with a stroller passes me and points to a sign that reads, NO ADULTS UNLESS ACCOMPANIED BY A CHILD. Yeah, no thanks.

South of uptown is midtown, home to the infamous and buzzing Times Square and a few other neighborhoods like Gramercy Park and Murray Hill. Apparently, there's not much to do in these areas except go to work or be a tourist. Thus, I can't be a midtown girl, because, a) I don't have a job yet and b) I don't even know if that type of girl exists. I've never heard a song with the phrase "midtown girl" in it.

Then there's downtown, home to a plethora of different neighborhoods. There's Chelsea, where the fabulous gays live, and the West Village, where the fabulous Sarah Jessica Parker and the not-so-fabulous I currently live, or rent—tomayto, tomahto. There's also Tribeca, home to uber-wealthy families who own uber-expensive strollers. Supposedly Beyoncé and Jay Z live in Tribeca, which means no way in hell can I afford to live there. At the most southern tip of Manhattan is the Financial District, which is buzzing with hot, rich bankers by day and, from what I hear, buzzing with absolutely nothing by night. Though this area offers high-rise buildings with amenities at lower costs, the fact that the hot hedge-funders hightail it out of there by five o'clock means a single woman like myself has no use for that part of town come sundown.

Also downtown are a few scattered neighborhoods along the East Side like the Lower East Side, where many recent grads live—meaning I'm too old to live there—as well as the East Village, which is apparently "grungy but hip." Though I don't know exactly what that entails, I do know that "grungy" is not a word I or anyone who has ever met me would use to describe me. Somewhere in between those two neighborhoods lie Nolita and Soho. A decent number of humans reside here as does every clothing store you could imagine, making this a potentially lethal neighborhood for me.

With all of this research, I'd narrowed my search down to a select few neighborhoods: Chelsea, West Village, Nolita, and possibly a quiet part of Soho. I'd made a list of a dozen or so available apartments that I'd seen on various websites and was able to schedule showings along with some open houses.

And so, just like that, one morning I found myself off to

Chelsea for my very first apartment showing. I followed my phone's GPS to find the bricked-over brownstone nestled between two other brownstones on a long residential street. As I wait on the small stoop, I notice the quiet and serene similarities this block has to the West Village. A few minutes pass before a slender blond woman arrives, wearing a black peacoat lined with an ostentatious fur hood that gives my trapper hat a run for its money in the department of fashion faux pas. "Hello, are you here for ze apart-a-ment showing?" she asks in a thick almost seductive-like Russian accent.

"Yes, hi!" I reach out to shake her hand, but her back is already turned toward me and she's unlocking the front door. *All righty, then.* I awkwardly tuck my lonely cold hand back into my pocket.

She ushers me through a hallway and up a staircase. By the second flight, I'm panting, wondering where the hell the elevator is until finally, we arrive at a brown door marked 3F. The paint is peeling off it. Not a good sign. Nevertheless, I decide to be open-minded and not judge a book by its cover—or in this case, an apartment by its door. The agent unlocks the door, and it swings open, narrowly missing the edge of the kitchen counter. It takes but two seconds to realize that when people say apartments in New York City are tiny, they aren't exaggerating. I've never seen something so small cost so much. The low ceilings and lack of windows certainly don't help. I can't imagine how much worse it will be once furnished. I'm waiting for there to be a secret door that leads to a palatial master bedroom, but instead there's just a kitchen with a half-fridge, a burner, and an empty hole for a microwave all nestled between brown rotting wooden cabinets that haven't met a can of paint in their lifetime. The kitchen leads into the only other room, which functions as "both living and sleeping quarters," as the agent puts it. There's no possible way both a bed and a couch can fit in this room, let alone a dresser, nightstand, television, dining-room set, and all the other shit that's currently collecting dust in my storage locker back in Atlanta.

"Vhat do you think?" *I think my American Girl dolls had more space in the miniature dollhouse my dad built me for my seventh birthday.* But her accent paired with a peculiar sultry look in her eyes has a way of enticing me to even consider living in this shoebox. She's good but not good enough.

"I'll think about it," I lie. There's no way in hell I'm taking this place. Not only could I never live in such small quarters, but I could never stomach spending so many quarters doing so.

"Vhy think? Vhat don't you like about it?"

She's angry. Oh, God, I've made the Russian angry. I timidly tell her it's a little smaller than I'm looking for.

"Oh, you vant bigger. I have a two-bedroom just down the street from here."

"Oh, yes, that's much more of what I'm looking for!"

"It's *Sven* a month."

"Sven?"

"Yes, *sven* thousand. A month. For the rent."

"Seven thousand?"

She nods. The repulsed look on my face is enough for her to know there is no way in hell I can afford seven grand a month. Before I can even reply, she is leading me back down the same three flights of stairs we just trekked up. Within seconds, she and her fur-lined peacoat are gone.

Standing alone on the stoop, in the cold, I feel less enthused and more poor than ever. Seven fucking grand a month! Where the fuck am I? Do these people have any idea what someone could get for seven grand a month back in Atlanta? Well, first off, they'd get a mortgage with that, but for seven grand, they could also get a sprawling mansion on a golf course, in a gated community, near great schools, that comes with a maid, a butler, a private chef, and a pool with a hot cabana boy. Seven fucking grand!

With thirty minutes until my next appointment, I decide to mosey around Chelsea until I find a coffee shop. I am just about to order my usual grande skinny vanilla latte when the words "seven fucking grand" flash through my mind. "I'll just take a small coffee, please."

Finally, it's time to make my way to the second apartment, which is in Nolita. It's another walk-up, but the street is not nearly as quiet or as charming as the one in Chelsea. Then again, who cares about charm if you're living in a coffin?

Waiting for me outside on the stoop is a middle-aged man wearing a black peacoat (of course). He reaches out his hand. "You must be Andi?"

"Yes, hi!" I shake his hand.

"George. Nice to meet you. Come on in."

He unlocks the entry door, and we make our way through a narrow hallway and up the stairs. Elevators must not be a thing in this city. Luckily, it's only two flights before we reach a black door, which is already unlocked. George opens it to reveal a small mudroom, and I instantly feel more optimistic. Unlike the last apartment, this one has an actual bedroom, with a door. Though I don't think it will fit a queen bed. The hardwood floors smell new, as does the coat of white paint on the walls. All seems to be going well until we reach the kitchen, where all my hopes and dreams go up in smoke. There in the middle of the kitchen isn't an island, a table, or a cute seating area. No, no. There in the middle of the kitchen sits . . . a bathtub.

Perplexed, I ask George when this will be installed in the bathroom.

"Bathroom? Technically, there isn't one. This is what we call bathing and cooking quarters."

"Excuse me?"

"It's not uncommon."

"Ummmm, so where's the bathroom sink?"

He points to the kitchen sink.

"That's a kitchen sink."

"And in this case a bathroom sink as well."

"What about the toilet?"

"Yes, right here." He slides open a pocket door, revealing one lonely little toilet.

He asks me what I think of the place, and I tell him I'm not sure but that I'll give it some thought. Of course this is a lie, but I don't have the guts to tell sweet George that he's got to be fucking kidding me with a bathtub in a kitchen.

"Fair enough, but I will need to know by the end of the day, because I've got another person coming to see this place later this afternoon, and it will probably get scooped up any day now."

Ummmm, okay, sure, let me know how that goes, George.

I exit the apartment, leaving George standing in the kitchen slash bathroom, and sprint down the stairs.

Two massively failed viewings have me heading back to the West Village feeling sullen and defeated. The rational adult part of me knows that it's only my first day of apartment hunting and there are plenty more apartments to see, but the emotional single woman in me is turning to the only two things that will soothe my pain: a glass of wine and a bubble bath. It's there that I find myself soaking in my own fear. It's there that I have my first New York City breakdown. I've almost made it a full forty-eight hours, almost. With tears streaming down my face and plunking into the bubbles, I can't help but feel as though I've made yet another monumental mistake. Did I really think that I was going to be able to pull this off? Did I really think that I was going to buy a one-way ticket and move to a new city and find a great place and actually somehow be happy again? Really?

I wasn't always this delusional. In fact, growing up I had a pretty good head on my shoulders. That is, until about a year ago when I went on a television show and got engaged to a loser in the most super-public way possible. When that didn't work out, I had to endure a breakup with said loser in an equally super-public way. So, one would think that a blunder like that would have brought me to my senses and cautioned me to look before leaping. You'd think I'd have learned by now that fairy tales don't exist. That you don't just pick up and move to a new city, and poof, all your problems have magically vanished, and you have suddenly been transported into a world of happiness. But sadly, it seems as though I haven't learned from my own mistakes. The truth is, just like I was blinded by love when I got engaged, I think I was blinded by heartbreak when I decided to move here. I'd fallen so deep into a hole as I grieved my broken engagement that I thought any place would be better than where I was. I thought maybe my breakup could be a chance to start anew. That embarking on the unknown could be a thrill. That I'd find peace in a new apartment in a new city. But just like when I got engaged, I guess it never occurred to me that there was a chance this wouldn't work out. And now as my fingers prune away, the bubbles subside, and the wine bottle empties, I wonder if what I thought was a leap of faith is really just a leap from one mistake to another. I wonder. . . . What the hell have I done?

broken

Luckily, by the next morning, both the red-wine buzz and my depression have worn off, and I awake feeling slightly renewed. I think I needed that first purge. I needed to cry away some of the fear that inevitably comes with picking up your entire life and moving it elsewhere. That's the thing with making bold decisions like these: they have a way of helping to dig you out of your dark hole, but once you do find the light, you eventually have to face the reality of your decision. I realize that as I sit on the couch of my enormous, unbelievably posh, drool-worthy, palatial rental, sipping my coffee. If I want to fully emerge into the light, I'm going to have to suck it up, put my grown woman panties on, and make this shit happen, because being depressed sure as hell isn't going to help me find an apartment. It's time to lower my standards and up my budget. Shitty apartments will not deter me from my newfound freedom. I decide to wipe the slate clean by writing out a new list of apartment must-haves, would-like-to-haves, and cannot-haves.

Must have:
1. Bedroom with a door
2. Bedroom with a door that fits queen-size bed
3. Elevator or maximum of two flights of stairs (maybe three)

Would like to have:
1. Dishwasher and garbage disposal
2. Washer and dryer
3. Floor-to-ceiling windows
4. Fresh paint job

Can't have:
1. Bathtub in kitchen

It doesn't take long for me to resume my search and find a handful of apartments that based on their photos and descriptions might have a chance of working out. Most of them are having open houses today and tomorrow, and for a few others I schedule showings throughout the week. As I look at the list of apartments, I actually crack a proud smile.

It's not long before I take that smile and head east to the first apartment, which is in the neighborhood next to mine. The listing describes its location as "the heart of Greenwich Village." It's a busy area; the streets aren't lined with trees like they are on Grove but instead are lined with Chinese restaurants, bars, and dry cleaners. I take a right on MacDougal, only to find even more dive bars. I can tell by the numbers on various buildings and doors that I'm getting close to my destination, a bad sign considering the more I walk, the more bars I see. Finally, I arrive at the building, which isn't so much a building as it is a door. A door next to a bar. A door next to a bar with an awning that reads, SHOTS! SHOTS! 5 FOR $10.

I press the button for the apartment number, and a real estate agent buzzes me in. I trek up four flights of stairs. The agent immediately greets me and hands me a flyer listing the details of the apartment. I take a quick walk-through. It's small like the last apartment, but nicer. And though it's not promising, based on the fact that it's above a nameless bar that sells five shots for ten dollars, the fact that I've found something somewhat accommodating and affordable slightly lifts my spirits.

It's off to the second apartment, which is just a few blocks south, near Washington Square. As I walk there, I can't help but notice all the young NYU students hustling around with their backpacks or smoking in groups on the corner. I'm not feeling particularly great about the area, but I go to see the apartment anyway. Another agent is there handing out flyers, and again I do a quick walk-through. A galley kitchen leads to a large bedroom that is bright and airy. The windows, though not floor-to-ceiling, are big enough to showcase the backsides of other apartments. It's quiet and rather peaceful. I even hear birds chirping. The agent must have seen the smile on my face, because she comes to personally show me back through the kitchen and into the living room. Everything about this place feels bright. That is, until she shows me the bathroom. And that's where I see perhaps the vilest thing my eyes have ever seen: atop the toilet lid sits . . . a sink. Positive that this is temporary, just like the apartment that had the bathtub in the kitchen, I rhetorically ask the agent when the sink is going to be installed.

"What do you mean?"

"The sink, on top of the toilet, that can't be permanent, right?"

"Yes, it's not uncommon. It's to maximize space."

And though I'm starting to understand this whole New York real estate agent lingo bullshit jargon, this one is beyond my comprehension.

"So let me get this straight. The sink is permanently affixed to the toilet."

The agent nods, confirming my worst fear.

"So I'd be using the same water to brush my teeth that I use to flush?"

"It's convenient, though," she says with a slight chuckle. At least she, too, knows that this is absurd. "It's a no-go?"

"Yeah, not gonna happen."

"I don't blame you. Listen, here's my card, with my website. Let me know if you see any listings you like on there."

I thank her before bolting out the door.

The next two days are like an apartment-hunting version of Groundhog Day. I wake up, check the internet for new listings, and head off to view an apartment. Each one seems, impossibly, to be shittier than the last. And each one makes me feel more hopeless.

One apartment has ants crawling in the bathroom. One has week-old takeout food strewn across the kitchen counter while a half-smoked blunt sits in the ashtray on the coffee table. Another one doesn't even have a kitchen. One apartment is *seven* floors up with no elevator. The only one with any real promise turns out to be a total scam.

Oh, yeah, that one was fun. I responded to a Craigslist listing and set up an appointment with the "agent." I arrive at a stunning brownstone with a staircase adorned with potted flowers and a freshly painted red-lacquered front door and press the buzzer, only to be greeted by a confused blond woman who asks how she can help me. When I tell her I'm there for the apartment showing, her confusion turns to annoyance, and she slams the door in my face. I should have known better, considering the place is fabulous, within my budget, in the West Village, and on Craigslist. That one leads me to call it quits for the day.

And with only six days left on my short-term rental, I find myself on the verge of panic. Despite there being a plethora of apartments available, even lowering my standards doesn't seem to be enough to find the perfect one. I've gone from searching for perfection to being willing to settle on livable. Oh, how the mighty have fallen.

To make matters worse, I'm still unemployed—and based on

something that happened yesterday, I might be that way forever. I'd gotten an email from an agent I used to work with, inviting me to go on a last-minute casting call for some new show that Amazon was developing. I'd never been on a casting call before. I always thought those were reserved for models and actors with actual talent. The closest I'd ever been was for a reality television show, and as you may know, that didn't turn out so well. I didn't know what the show was about or if it was even something I'd be interested in, but I knew I needed an apartment, which meant I needed money. So I said yes. Moments later, a follow-up email arrived with an address and a list of instructions. The first was to come "camera-ready," the second to come looking "stylish," the third was that the audition would be tomorrow.

Come the morning of the audition, and I'm frantically rifling through my suitcases. Of course, like every other woman, I have nothing to wear. A mountain of clothes on the floor later, I concede and settle on a basic black A.L.C. dress I happened to pack just in case I got invited somewhere cool. I jazz it up with a pair of emerald-green stilettos I also packed just in case, taking it from regular basic to something more like Pinterest basic.

My basic self arrives shortly after noon, camera-ready, to the address given in the email. As I exit the elevator, I am expecting a lobby and a receptionist, but all I see is empty office space. Assuming I'm in the wrong place, I walk down the empty hallway until I find an open door, inside which a blonde sits on a couch typing on her computer.

"Hi, I'm here for the casting call. Do you know where I go for that?"

She looks up from her computer. She's super-chic, wearing a cream-colored one-shoulder ruffled top, her sleek-straight hair with a perfect middle part. "Sorry, I don't work here, but I think it's all the way down the hallway."

Shit, it's Whitney Port from that MTV show *The City*. Though she was never the most dramatic or extravagant character, I remember liking her because she managed to go on a reality television show, maintain a decent reputation, and catapult her newfound fame into quite the career for herself. And now here I am mistaking her for a receptionist. Mortified, I continue walking down the hallway until I find a short brunette wearing an earpiece and a walkie-talkie on her hip. She *has* to work here. I repeat my exact words, hoping not to eat them this time.

"Hi, yes, all the way to the back, last door on the left."

My shoes are already painfully rubbing the back of my ankles as I make my way down the hall to the last door on the left. I walk into a room of no fewer than fifteen women sitting in folding chairs along the wall. All silently reading the blue index cards in their hands. All of them are camera-ready and dressed to the nines, some in trendy culottes and chic blouses, others in harem pants and skater dresses. As I scan the room, I notice that everyone's style is different, but everyone has style. Except for me. I'm so fucking basic it's appalling.

I take an empty seat and wait until a lady comes into the room and calls out my name. She introduces herself as one of the producers of the show and takes me back to hair and makeup to get touched up. While I'm in the chair getting powdered, she gives me the rundown of what the hell it is I'm actually doing here.

"So what we'll do is partner you up with someone . . ." She looks down at a stack of papers and flips through them. "I'm not sure who yet, but I'll have that shortly. The segment will be about fifteen to twenty minutes long. These are the topics." She hands me a stack of blue index cards. "And obviously, you can just read off the teleprompter, but feel free to ad-lib. And most important, lots of energy!"

"Teleprompter?"

"Yeah, a teleprompter will be there, so no worries if you forget anything."

"Shit, I've never used a teleprompter."

"It's easy. Also, no cursing." She laughs as if she's relieved to finally see someone who doesn't have her shit together.

"Oh, right, sorry."

"Don't worry, it's not that hard, honestly. Plus, all we're looking for is chemistry and lots of energy! Lots and lots of energy."

Needless to say, I didn't get a callback. I guess being stylish and having lots of energy are not my strong suit. Then again, I could have told you that before humiliating myself on camera.

That evening I return yet again to my sprawling rental (which I think is growing bigger by the day), where frustration leads me back to my usual remedy: a glass of wine (or two) and a bubble bath. Once again, while my body soaks in bubbles, my mind soaks in the anxiety of my decision to move here. I do give myself credit, though, for not shedding any tears this time. But I realize what I'm missing. Gone are the comforts of Atlanta. Gone is the short drive to my parents' house for Sunday dinner. Gone are the familiar roads and shops. Gone are all my friends. I'm in a city of millions of people, yet I feel more alone than ever.

It's not until a day later when I get a random text that my loneliness subsides. It's from an old friend from back home, Michelle, and she's asking me if I want to grab dinner. She must have a sixth sense when it comes to lonely Atlanta girls living in New York.

I use the term "old friend" loosely, since Michelle is really the best friend of one of my best friends, and we've only hung out a few times in Atlanta, but I'll take what I can get. She had moved to the city years ago so she could become a personal stylist. Tonight, she is sitting in the back corner booth of Rosemary's, a cozy neighborhood restaurant on the corner of Greenwich and West Tenth. I walk in and we embrace like the long-lost friends we kind of are but kind of aren't. She looks the same as I remember: petite frame, shiny beach-waved blond hair that rests slightly above her shoulders, and bright red lipstick. Still as chic as ever, and she now has a city-girl vibe to add. She never was the Atlanta type of girl. In a world of pink and green Lilly Pulitzer dresses and matching Jack Rogers sandals, Michelle has always stood out with her rocker-chic leather jackets and studded booties. She is the type of girl who probably just wakes up cool.

Over pesto-infused burrata, tortellini, and plenty of red wine, we gossip away about what we've been up to, including my now infamous breakup, which continues to haunt me thanks to the weekly tabloids. Gag. She gives me the lowdown on all the hot spots to party at and a list of her favorite restaurants, as well as her love life. Turns out the party-girl-make-out-with-a-random-guy-at-a-bar Michelle whom I used to know now has a boyfriend. She even lives with him. His name is Pete, he works in finance, blah, blah, blah. All I really hear is "boyfriend," and then I tune out. Despite her not being single anymore, there is still a familiarity with Michelle that evokes the comforts of home and makes me momentarily escape the reality of my apartment-hunting shitstorm. I say momentarily because, of course, she asks me where I'm living.

"Oh, don't even get me started."

She rolls her eyes and nods in agreement as if she knows exactly what I'm going through.

"Long story short, I'm in a short-term rental right now while I search for a place. It's a total shitshow trying to find something decent."

"Oh, girl, tell me about it! It's insane."

"And expensive!"

"Fucking extortion." She takes a swig of wine. "My first apartment was a shitty shoebox on the Lower East Side. Now we live uptown." Of course they live uptown; they are a couple.

"How shitty?"

"Shitty shitty!"

"Fuck!" I have no chance.

"Yeah, we're not in Atlanta anymore, girl. What neighborhoods are you looking at?"

"Well, so far, I've seen a place in Soho—"

"Hell no!" she interrupts.

"One in Chelsea."

"Not bad. Not bad at all, actually. Just stay away from the Highline. God, that thing is such an eyesore and a total tourist trap."

"But I really like where my place is now, in the West Village."

"Duh, *everyone* likes the West Village. It's the best. And the most expensive."

"So I hear."

"Just know that stuff moves really quickly, so if you find something you like, be ready to say yes. Nothing lasts more than twenty-four hours. Nothing good, at least."

We finish dinner after making plans to hang out again soon. It feels nice knowing that at least I have one friend here. Plus, Michelle is a ray of hope I desperately need right now. She's living proof that even girls from the quiet suburbs of Atlanta can make it in the Big Apple.

I start walking home, breathing in the chilly air, which feels slightly warmer thanks to a night with a familiar face. That and the two bottles of wine in me. I'm strolling through the quiet streets of the West Village, when out of nowhere a sign hanging above a stoop catches my eye: APARTMENT FOR RENT. Hmmmm. I look around the street. It's serene and beautiful. The brownstones are pristine. Some of them even have colorfully painted lacquered doors. And there's no Chinese restaurant or bar selling two-dollar shots in sight. I take my phone out of my leather cross-body and type the phone number into a new note so I can call in the morning.

I'm just about to turn onto Grove Street when a muffled voice starts shouting at me. "Hello! Hello? Can you hear me?"

I look around to see where the voice is coming from, but I'm alone on the street.

"Helllllooooooo!" The voice gets louder and angrier. Fuck, the sound is coming from my purse.

I dig back into my cross-body. Shit! I've just pocket dialed a stranger. "Hello! Hi, I'm so sorry. Can you hear me?"

"Who is this?"

"Ummm, hi! My name is Andi, and umm—"

"Are you calling about the apartment?"

"Yes, actually, I am!"

"Which one?"

"Ummm, one second." I run to the nearest corner to find out what street I'm on. "Perry, the apartment on Perry."

"Hold on, let me look. Yes, it's available. Do you want to see it?"

"Yes, please!"

"Tomorrow at noon?"

"Perfect. See you then!"

And just like that, I've (well my pocket really) scheduled yet another apartment viewing. Go, me! Despite the fact that I don't know how big or how much a month the apartment is, I feel a buzz coming on and it's not just from the wine.

a new lease on life

The following morning, I retrace my steps from the previous night, making my way down Perry Street for a few blocks before I finally find the familiar sign. The short brunette (in a black peacoat, naturally) standing on the stoop scrolling through her phone means I probably have the right place.

"Hi. I'm Andi, here for the viewing."

"Sheila. Nice to meet you! Come on in."

Sheila is much peppier than most of the other agents I've met. Though I should have realized that when she took my phone call last night at ten o'clock. She's quite petite, even in her bundled-up Canada Goose coat. She opens the door that leads into what she calls the "foyer," which is really just another narrow hallway, and I follow her up the stairs. As we climb, she rambles on and on about how the building is from the 1800s and how it's been kept up so well and is in the best neighborhood. Unbeknownst to her, I'm an apartment-hunting pro who knows none of the shit she is saying matters if there's a bathtub in the kitchen or a sink attached to the toilet. I'm relieved when it takes us only one flight of stairs to reach the slightly ajar door labeled 2C. The instant it flings open, a whiff of fresh paint fills the air. Straight ahead is a wall adorned with an adorable small white-brick fireplace. The kitchen isn't so much a kitchen as a ten-foot wall, but the black granite countertops and wooden cabinets look new.

"All of the hardwood is original," says Sheila.

She's starting to tell me something about the number of units in the building when I blurt out, "Is there a dishwasher?"

"No." She chuckles with a this-is-New-York-honey kind of laugh.

"Not a common amenity in this city, is it?"

"Not unless you're a millionaire."

I ask about the laundry situation, and she tells me there are washers and dryers downstairs. We move into the bedroom. I use the term "bedroom" very loosely in this instance, because again, there is no way in hell a bed could actually fit here.

"How in the world does a bed fit in here?"

"It's definitely on the small side, but you could do a Murphy bed."

Me, a Murphy bed? No, no, and hell fucking no.

We make our way back past the kitchen wall (a whopping twelve feet) and toward the two large windows that reveal the backs of a dozen other brownstones, all with small yards separated by wooden fences. It's a large space, and the high ceilings make it feel even larger.

I start thinking aloud. "What if I somehow sectioned this part off and made it the bedroom?"

Sheila reaches for her purse and takes out a piece of paper with the floor plan on it. She starts spouting out square footages before telling me what a great idea that would be.

I take a few laps around the apartment, envisioning where I could put my furniture and how I could decorate the walls. This could work. This could really work! After everything, could it be that one accidental pocket dial may be the golden ticket to my new pad?

"I forgot to ask, what's the price?"

Sheila looks back at her piece of paper and reads off the listing price. I black out. This is *not* going to work. Seeing the expression on my face, Sheila starts telling me what a great deal this place is for the location, and she's so sweet and convincing that I actually start to believe her. She's different from the previous agents. She actually seems to care. That is, until she hits me with the "broker's fee" speech.

"And . . . then . . . there's the broker's fee on this property, which is twelve percent of one year's rent."

"Broker's fee?"

"Yeah, broker's fee. Every unit has one."

"Is that like a security deposit?"

"No, it's in addition. I could do ten percent for you, but that's the absolute lowest."

I go silent. Sensing something is off, she asks me what I'm thinking.

"It's just a little more than I want to spend." Actually, it's a lot more than I want to spend.

"I understand. Living in this city is expensive. If you're looking for something cheaper, I'd suggest Soho or the Lower East Side. Maybe even Brooklyn."

"I know, but I really like this neighborhood. Can I have some time to think about it?"

"Of course! But it just came on the market, and I can't see it staying available for long. And unfortunately, I can't hold it for you. But take my card and think about it. Also, if you do want it, there will be an approval process. I'll need to see your credit information, tax returns, all that stuff. Also, what do you do for a living?"

Fuck, the dreaded occupation question. "I'm a blogger," I lie.

I can't tell her the truth, which is that I'm a former attorney who went on a reality television show, who is surviving on odd jobs like attending events that I really have no business attending, and getting paid to post on social media. I know she'll roll her eyes and mutter "Damn millennial" under her breath, I just know it. Luckily, my little blogger fib seems to appease her enough to forestall any follow-up questions.

We leave the apartment, and I tell Sheila that I'll be in touch. Immediately, I call Patrick, my cousin's boyfriend, who is a real estate agent in the city. "Okay, so I just saw a place on Perry Street—"

"Great street," he interrupts.

"Sooooo great! It's a one-bedroom, but I could kind of convert it into two. Only problem is, it's expensive as fuck."

"Welcome to New York City!"

"Why does everyone fucking say that? And get this, there's something called a broker's fee that she's trying to charge."

"Yeah, typical. What percent did she say?"

"Twelve, but she could do ten."

"That's a steal!"

"A steal? Why am I paying a broker fee when she's not even my broker?"

"She's the landlord's broker. That's how it works here."

"So basically, I'd be paying her ten percent to what? Open the unlocked door?"

"Yup! Welcome to New York."

"You said that already."

My head drops in defeat as I realize it's just another day in the city and I am once again sitting on the couch of my luxuriously spacious, unbelievably extravagant short-term rental. But at least this time I'm not pondering depression, rather I'm pondering Perry Street. It's really a stretch budget-wise, but it's so cute, and it's on Perry Street! The same street Carrie Bradshaw lived on in *Sex and the City*. That makes it the ultimate bachelorette pad, and Lord knows I could really use that right about now. But it's so damn expensive. I'd need to get a steady job, start budgeting, and stick to ramen and two-dollar pizza slices for dinner. But I could do it. Maybe.

Instead of recklessly saying yes, like I did about moving to this city, I decide to go back on the internet to see if anything new has been listed. I'm scrolling through the same apartments I've scrolled through a dozen times, when I suddenly see something new. I zoom in on the location to see that it's right around the corner on Hudson Street. I flip through the pictures and see that it's not terrible. It's no Perry Street, but it is much more afford-able. And the fact that there's an open house tomorrow is making it seem less terrible and more tempting, almost as if it's fate. With Perry Street still on my mind, I make a deal with myself: I will go to the open house on Hudson tomorrow with an open mind, and if I don't like it, I will call Sheila. If she says Perry Street is avail-able, then I'll take it as a sign that it is meant to be, and I will pull the trigger and officially become a renter. It will all be out of my hands. I will relinquish control to the New York City rental mar-ket gods and hope I end up with a roof over my head by the end of the month.

I wake up the next morning with one thought on my mind: Perry. With four more hours until the open house on Hudson starts, I look it up again. Photo by photo, Hudson is losing its appeal. It just doesn't compare to Perry. I'm torturing myself as I look at the clock. An hour passes, then another fifteen minutes. I can't take it anymore. Fuck it. I cave and call Sheila.

"Hey, it's Andi. Is Perry Street still available?"

She tells me it is.

"Ten percent broker's fee?"

There is a long pause.

I cross my fingers. *Please say yes, please say yes.*

"Sure." She definitely didn't want to say yes.

"I'll take it!"

We set up an appointment for the following afternoon for me to come by and fill out the application, sign some paperwork, and, most of all, cut her some checks. I can't help but prance when I walk into her office. I'm seated across from her, making small talk and trying to hide my excitement as she's clicking away on her computer and the printer spits out page after page.

"Start by filling out this basic info page," she says as she hands me a pen and the first of many forms. "There will be a security deposit and first month's rent due today, so if you can, please write two checks according to the amount listed on that third page. Also, I'll need your tax returns, because the building requires the tenant to make ninety times the monthly rental amount."

The pen falls out of my hand and onto the desk. "Huh?"

"Last year's return needs to show that you made ninety times the monthly rent. It's usually forty to sixty times, but the better the neighborhood, the higher the number. It's because of the eviction laws in the city and, honestly, controlling what kind of people live in the building."

"Wait. Ninety, like nine-zero?"

She nods.

"Ummm, yeah, I didn't make ninety times the rent last year. Pretty sure I'd be living in Tribeca if I did."

"It's okay, because you can have up to two cosigners. Maybe your dad or another family member?"

My worst nightmare has come to fruition: I'm a grown woman, and I need Daddy to cosign on an apartment for me. I know he'll do it, but I really don't want to have to ask him. I have no other option, though. Kill. Me. Now. I step out of Sheila's office and into the lobby to make the dreaded call.

"Hey!"

"Hey, Dad!"

"What's going on? How's New York?"

"Great. Well, cold but great. I actually think I found an apartment!"

"That's great, honey."

"But there's one thing . . . I'm actually with the broker right now, and basically, in order to get the apartment, I have to show that last year I made ninety times the rent."

"Ninety times. What the *hell*? You livin' in a damn penthouse or somethin'?" He's resorted to his ultra-redneck Southern twang, something he always does when he hears something is expensive or chic.

"More like a shoebox."

I don't say anything about needing him to cosign or borrow money. I don't have to. The next sentence out of his mouth is, "Okay, well, send me the documents, and I'll cosign if you need."

"You don't have to. I can figure out a way—"

"Andi, stop. Send me the documents."

"I really didn't want to have to ask you, Dad."

"I know. But you didn't ask me. I just offered."

"I didn't think I'd have to ask you to do this for me."

I'm on the verge of tears. Not because my ego is bruised but because my father is quite simply the best. He's here for me. He's been here for me through it all: the ups, the downs, the tears, and the embarrassing moments on reality television. And even though I don't want to need him right now, the fact that I don't have to say out loud that I do makes me overwhelmingly grateful to have a father like him.

"Andi, listen to me very carefully. You need to learn that sometimes it's all right to ask people for help. It's not a sign of weakness. You asking me to cosign because of some absurd nine-hundred—"

"Ninety."

" . . . some absurd ninety-times rule. The point is, it doesn't make me think of you differently. I know you can hold your own and take care of yourself, and I'm very proud of you for that."

My eyes well up with tears. I'm too choked up to say anything except a soft whisper. "Thank you."

"And also congratulations. I love you."

"I love you, too, Dad."

I regain my composure and walk back into Sheila's office with my two thumbs up. "Good to go!" I finish filling out the forms without any hesitation, until I get to the final page of the lease agreement. I've initialed nearly twelve pages, and now all I need to do is simply sign my name. I pause. Am I really ready to do this?

I feel the same reluctance that I felt months ago, back when I was looking to lease an apartment in Atlanta. I'd seen a ton of places that were perfect for me, and yet I never could manage to sign on the dotted line. Deep down, despite the apartments being perfect, they just never felt right. Now I'm hesitant again but not because this place doesn't feel right. In fact, it feels so right. I know *this* is my apartment. But I also know that this one signature is going to change the rest of my life. Because to me, in this moment, it's not just a signature. It's more than that; it's a commitment. It's a commitment to following through on that one-way flight, a commitment to myself to move on from my past and leave heartbreak behind. I spent so many months withering away because of the painful ending of my engagement, waiting for the time when I would eventually crawl out of that dark hole. And now "eventually" has arrived, and instead of feeling empowered, I feel terrified. It's interesting how sometimes we find ourselves sad for so long that we become resistant to happiness.

I'm one signature away from potential freedom and yet my hand won't move. I take a deep breath and close my eyes. A moment from a few weeks ago plays in my head. It was Kelly sitting on my bed telling me how proud she was of me for moving to New York.

We were clutching each other's hands, crying tears of achievement and pride.

I open my eyes and realize I can't let her down. I can't let her or my family or any of my other friends down. And most of all, I can't let myself down. I've come too far to sabotage myself now. I can do this. I *need* to do this.

I grasp the pen and, with a pulsing heartbeat, sign my name.

"Congratulations!" says Sheila. "Now I'll put you in touch with the super, and you two can figure out a move-in date and time. Her name is Mary, and by the way, I should warn you, she's, ummm, how do I say this? She's interesting."

"What do you mean?"

"Totally harmless, just talks a lot. You'll see what I mean."

I leave the office feeling a little poorer than when I came in. But a little fuller, too, as if I'm not so alone anymore. I have a new man in my life, and his name is Perry. And most of all, for the first time since arriving in New York, I feel a sense of pride. I did it. I actually took that leap of faith. I signed on the dotted line, and in doing so, I didn't just lease an apartment. I signed a lease on a new life.

air mattresses and fire escapes

I'm on a hot streak. Not only have I nailed down an apartment, but I might have nailed down a new job. The other day, out of the blue, I got a call from a literary agent asking me about working together. Well, I guess it wasn't completely out of the blue because shortly before I moved to New York, I let Kelly read the journal I kept throughout my breakup. I didn't really *let* her, it was more that she insisted I show her what I was writing all the time. And since I was living in her house, I couldn't exactly say no. Over plenty of wine, she'd laugh aloud as she read my entries, and then one night, somewhere between our second and third bottle of wine, she suggested I turn the journal into a book. I scoffed at the idea, all the while sort of secretly loving it.

Maybe it was the wine or maybe I just had nothing else to do, but for some reason I contacted a literary agent recommended by my cousin, who once worked in journalism. I didn't think anything would come of it. In fact, I'd kind of forgotten about it until this call.

Anyway, the agent introduces herself, and I tell her how I just moved to New York and all about my breakup and the fact that I journaled about it. There is a distinct pause on the other end of the line.

"Listen, I don't usually do these types of books, no offense. But I think you might have something here."

"Thanks. No offense taken. I totally get it."

"Why don't you put together a proposal, and I'll look it over, and we can talk about sending it out to publishers?"

"Absolutely!"

Later that day, I can't help but think how the timing of this phone call could be a stroke of luck. Here I am a month into my new life in New York City, and hardly a thing has gone right. From my apartment search to the embarrassment of my first, and I hope last, casting call, this phone call is a ray of sunshine in the midst of my new-life storm.

I search Google for "book proposal template." I quickly realize that writing a proposal isn't as easy as writing a book report back in middle school. But at least it's given me something to do. And most of all, it's given me a bit of purpose. It probably won't go anywhere, but I figure, fuck it, what do I have to lose? Plus, I may have landed an apartment, but I still need a job to stay in it.

Speaking of my apartment, today is the day! It's finally time for me to move in, which means my new man, Mr. Perry, and I are hours away from becoming an official couple. I've spoken to the superintendent of my building, Mary, a couple of times over the past week. Sheila was right about her—interesting, to say the least. She's the talkative type who seems to have a few screws loose up in there, but nevertheless, we managed to schedule a move-in date and time so she can show me around the building and give me my keys. I splurged and hired some last-minute movers to bring my furniture up from Atlanta. In hindsight, it would have been cheaper and more fun to buy new furniture, but I justified the shipping cost by telling myself having my old furniture will make me feel more at home.

Ecstatic to finally have my own place, I arrive at the Perry Street apartment at exactly nine in the morning, as scheduled, with my two suitcases in tow. I enter the first set of doors into the small foyer, which I didn't notice until now is lined with small silver mailboxes, each labeled with a last name. Next to the mailboxes is a call box, also with a list of last names and corresponding numbers. I find Mary's name and press 1A.

"Hello!" screams a muffled voice over the intercom.

"Hi, Mary, it's Andi. I'm here to move in today."

She lets out an audible sigh. "Fine, be right there." Her surprised and annoyed tone has me a little baffled.

Suddenly, through the window in the door, I see a small dog sprinting toward me. Behind the dog is a short middle-aged woman wearing an oversized rainbow tie-dyed T-shirt, black track pants, and no shoes. This must be Mary.

She opens the door. "Lucy, stay!" she barks. "Come on in."

I can immediately tell that not only is this woman not so keen on shoes, but she smells like she's not so keen on showers either. Her gray hair is short, greasy, and a tangled mess. She's giving me a cat lady with a smoker's laugh meets hippie dippy vibe. Her bare face could use some foundation and contouring, but she has good bone structure. Twenty years and a few thousand cigarettes ago, I can see her having been really pretty.

"Lucy, back in the house!"

Poor thing. You know how sometimes dogs resemble their owners? Well, Lucy is undoubtedly related to Mary. She is a small terrier-looking dog who, other than the stray brown hairs around her mouth (which I don't even want to think about), also has short, greasy gray hair. She's looking up at me with the saddest little doggy eyes I've ever seen, silently screaming, *Help me, help me!*

"Here, let me help you with your bags," offers Mary.

"Thanks, but they are very heavy."

"Well, I'm very strong." She chuckles creepily as she flexes her right arm.

I'm grateful for her generosity but also not sure about being left in the same room as her. She effortlessly lugs one of my suitcases up the stairs while I not so effortlessly follow her.

She opens the unlocked door to my new apartment and places the suitcase in the middle of the empty living room before digging into her pocket. "Here are your keys, but the lock doesn't work."

Confused, I ask what she means.

"Well, something is wrong with the lock, so like I said, it doesn't work, duhhhhh!" It's confirmed, Mary has an undeniable case of the crazy eyes. "The locksmith can't get here for a day or two. But it locks from the inside."

I raise my eyebrows. "So what do you suggest I do?"

"Well, I didn't know you were moving in *today*."

What the fuck? How did she not know? We've talked about this for an entire week.

She looks around for a second and then points to the back window with a solution. "There's a fire escape you can go up and down. It leads to the basement where the laundry room is, and this key right here unlocks the main door."

"Ummm. Okay . . ." I'm trying hard not to ruffle her feathers since it's my first day here, but inside I'm fuming. Does she seriously expect me to fucking climb up and down the fire escape? Of course, I say nothing to this effect, and instead, like a coward, I stay silent.

"Also, I live in the apartment below you, so please, no heels in the house. This key is for the mail. Laundry is downstairs. I'll take you down there now."

I follow her down two flights of stairs into the basement, where a few washers and dryers are lined up against a blindingly bright yellow-painted cinder-block wall.

"The machines only take quarters. Also, the trash is down here." She points across the room to a corner, where I see seven or eight trash bins. "You *must* recycle. We get fined if you don't. Plastic goes in one bin, paper in another, and then food and any other garbage that can't be recycled goes in the blue one."

When the tour of the basement is over, I follow Mary back upstairs. I can hear Lucy barking from inside her apartment. Great, just my fucking luck. I finally find an apartment, and of course, it's above a super who is a bit crazy (I had quickly upgraded the agent's "interesting" and secretly nicknamed her "Mad Mary." She'd probably kill me if she knew.) with a barking dog. No wonder the agent let my dad cosign for me.

Mary goes into her apartment, and I hear her scream at Lucy to "shut the fuck up" just before the door slams shut.

I walk back up the stairs and into my empty apartment, letting the door with no lock close behind me. I stand in the living room for a moment, looking around and thinking how much smaller the place is than I remembered. My visions of a grand foyer, a dining area, and a large bedroom have been instantly squashed. Why did I remember this place being so much bigger? Have I let my infatuation blur my reality yet again?

I'm sitting in my empty apartment, using up my data plan because the internet guy doesn't come until tomorrow, when I realize it's noon, which means the movers are an hour late. I call to see what the holdup is. The line is busy. I dial again. Still busy. I wait a few minutes and try again. A woman answers.

"Hi, I'm calling to check on the status of my movers who are scheduled today."

She asks for my confirmation number, and I read it to her. "Hold, please." I can hear her talking to a coworker about my reservation number. "Ma'am, your move has been delayed due to bad weather."

"Excuse me?"

"I said your move has been delayed due to bad weather."

"No I heard you, but what do you mean?"

"Looks like there's a snowstorm, and so the movers are delayed."

"Okay. So what time should I expect them?"

"Hold on. Let me call the driver." I'm on hold for a solid three minutes before she comes back on the line. "It's delayed by two days."

"Two days!"

"Yes, the movers are in Virginia, but there's bad weather, so hopefully they'll be there in a couple of days."

"Ummm, why didn't anyone bother to tell me this?"

"You should have received a call."

"Well, I didn't."

"Well, you should have."

"Well, I didn't. Do you have a supervisor?"

"I *am* the supervisor."

"Well, again, I didn't get a call. What am I supposed to do? I'm at my apartment right now!" I'm frantic and on the brink of tears.

"There is nothing they can do. There's a snowstorm. Do you want me to cancel?"

"Cancel? You just said they're in Virginia. They have all of my furniture with them. I can't just cancel. What happens to my stuff?"

"Well, if you're unhappy with your service, I can cancel it, and you can hire a different moving company."

"Are you serious?"

"Yes, you are more than welcome to cancel."

"No! I don't want to cancel. I want my furniture!"

I'm audibly crying now, which sparks enough sympathy from the woman to turn her bitchy tone into a softer more apologetic one. "Well, I'm sorry. How about this? I can give you a call tomorrow and give you an update."

I hang up the phone and my crying turns into a full-blown wail as I realize there is absolutely nothing I can do to get my furniture here. There is no amount of sweet-talking, eyelash batting, or money throwing that will solve this dilemma. There is no way I'm getting my way on this one. I am simply shit out of luck.

And that shit luck has me now searching Travelocity for the nearest hotel to stay in. I realize my luck has just become even shittier (if that's even possible) when the cheapest hotel within walking distance is four hundred fifty dollars a night. I can't do it. I immediately go into survival mode. Something I have to say I'm not terrible at. What I lack in emotional strength, I've always made up for with instinct. Growing up my sister and I used to play this game we called "Zombie Apocalypse." Basically, you choose who in your life you'd want by your side if the world was coming to an end and you needed to survive. You could also play this along the lines of being stranded on a desert island if you're less morbid than we are. My sister always says that she would choose me, and I usually rack my brain trying to think whom I'd choose, but I always come up with the same answer: myself. I figure everybody I know, including my sister, whom I love dearly, would just slow me down. I'm actually glad my answer is myself, because right now, that's all I've got. Me, myself, and no furniture.

I look up the closest Bed Bath & Beyond and call to see if they have any air mattresses in stock. They do! "Can you please put one on hold for me? I'll be there soon," I beg the operator.

Of course, before I can be there soon, I must climb down the fucking fire escape. Careful not to slip, I make my way down it and walk the seven blocks in the freezing cold to Bed Bath & Beyond, where I'm delighted to see they've put a full-size air mattress on hold for me. I put it in a cart, along with a set of sheets, a blanket, two cheap bath towels, one pillow, and a four-pack of toilet paper. One hundred eighty-four dollars later, I'm trekking back to Perry Street with my new bed. On the way, I stop at a place on the corner to pick up a bottle of Cabernet and a corkscrew (since I know that's in a box somewhere along with my furniture). My arms are exhausted as I make my way through the basement/laundry room. I drop the bags on the pavement at the bottom of the fire escape. I haul the first load up the escape, through the window and into the empty living room. I make my way back down, hauling another two loads back up. When I'm finally done hauling, I close the window behind me and open the bottle of wine. I order food from the closest Chinese restaurant with decent Yelp ratings and begin blowing up my new air mattress. I have no furniture, no kitchen appliances, no nothing.

It's halfway comical and halfway pathetic; I'm sitting on an air mattress in a bare apartment that I can barely afford, eating sesame chicken in between sips of wine, as I plow through my data so I can stream the latest episode of *Scandal*. It's déjà vu. Barely a month ago, I was doing this exact same thing as I attempted to mend my broken heart. This time, though, I'm not sprawled out on a plush Tempur-Pedic queen bed at Kelly's house but in a glorified cell of solitary confinement. And while I knew this wasn't going to be all rainbows and sunshine, I didn't know it was going to be a goddamn tornado. Mr. Perry is just like every other man I've had in my life. From the outside, they look good, but once you find your way inside, you see it was all just one big facade.

My luck seems to be coming and going in waves. And it doesn't stop when my furniture finally does arrive. When the movers can't get the couch through the door, I'm reminded just how small my apartment is. They try to jam it in every which way they can, but despite their valiant efforts, there is no hope. Apparently, this whole couch-not-fitting-through-the-door situation isn't abnormal in New York. In fact, it's common enough that one of the movers gives me a business card for a company named "The Couch Doctor." While they continue moving the rest of my furniture in, I call the number on the card. A lady answers the phone and quotes me a rate of six hundred fifty dollars, which is more than the outdated couch cost in the first place, so I decide to toss it.

Well, first I go downstairs and knock on Mary's door. She opens it just enough for me to see only one of her crazy eyes. *The Price Is Right* is playing in the background, and she seems in no mood to talk, so I cut to the chase.

"My friend wants to know what she should do if her couch doesn't fit through her door."

Mary doesn't take the hypothetical bait. "Tell your movers to put it on the curb. Someone will pick it up."

She closes the door before I can say a word, and for two straight days, through rain and cold, my old couch sits outside on the curb of Perry Street, until one day it simply vanishes. And when it does, I can't help but hope it takes my bad luck with it.

a pulitzer and a hooker

Though my move in was a complete and utter disaster, my luck is trending up this week. Actually, this week is the best one I've had since moving here. Hell, it's the best week I've had in a very, very long time. As it turns out, that one random phone call from a literary agent led to me writing and finishing a proposal, which led to the agent liking it enough to take a meeting with me and sign me as her client. She pitched my proposal to the "Big Six" publishers, who-ever they are, and to my surprise, *five* of them were actually interested. So my agent set up a two-day book-shopping spree where we met with each of the five publisher teams. Some were more enthusiastic than others. Some had their shit together more than others. And some, I think just wanted to meet a former "Bachelorette," so they could tell their friends about it. And in the end, the publisher I really liked came out as the highest bidder. Yes, just like that, I am happy to report that I am officially . . . employed. Though I'm sure writing a book won't be as easy as it sounds, I can't bring myself to think about the daunting task just yet. I'm on too much of a high. I need to celebrate! I need to *shop*. I need Bloomingdales, Aritzia, AllSaints. I need to walk to Soho.

Well, that was the plan, at least. Instead, I found myself having made the fatal mistake of walking down Bleecker Street, home to all the high-end luxury designers that use their storefronts not for revenue but for advertising. And as I'm strolling, I see *it*. There in the window of Burberry, draped over a white mannequin, is the most beautiful black peacoat I've ever laid eyes on. I need it. I *deserve* it. Seven hundred and fifty dollars later, I am toting an obnoxiously large brown bag with a gold Burberry label on it. I know I can't afford to go to Soho now, but I still crave just a little more celebration. Enter . . . a cute little wine shop on Hudson. After all, what's a celebration without wine? As I meander through the store, I am desperately trying to avoid knocking over any bottles with my enormous Burberry bag, when from beneath the register, out pops a short elderly man.

"Hi there! Can I help you with anything?"

"Hello. Just looking for a nice bottle of Cab."

"Cab, during daylight?" He pauses. "My kind of girl! Follow me."

He leads me toward the back of the store, where endless bottles of red wine sit atop wooden shelves. We start talking about wine, what we do and do not like, what's a rip-off and what's not, blah, blah, blah.

"I'm Antonio, by the way." Antonio is flamboyant, most definitely gay, and seems like one of those "queens of the West Village."

"Andi. Nice to meet you."

"Okay, I'm dyyyiinng! What's in the bag?"

I proudly untie the dark green ribbon, unzip the tan garment bag, and pull out my new peacoat.

Antonio eyes it approvingly. "Fabulous. Classic, but the collar gives it some edge. I knew I liked you." He strokes the wool up and down as I preen. "Do you want to try out some wines that I just got?"

"Ummm, yes. Don't threaten me with a good time."

Our shared affection for Burberry and good wine mean that after an hour, I am still in the wine shop, teetering on the verge of drunkenness. It is the most randomly perfect celebration a new author could ask for.

"Goodbye, my new favorite Village girl!" Antonio shouts as I walk out the door.

" 'Bye! See you soon!"

I find myself walking home with a sense of glee that I have not felt since moving here. I realize that Antonio has just given me my first compliment as a New Yorker. A *Village girl*, I think to myself. He's right.

Little does Antonio know that I still can't navigate the streets of my own neighborhood without getting lost. It's not entirely my fault though. I quickly discovered that Manhattan is made up of avenues that run north and south and numbered streets that run east and west. I even made up my own helpful rule that odd avenues go south, evens go north, odd streets go west, evens go east. I think it's right; at least, so far it is.

However, these rules of the road don't apply to the West Village. It turns out my neighborhood is "off the grid," meaning instead of adhering to a sensible layout like every other neighborhood, the streets here make no sense at all. It's as if someone decided to just fuck with everyone and start paving roads that zig and zag, split and merge, and randomly turn into different streets for absolutely no reason. Hudson *Street* technically should be an avenue because it runs north, but it's not. Bleecker Street is parallel to Hudson, so it, too, should be an avenue, but of course, it isn't. Instead, it runs diagonally through the Village before eventually turning *into* Hudson, which I think at some point does, in fact, turn into an avenue. Eighth, I think? Which makes me wonder why the hell it just isn't Eighth Avenue in the first place. The cross streets are just as fucked up. Instead of the numbering system, these streets are named; there's Christopher, Perry, Charles, Barrow, Morton, and so on. I blame this entire clusterfuck on whatever rich white dude probably developed the neighborhood and decided not only to be difficult but also to name every street after his rich white friends. Other than occasionally screaming at my GPS, I'm really loving the area. It's got this friendly vibe to it that you wouldn't expect in New York mixed with an unfriendly attitude that's completely expected.

I'm definitely not in the South anymore. That's pretty evident by the size of my apartment, which is more like a jewelry box than a shoebox. But, I must say, now that I've bought a new couch and painted a few accent walls, I find it to be small but charming. Yeah, around here, everyone seems to live, work, walk, and breathe on top of one another. Well, everyone except the people in the brownstone directly across from my bedroom window. Instead of the building housing tenants like me who live in one of four apartments on each of five floors, the whole thing is occupied by one family: a mom, a dad, two young girls, a toddler boy, a chef, two nannies, a housekeeper, and a gardener. Apparently, the home used to belong to a movie star couple before they got divorced and sold it. I often hear the kids playing in the six-by-six-foot backyard by day and occasionally stare into their kitchen at night. Not in a creepy way. I really just like watching the chef cook nightly dinners in the pristine white-marble kitchen that boasts an island and a custom black and gold Viking stove. Okay, maybe I am creepy, but it's not like I watch the family eat dinner; I just watch the chef prepare it.

And with small spaces come loud sounds. I can hear *everything* that *everyone* does. There's a dog that barks at least once a week at precisely seven o'clock in the morning because someone let it out but forgot to let it in. Someone from another apartment usually yells, "Hey, asshole, let your dog back in!" and the barking stops. A noise that doesn't stop, however, is the moaning and groaning and "Yeah, Daddy" and "Oh, yes, baby" that come from some chick who, based on the decibel level, must live in or very close to my building. Whenever I open a window, at any time of day or night, there is a seventy-five percent chance that I will hear this woman having sex. She's not doing it alone, either. I can hear a man's groans, too, though they aren't nearly as loud as hers. I think she's a hooker.

She has sex morning, noon, and night. The same woman, the same sounds. All the damn time! Who the fuck yells *that* much *that* loudly during sex *that* often? Hookers. That's who.

And I'm not so quiet myself, at least not according to Mad Mary. She happens to be a stickler for this "eighty percent carpet rule," which, according to her, is in my lease and requires eighty percent of my apartment to be covered by rugs. She's already reiterated this rule upon two separate occasions when she came upstairs to yell at me for dropping something. One night, I dropped a brand-new Jo Malone candle straight from the box. Before I could even sweep up the shattered glass, an aggressive knock is beating on my door.

"What the hell was that noise?" shouts Mad Mary.

"Sorry, I just dropped a brand-new candle on the floor, and it broke."

"I don't care what you dropped, it woke me up!"

I contemplated explaining the magnitude of dropping a brand-new overly priced candle, but I didn't think she was the candle-loving type who would understand.

"You are always dropping stuff, and it is always waking me up."

"I'm sorry, it's not like I mean to. Plus, your dog is always barking early in the morning, waking me up. You don't see me banging on your door, do you? It's New York, what do you expect?"

Instead of answering, she poked her head into my apartment. "And you know what I said about eighty percent of the apartment has to be carpeted."

"I ordered rugs, okay! They're on their way. Good night." I closed the door, feeling like a real New Yorker now that I'd somewhat stood up for myself against the self-proclaimed mayor of Perry Street.

Luckily, Mad Mary is not one to hold on to a grudge. I learned this the following day when I saw her in the basement when I was taking out the trash, and she acted as if our fight the previous night had never even happened. That's the thing I've learned when it comes to New Yorkers; they are confrontational as hell, but they say what they want and then they're over it.

Though I don't think this mini tenant-super war is over just yet. She's also a snoop. Yesterday she yelled at me for throwing my container of soy milk into the trash bin and not the recycling one.

"How do you even know it was me?" Even though I knew it was me.

"Because I can tell everyone's trash. Like this . . ." She walked a few feet over to her storage unit. "I know this belongs to that girl upstairs." She was waving around a light blue dildo. Yup, definitely a hooker living in my building.

But as annoying as the sounds and lack of space and even Mad Mary might be, there's something hypnotic about it all. There's something so melting-pot-ish and enthralling about this city. So many people living on the same block, sharing the same streets, but leading such different lives. All with their own stories to tell, their own reasons for being here, their own lives. And for the first time, I feel like I have my own, too. After all the disastrous apartment viewings and move-in mishaps, I finally feel like I made the right decision moving here. I have a job, I have an apartment, and I have the beginnings of a new life. And though I don't have a man, I find myself living blissfully. I take pleasure in the oddest moments. Like when I flip my hair as I cross Seventh Avenue or randomly but naturally drop an f-bomb mid-conversation. I smile every time I see tourists taking photos, because I realize I'm living in a city so special that people from all over the world come to visit. I'm actually here. Could it be that a girl from the South who bought a one-way ticket thanks to a broken heart is actually beginning to morph into a true New Yorker?

a new number one?

Not only did I begin writing the first chapter of my book this week, but I've also begun the first chapter of my new life as a single woman. It all started with another first: my first subway ride—which I'm pretty sure is also going to be my last. It's all Michelle's fault . . . *all* of it.

First, she invited me to come have dinner with her and her boyfriend, Pete, at their place uptown. They get to live there because they are a couple, unlike me. I called Michelle to get directions to her place via the ominous subway that both terrifies me and intrigues me. It just feels like such a native New Yorky thing to do. I've heard everyone takes the subway and that sometimes you can even spot celebrities on your train.

"Just take the one to Seventy-Second Street, then follow your map with the address I'm about to text you." She makes it sound so easy.

"Do I need to purchase a ticket ahead of time?"

This makes her laugh. "You're hilarious. Yes, buy a card at the station on Fourteenth. You'll see the stand; you can't miss it."

Later that evening, I walk a few blocks to the corner of Fourteenth Street and Seventh Avenue, where, just like Michelle said, a staircase leads to the station below. I see the kiosk she was talking about and walk over to it. I press "Start" and proudly select the option "Buy a Card." I add forty dollars to it, and a credit-card swipe later, I have my first yellow "MTA" card. I take a minute to observe the other passengers as they swipe their cards and then promptly push through the large metal rotating door. Swipe, then push—next—swipe then push—easy enough. I walk to the turnstile, where I follow suit and swipe my own card. A green light goes off, and the reader indicates my new balance of $37.25. I push through the turnstile, but it resists. Fuck, which way does the turnstile thing go? Fuck, now a red light is blinking, and there's a beeping sound going off. I'm trapped. Fuck, fuck, fuck! Someone is yelling "C'mon!" behind me, I don't know what is happening! I swiped it, it was green, it should be letting me through. I reach my hand back and furiously swipe my card a few more times, I keep pushing, but it's not letting me through. I swipe again and try to push the other way. Finally, I break free.

Traumatized and having just spent more money on all those swipes than an Uber would have cost me, I follow the signs and make my way to the platform. It isn't long before I see a train speeding toward me with a red digital circle and the number 1 on the front. I step onto the train and take a seat. It smells as if someone has just urinated nearby. Everyone looks grumpy. People aren't singing and asking for money, nor are they talking to the people beside them. I definitely don't see any celebrities. This is nothing like I imagined.

Upon arriving at Michelle's, I immediately wash my hands, despite having doused them with half a bottle of hand sanitizer already. She asks how my first ride went, and I tell her how disgusting I feel and that it will be both my first and my last time ever taking the subway.

"Yeah, we'll see about that," she challenges.

Michelle has not only cooked a nice dinner of chicken, steamed broccoli, mixed green salad, and wild rice and orzo, but she's also set the table with real silverware and floral linen napkins. I don't know if it's New York or her boyfriend, but something has turned her from the partying train wreck I once knew into a gourmet chef who owns real napkins. Who would have thought?

Pete gets home from work shortly after my arrival. He drops his briefcase on the couch, and Michelle immediately walks over and moves it to the table in the entryway.

Without saying a word, he grabs a beer out of the fridge, pops the top, and takes a gulp. "So Michelle tells me you are friends from Atlanta?"

"Yeah, from back in the day." I'm trying to give him the benefit of the doubt but so far his first impression isn't a great one and my semi-disgusted tone probably makes that obvious.

"Nice, and you've just moved to the city?"

"Yeah, bought a one-way ticket, and here I am."

"How are you liking it?"

Before I can answer, Michelle interrupts to say that dinner is ready. We take our seats around a round glass table. At some point after talking about the vast differences between Atlanta and New York, the conversation turns to the topic of dating.

"Okay, don't get mad at me," Michelle says, "but I have a great guy I want to set you up with!" She's annoyingly excited.

I take a large gulp of wine. "Like as in a date?"

"Well, yeah!"

The look on my face sends her into a two-minute monologue of profuse apology. She fears she's overstepped and feels terrible for assuming I was ready to get back into the dating game and can't believe how she could be so insensitive.

I can't help but laugh. "No, it's not that at all."

"Oh, whew! So what do you think?"

"Ehhhhh, who is he?"

"He works with me," Pete says, "but I don't really know him that well. He just started, but he seems cool." From the chugging of the beer upon his arrival home to the simple description of this guy, it's obvious that Pete is very much a dude-ly dude.

"He's very, very cute," Michelle adds.

"Cute or hot?" I need clarification.

She looks at Pete. "He's hot," he admits.

"Hmmm, I don't know," I say. "I'm not sure if I feel like going on a blind date."

"I think it would be good for you, Andi. I know you don't *need* a man, but you never know. You could meet him and it's great, or he's not the guy for you and you find yourself right back where you are now."

She has a point.

"Come on, do it for me! Pleeaaase?"

"Ughhhh. I don't know. A finance guy? I've heard about them." I say it in a way that makes it clear what I've heard about them is not particularly glowing.

"Hey, now."

Shit, I forgot Pete is in finance. "You're different."

Truth is, I really don't know much about New York finance guys or if Pete's really different from them. All I know is they have a reputation for being assholes, and apparently ninety-nine percent of them are pompous douchebags with nothing but a pocket full of money and a superiority complex. They're the kinds of guys who've never had to struggle in life, the rich kids, quarterbacks on the high school team, who go on to become rich frat brothers wearing seersucker suits and Costa sunglasses to college football games, only to become the even richer kids living in penthouses in Tribeca next door to celebrities like Beyoncé and wearing tailored Hugo Boss suits and Ferragamo loafers. Actually, I'm not sure that Pete is really different from them, except that he lives on the Upper West Side and has a girlfriend. But, given the fact that he's the boyfriend of my only friend here, I need to give him some leeway.

As Michelle continues to beg me to accept, I realize I'm not going to hear the end of it unless I agree. Plus, I'm thinking I should find a man soon to help me change some lightbulbs and hang the rest of my picture frames on the walls. But knowing that if I outright say yes I'll feel obligated to actually go out with the guy, I decide instead to compromise and tell her that I will definitely think about it. This leads her to do a celebratory fist pump. God, I love her.

Then, two days later, I get a text from a 917 number I don't recognize. The texter introduces himself as Ryan, Pete and Michelle's friend, and asks me how my Friday looks to grab dinner or drinks. Fucking Michelle, I'm going to kill her. I'm reluctant to respond. Do I really want this? It's been a while since I was blithely dating twenty-six men on national television. Am I really ready to start all over again?

I ponder for a few hours before I send a text back, and tell him Friday will be good. He tells me he has to go to a happy hour event after he gets off work but that he can meet me for dinner as soon as he's done. We make plans to meet at eight o'clock at a restaurant I've never been to called Bell Book & Candle. And just like that, here goes nothing.

Fast-forward to seven o'clock, and I'm demolishing my closet in an attempt to find the perfect outfit for my first real date as a New Yorker with my new Number One. Hell, it's my first real date since being engaged. Yikes, that stings a little bit. It's not that I haven't had the opportunity—well, I haven't, really—but that isn't what has me in a tizzy. When it comes down to it, I absolutely despise first dates. If I could somehow magically land a man without having to go on another first date for the rest of my life, I'd give up wine. (Just kidding, I'd never do that. But I would be forever grateful.)

Long ago, in my early twenties, I didn't mind dates so much

because they meant a free meal. I put up with some brutal Friday nights just to get a complimentary buzz and a juicy medium-rare steak. Maybe it's because I can afford my own food and booze these days that I don't feel those sentiments anymore. Or perhaps it's the fact that I went on twenty-six first dates on national television. Whatever the case, I despise first dates. They rarely lead to anything, and they're just so damn awkward. I never really know how to act when I'm on a first date. Like every other single woman, I've read the dozens of advice columns that talk about the dos and don'ts of first dates, but I'm still flustered. Some say a kiss is appropriate, some say it's not. Some say not to talk about this or that, some say talk about whatever you want. Personally, I prefer transparency, because I figure sooner or later, if he makes the cut, he's going to figure out the real me anyway. Then again, maybe that's why I'm still single.

Perhaps the worst part about first dates is the shallowest part: picking the outfit. Men have it so easy; they throw on a pair of pants and a shirt and they're done, while we women have to put in all the effort, as usual. It's bullshit. This outfit conundrum is clearly evidenced by the pile of clothes mounting on my closet floor. Nothing looks good on me, I have no idea how dressy this restaurant is, how tall or short he is, what style he likes. Fuck, why is dressing for a date so difficult? It shouldn't be. I feel like when it comes to style, there are essentially three looks. Number one is the no-makeup, yoga-pants, just-rolled-out-of-bed look. Men seem to love this one, especially when you're rolling out of *their* bed, but it's not first-date appropriate. Then there's look number two, with maybe some foundation, eyeliner, mascara, and jeans. Good for a Saturday stroll, but if you wear this on a first date, your second date is bound to be somewhere as mundane as your look. And finally, there is the dressed-to-the-nines, red-carpet, full-hair-and-makeup, Momma-is-ready-to-get-her-some look. Obviously, category three makes you look like you give too much of a shit. Plus, it sets him up for unrealistic expectations of what you *won't* be looking like come morning.

In addition to categorizing looks, I have this "rule of seven" when it comes to dressing for dates. Basically, it is the only time in my life where, on a scale of one to ten, I allow myself to publicly look like a seven. This ensures that I put some effort in but not too much and that I was neither overdressed nor underdressed. However, that rule doesn't seem to be solving my current issue. So I pour a glass of wine, take my phone off the charger, and look up "date-night outfits" on Pinterest. As I scroll, one outfit catches my eye: black leather leggings, a white top, and a moto jacket. *I have all three*, I think to myself. I dig in the pile of clothes on my closet floor and find the leather leggings I already tried on, then put on a white top and my black Joie leather jacket that I got a week ago at a sample sale and, of course, my new Burberry wool coat. I take a look in my full-length mirror and decide this will do. The clock says it's five after eight, which means I guess I'll pack my clutch and start heading over to the restaurant, which is only a few blocks away. I'll be about ten minutes late, which I think is appropriate but not offensive for a first date.

When I arrive, I check in with the hostess, who tells me the other person in my party isn't here yet but offers me a spot at the bar. Apparently, fashionably late is a gender-neutral thing in New York. It's now twenty minutes past eight, and I'm dying to order a glass of wine, but I don't want the first time this guy sees me to be with alcohol in my hand. Although at least it would give him a preview of what life with me is really like. I decide instead to text him.

"Hey, just got to the restaurant, what's your status?" I lie so I won't seem desperate. Three minutes of wondering if I'm getting stood up go by before my phone chimes.

It's him. "Oh, shit, totally got stuck at this work thing. I'm leaving now and headed to meet you."

"Oh, no worries. Do you want to reschedule?"

"Nah, I'll be there in five."

Ummm, okay. What the fuck?

Fifteen fucking minutes later, I get a tap on my shoulder. "Andi?"

"Yes?"

A tall, blond-haired, brown-eyed man reaches out his hand and shakes mine. Pete was right, he's hot. His tailored navy suit, sans tie, has me feeling way underdressed. Shit, he's *really* hot. But he also *really* smells like booze. Strike one. We've barely said five words to each another, and already I feel that I might be secondhand drunk off his breath. I follow him to the hostess stand, taking note of his great ass. The hostess brings us to a table along the wall and without hesitation, he takes the banquette, leaving me to sit in the wooden chair. Strike fucking two.

"So. How was your day?" he says after I've taken my uncomfortable seat.

And for the first time, I actually see his full face. His eyes are barely open but appear to be bloodshot. He keeps sniffling. Something is going on, and it's more than him being a little tipsy. The waitress comes over and asks if we'd like something to drink. He looks up and orders tequila on the rocks. And that's when I see his nostrils. Oh. My. God. They have remnants of white powder around them. Holy fuck, this guy is not only drunk, he's drunk *and* high on cocaine.

After ordering a glass of wine, I try to ignore the fact that I'm on a date with a drunk, coked-out, tardy asshole who took the good seat. I ask what he does for a living. Cue the slurring as he goes on and on about hedge funds. Wall Street, banking, business school— the buzzwords start to nauseate me. My drink has come, thank God. As he continues on and on about his pretentious career, I start to play a drinking game with myself: every time he says the word "million," I will drink. I'm almost done with my first glass, and we haven't even ordered the entrée, when in walks an obstacle.

"Hey, you!" a female voice shouts from behind me.

His eyes light up as he stands. I turn around to see the voice is coming from the slender blond bartender who kept asking me if I wanted a drink while I was waiting. He gives her a hug, and they start to have a full-blown conversation with each other above me as if I'm not sitting below. I can hear the tone; it's more than friendly. They definitely have a past. And from the look and sound of it, that past is still very much part of the present. A few minutes and no introduction later, she disappears.

"Friend of yours?" I ask.

"Yeah, we dated, not gonna lie."

He's too drunk even to notice the shift in my demeanor. We continue talking, but within minutes, he excuses himself to go to the bathroom. A few more minutes pass, and he has yet to return. I've ordered my second glass of wine. When I turn around to see him not standing in line for the bathroom but standing at the bar talking to the blonde. He's flirting with her. She's laughing. He's laughing. They are laughing together. They're taking a shot together.

He heads back to the table and immediately pulls out his phone. The meal arrives, but he doesn't notice. How could he? His eyes have yet to leave his phone. A smirk has made its way to his face, right below his coked-out nostrils. Suspicious, I turn around. The bartender is on her phone, too, the light of the screen spot-lighting the grin across her face. I look back at him and back at her. Back at him, back at her. Holy shit, now they're not just flirting in front of me, they're texting in front of me! He's literally texting on our date . . . with the fucking bartender. The entire situation is part horror, part comedy. Is this really happening? Is this really how my dating career in New York City starts?

I can't stand to be here any longer. I've barely touched my meal when I lie and say, "I'm not feeling great. Would you mind if we call it a night?"

He looks up from his phone. "Oh, no worries. Do you want me to walk you out?"

"Sure. Should we get the check?"

"No, I'll just come back in and pay it."

I stand up and tell him it was nice to meet him and that I can walk myself out. I don't even bother being polite by giving him a hug or telling him thanks for the worst three glasses of wine of my life. He's so drunk he won't remember anyway. Plus, I am one hundred percent certain he's going home with the bartender tonight.

As I walk the few blocks home, alone, I text Michelle. "Your ass is grass. Call me in the morning."

ménage à nah

Not only have I never done a threesome, but in twenty-eight years on this earth, no one has ever even asked me to participate in one. That is, until this weekend. I don't know whether to be proud, mortified, perplexed, or all of the above. And the way it went down (pun intended) makes it even more . . . even more . . . I don't even know what it makes it, honestly. Then again, based on the worst first date in history, I don't think I really know what to say when it comes to men or threesomes for that matter.

Flashback to how this all came about. Long story short, I'd been invited by a charity event on an all-expenses-paid trip for me and a plus-one to attend the Kentucky Derby. Now, I get that everyone knows how legendary this event is, but you have to understand, to a Southerner like myself, the Kentucky Derby is more than legendary— it's the mecca of sporting events, the once-in-a-lifetime-if-you're-lucky, must-do-before-you-die event. And now here I was, getting my chance to go for the very first time and for free. I couldn't wait to sip mint juleps by day and attend the legendary parties by night.

I'd bought myself a tacky black wide-brimmed hat, which I adorned with a DIY brooch that was really just a cluster of peacock feathers and pearls that I'd found at a store in the Garment District and hot-glued together. And although I didn't have a hot guy in a seersucker suit as my plus-one, I had something better: my child-hood friend Kristen.

Kristen is the type of woman who is hard to describe in words alone. She was always the "developed" girl growing up; she got boobs before anyone else did, got highlights before anyone else did, had sex before anyone else did, even got her belly button pierced before anyone else did. After college, she moved to Los Angeles, which was no surprise to anyone. She belonged there and nowhere else. She's the kind of woman who has no qualms about saying what is on her mind, regardless of how politically incorrect it is certain to be. When she walks into a room, she owns it, and you want to hate her for it, but you don't. Probably because she's the type of woman who is hot but in a messy kind of way. Basically, the only thing you know for certain you'll be getting when it comes to Kristen is guaranteed entertainment.

So, with my hat packed in a round box, I find myself in the Louisville airport, where I'm greeted at the baggage claim by a pe-tite lady who introduces herself as Katherine, a member of the board of directors for the charity that was hosting me. Beside her stands a tall, young, blond stud of a police officer, whom she introduces as Officer Stone, my "escort for the weekend."

Yes, he sure will be, I thought silently as I scanned him from head to toe, checking out his equipment (gun and baton, of course). Yummy! Check, check, and—*there* it is, the fatal flaw. A shiny gold ring on the wedding finger. Dammit. One piece of jewelry, and instantly his stock plummeted. It's amazing how that can happen. I know some men say a wedding band actually makes women want them more, but I think that's just their egos talking. There is no single bigger turnoff for me than a man in a relationship. It's just not my thing, never has been, never will be. I'd like to say it's based solely on my morals, but I'm not gonna lie, it's also based on prac-ticality. I just think with plenty of men in the sea, why would I need one who comes with the drama of a wife or a girlfriend *and* the moral hangover? But married or not, having my very own police escort for the weekend had me feeling like a badass. Plus, I was pretty sure this was my automatic get-out-of-jail-free card for the weekend, right?

A short drive later, and hunky, married Officer Stone and Katherine are escorting me to my room. Katherine reaches into the gift bag on my bed and reads from a printed itinerary of the weekend plans, which consist of a gala, some optional after-parties, the Derby, and a party to watch some big boxing match between two guys I'd never heard of.

After they leave, I spend the next few hours relaxing until I hear a knock on my door. It's Kristen. She hugs me as she delivers two air kisses on each cheek while saying, "Mwah, mwah, so good to see you, dahhhhling." Immediately she spots the gift bag and begins rifling through it. I'm doing my mascara when I hear her pop a champagne bottle she must have found in the bag. I swear, I think Kristen has a sixth sense for finding alcohol.

"Tell me everything! How's New York? You look so skinny! Are the men hot? You look so skinny! Can you tell I got my lips done? Do they look too big? Where are we partying tonight?"

Her lips were enormous! Like she'd come straight out of a goddamn cartoon. But I couldn't tell her this. I mean it wasn't like it was a bad shade of lipstick that she could just blot off. No, it was going to take a lot more than some tissue to blot out whatever the fuck had been injected in there. So, instead, I told her they looked great and read off the itinerary. In between sips of champagne, she approved with her trademark "Amazeballs!"

We are both all dolled up as we make our way down to the lobby, where Officer Stone is waiting for us. Kristen gives him two air kisses and then takes a step back. She blatantly checks him out while saying "Mmm-hmmm" and "Yassss." If we were in a work environment, Kristen would have just earned her first of many sexual-harassment complaints.

We are escorted to the ballroom, where the gala was being hosted, and to our table. I'm seated between Kristen and a particularly petite man who I assume to be a jockey when suddenly, I feel a tap on my shoulder.

"Heeeeeyyyyyyy, you!"

It's Sarah Hyland from *Modern Family*. I'd met her about a year ago at the Billboard Music Awards, but I didn't think she'd actually remember me. And if she did, I would have expected her to be like most celebrities who pretend never to have met you before.

"Hey, girl!" I say back as we hug each other.

We chat for a little bit, I introduce her to Kristen, and Sarah introduces me to a gal pal who was her plus-one.

The gala officially is in full swing once the host takes the stage and begins doing some presentations and introductions of who I assume to be important people. My stomach is rumbling as I look at the empty plates. A server comes around with a bread basket and places one baguette on each person's plate, which I promptly devour. Speaker after speaker, and still no sign of any food. I turn around to see the baguette untouched on the jockey's plate.

Don't do it, Andi.

He's not going to eat it. He would have done it by now.

Don't do it. Be classy.

A PowerPoint presentation began to play. Fuck me! I can't take it! I see out of the corner of my eye that the jockey is completely fixated on the presentation, so stealthily, without moving my head, I reach back with my right arm and steal his bread. A girl giggles. Shit, I'm caught. I look out of the corner of my eye to see the source of the laughter. It's a young blond woman wearing a crown. She has a sash on. It reads MISS USA. Oh, God! Miss USA just caught me stealing bread.

Cut to the next morning after we've finally eaten and proceeded to dance the night away and I am awaking from a four-hour "nap." I hop into a cold shower, dry off, and look in the mirror to see last night's mascara running down my cheeks. My head is pounding, my eyes are bloodshot, and I have what I'm pretty sure is the remnants of pizza sauce stained on the corners of my mouth. Kristen is moaning as she rolls around on what might become her deathbed. We are both train wrecks. Train wrecks in need of Gatorade. I rummage through the gift bag, only to find an empty miniature bottle of bourbon that Kristen must have drunk while I wasn't looking, along with a coozie and a plastic sleeve of Planters peanuts, none of which is going to do the job. Gift shop it is.

I throw on a hat and some sweatpants and take my hot-mess self down the hall to the elevator. The door opens. And there inside the elevator stands the most beautiful sight I'd ever laid eyes on. Fuck the Burberry peacoat, this was better. This was a tall, athletic, godlike creature straight from a dream, leaning against the wall. This was a clean shave that showed off a sharp jawline, which showed off a pair of piercing blue eyes, which for a second caused my heart to stop beating. I closed my eyes and opened them again to make sure that I was, in fact, seeing what I thought I was seeing. Yup, it was Tom fucking Brady.

"What floor?" he asks.

I go numb. I open my mouth to speak but nothing comes out. Finally, I just shake my head in defeat and say, "No idea."

He laughs. "What do you mean?" God, not only was he hot, but he was sweet, too.

"I—don't—even know."

He'd clearly seen this reaction before, because not only was he completely unfazed by my inability to take my eyes off him, let alone form a complete sentence, but he knew exactly how to revive me.

"All right, well, let's see. What are you looking for?"

You, I want to say. "Gatorade."

He laughs again. "I see. Rough night?" I nod. "Pretty sure that's in the lobby." His forearm brushes against my shoulder as he reaches over me and presses "L."

I'm never washing this shirt ever again.

Two floors later, he gets off, leaving me alone, with wet hair, no makeup, and my hungover puffy face hidden underneath a floppy hat, wondering if my shower had been enough to wash away the scents of last night's booze and pizza. Of course, *this* would be the time I meet Tom fucking Brady. Of fucking course.

A lot of pride lost and a few hours later, we'd made our way to the racetrack, where I walked the red carpet and did some quick interviews about my excitement at being at the Derby (which was actually true, despite a raunchy headache). Officer Stone escorted us to the club level, which was a large room filled with various buffet stations and several makeshift bars along the walls. Large round tables circled the betting kiosk in the center of the room. Several balconies gave us an incredible view of the track. I soaked up the energy as I peered down at the crowds. *Ahhhh, this is the good life*, I thought to myself.

Suddenly, a shot was fired, and just like that, the horses began running down the track. *This is it! This is it! This is the Kentucky Derby!* Wait, why was no one into it? Seriously? The stands were not even halfway filled, and the cheers were so faint they were embarrassing. Seconds later, the winning horse crossed the finish line. A few more cheers but not much.

"Ummm, that was kind of anticlimactic," I said to Kristen.

"Well, it's only race number three. There's like ten more to go before the big one."

"Big one?"

"Yeah, like the actual Derby. These are just the small races before."

With that in mind, I began alternating races with trips to the bar to refill my mint julep. In fact, I think it was somewhere between mint julep numbers four and five, or perhaps even five and six, when I met a young couple from New York. He was on the shorter side, with dirty-blond hair and one of those beards so pristinely groomed that you don't quite trust the man behind it. His wife was more subtle in her appearance but beautiful nonetheless. Taller than he was, she wore a tight black dress that revealed her ample cleavage. Her minimal makeup complemented her wavy brown locks. The total effect was one of effortless sophistication that also oozed sex appeal. They immediately give a bio of themselves: married for six years, no children, split time living in New York City and Malibu.

"Do you have a boyfriend?" the husband asks me but not Kristen, who was standing right next to me.

"No way!" I laughed.

"Really? A beautiful girl like you is single? That's hard to believe."

Umm, okay, that's a little weird considering his wife is next to him. But there was no way he was hitting on me, right? It's not until later when I find myself standing among some guests that shit really starts to get weird.

The husband comes and stands right next to me while I'm listening to a guy in a seersucker suit (of course) tell us a story about bourbon (of course). His wife is nowhere in sight.

"You *really* are beautiful," he whispers creepily into my ear.

It's confirmed: he's hitting on me.

"Thank you." I cringe and take a small step away from him.

Moments later, his wife joins the conversation (thank God). We begin talking about fashion and our favorite places in New York. She seems completely normal, unlike her husband.

"We should get together in the city," she says.

I lie and say, "Definitely."

Then she asks me when I'm heading back to New York.

"I fly back tomorrow, you?"

"So are we. What time?"

"Oh, I've got a layover in Atlanta because there weren't any other options."

"Oh, that doesn't sound very fun."

"I know. The things you endure to come to the Derby." I chuckle.

"True." She giggles. "Wait a second, why don't you just fly back with us? We have a plane and extra seats."

"Oh, no, thank you, but that's too kind. I can't."

"Seriously, we are more than happy to give you a ride. We can drop you off on our way into the city." She said it so damn casually it was as if she was just splitting an Uber with me.

"Are you sure? I don't want to impose."

"No, really, I insist. What hotel are you at?"

And just like that, my layover turned into a direct flight . . . on a private jet. Sure, it was a little strange, but I'd been in New York long enough to know (a) people here have money, money, money, money, (b) people here like to spend their money, and (c) when you have money, you don't fly commercial. Plus, I already seemed like a badass thanks to Officer Stone's escort; why not add a private jet ride?

Later that evening, I get a text from the wife asking me for my date of birth, weight, and number of bags I had. I turn to Kristen to tell her that the weird couple at our table offered me a ride home on their private jet.

"That's fab!" Kristen exclaims.

"Yeah, but I don't know. Was it just me, or did you—"

"Get a weird vibe?" she interrupted. "Oh, for sure. Probably swingers."

"You think?"

"One hundred percent. But fuck it, a private jet is a private jet."

She was right. I reply to the text: "April 3, 1987. 115 pounds. 2 bags." (The weight part might have been a little bit of a lie.)

She immediately replies, telling me to meet in the lobby at noon. I turn to Kristen to ask her what to do when you get invited on a jet. I'd never been in this situation before, but I was all but certain Kristen had been. Should I be offering to pay for this? If they had a jet, they certainly didn't need my money, but my mother would kill me if she knew I didn't offer to pay for something. That's very much outside the Southern code of conduct. But then again, what if I offer and they take me up on it? I can hardly afford my rent; a private jet would be the end of me. Kristen reassures me that I don't need to offer to pay, nor do I need to feel anything but bad-ass about the entire situation, which, like I assumed, she's been in a number of times herself.

The following day, I nervously meet them in the lobby as planned. We walk to the front of the hotel and into a waiting Cadillac. We'd barely reached the highway when the wife turns around from the passenger seat and asks me, "So, just out of curiosity, are you into threesomes?"

"Huh?"

"Sorry, that's probably forward, but we are both *very* open and nonjudgmental, aren't we, babe?" She strokes the back of her husband's neck.

He looks in the rearview mirror at me. "Have you ever tried it?"

What the fuck! What the fuck! What the fuuuuuccckk! Think, Andi, think. If I tell the truth and say no, they're probably going to ask me why not and tell me I should try it. If I lie and say yes, they'll either leave it at that or ask me details, at which point they might find out that I'm lying. Fuck!

I go with the most minimal lie I can muster up. "I've dabbled."

"And?" the wife asks.

"Not for me."

"Oh, well, that's too bad."

"Well, we think you're gorgeous, so if you ever did want to try it . . . " the husband chimes in.

I awkwardly thank him for the "offer."

"So is it the girl-on-girl thing you don't like or the sharing or what?" the wife asks.

"Yeah, like, would you do girl-on-girl?" he adds.

"No. Yeah. Ummmm, it's both—the girl-on-girl and the, um, the, um sharing." My mouth can hardly utter the words "girl-on-girl."

"That's too bad. I think you'd be fun," he says seductively.

Meanwhile, I'm dying in the backseat and know I need to shut this down immediately, so I try to change the subject. "So what do you do in the city?"

The two of them start talking as I hysterically text Kristen: "SOS CALL ME ASAP."

Within seconds my phone rings. "Spill. What the fuck?"

I begin a conversation with Kristen that basically consists of her asking me every question imaginable while I answer in yes or no form.

"Are they swingers?"

"Oh, yes, *absolutely*!" I say to Kristen in my most cheerful voice.

"Shut the fuck up! I knew it! You're in the car with them, aren't you?"

"I am. I can't wait—it should be great."

"God, you're good at this, almost too good. Holy fuck! This is just—this is amazeballs. You win. Okay, text me when you get to the plane. Guard that vagina!"

"Will do! I'll give you a shout when I get back to New York."

We pull up to the private hangar, where two valets take our bags and escort us to the check-in desk. I make a beeline for the bathroom and lock myself in a stall. *Think, Andi, think.* I take a seat liner and place it on the toilet seat and sit. My hands are rubbing my temples as I replay the conversation in my head. *Am I into threesomes? What the fuck!* I am panicking. *What am I going to do? I cannot for the life of me endure two and a half hours in a jet with them. What do I do? Do I abort and just make a run for it? Fuck, they already have my suitcases loaded on the plane. Do I just suck it up? I mean, after all, it really is saving me a ton of time and a layover in Atlanta. I can do this, right?*

"Time to board," the wife shouts into the bathroom.

I guess I'm doing this.

We board the jet, where I find myself sitting next to the wife. I dig in my purse and open up the magazine I'd already read on the flight over but forgot to throw out, and I pretend to read. We are just about to take off when I get a text from Kristen.

Kristen: "Holy fuck! Look up the wife's name on Google."

Me: "Can't right now I'm sitting next to her on the plane."

Kristen: "Trust me you need to."

Me: "I can't what is it?"

Kristen: "She's a Hollywood madam."

Me: "WTF! What do you mean?"

Kristen: "She sells girls as sex slaves to rich millionaires."

Me: "WHAAAAT?"

Kristen: "Oh yeah got busted a few years ago and changed her name."

Me: "Like sells them how?"

Kristen: "I don't know but just FYI."

Me: "WTF!!!!"

Kristen: "Just don't take any drinks they offer you."

Me: "WTF what do I do?"

Message failed to send.

Fuck. We are airborne now. *I'm screwed, figuratively and quite possibly literally.* Here I am, aboard a private jet bound for New York City, sitting next to a swinger and his madam wife, thinking this is how it is all going to end for me, isn't it? I am going to wind up shoved into the trunk of a car, only to wake up in a brothel somewhere in Russia where I'll be auctioned off to the highest bidder and live out the remainder of my life as a sex slave. Or the plane will crash and I will die, and nobody will even care. The headline won't read, "Former Bachelorette dead at twenty-eight in a fiery crash." No, the *New York Post* won't give a shit about me. Instead, the headline will be "Hollywood madam goes down in flames."

It's taken twenty-eight years, but now I finally understand why my mom always told me never to take rides from strangers.

a charitable act

Apparently charity events in New York City aren't just for supporting worthy causes. They're also grounds for man hunting. I'd been invited to attend an event uptown supporting the New York Police Department, my first as a New Yorker. Though I didn't expect much in the man department, other than perhaps some cute police officers, I was pleasantly surprised when I walked into the event and found it filled with good-looking men. And not just good looking, but well-dressed and well-groomed. It was as if the stock market had packed up, traveled uptown, and turned itself into a single woman's meat market. So there I am sipping my champagne when a guy comes up and introduces himself. The epitome of boyish all-American good looks, he had short salty-blond hair, pale skin, light eyes, and a freshly shaved face. I quickly learn that he isn't a stockbroker but rather a writer, like me. An Ivy League graduate no less. And unlike the last two men I encountered, he doesn't appear to be drunk and coked out or interested in a threesome. Thus when he asks for my number, I give it to him.

Later that week, he invites me for a casual night of drinks at Employees Only, a trendy cocktail lounge in the West Village that is apparently impossible to get into. We meet there and sit at the bar, where we begin the typical first date conversation consisting of mundane topics like where we grew up and how many siblings we each have. And although I don't find myself physically attracted to him, the more I drink, the cuter he becomes. Here is a smart, funny, well-mannered guy, something I thought after my first disastrous date might not exist in this city.

"Can we have one more round?" he asks the bartender, who shoots him an atta-boy look.

I've always wondered what the view must look like from the vantage point of a sober bartender. It has to be comical for them to watch the progression of two strangers walking into a bar, getting more and more buzzed, inching closer and closer, until finally their hands find their way onto each other's thighs, like ours are.

We finish our last drink and make our way onto Hudson Street. It's three in the morning, and we're both starving, so we decide to walk to Bleecker Street for pizza. As we walk, his hand gently brushes against mine for a brief second. We keep walking. His hand brushes up against mine again, this time for a bit longer. Finally, he grips my hand. I don't resist. We turn the corner. His grip goes from timid to confident. Suddenly, without any provocation, he gently but authoritatively pushes me up against a brick wall covered in graffiti. His eyes gaze into mine as he leans closer. And there, at three o'clock in the morning, up against a dirty brick wall . . . I have my first New York City kiss.

It turns out that what he lacked in hotness he made up for in the way his lips move over mine. It's incredible the way a good kiss can bring up a man's average. And kiss we do, the entire way down Seventh Avenue, in fact, until we arrive at Bleecker Street Pizza. There we sit at a table and drunkenly share a greasy pepperoni pie. I'm feeling more satisfied than ever until I'm on my way out of the restaurant and catch a glimpse of myself in the mirror. Thank God it's still dark. He walks me the few blocks back to my apartment, where we find ourselves kissing once again, when suddenly, things start to brighten. The sunrise is breaking.

"Holy shit!" I look at my watch, "it's six in the morning."

"What do you want to do?" he asks.

I know what this means. I know what he's wanting. He wants to come up. And the time has come to decide whether or not I want him to. Even with a little buzz, I rationally debate it in my mind. On one hand, maybe I need to rip off the Band-Aid and go for it. On the other hand, deep down, I'm not ready to have a new man in my bed. I've just had my first kiss since my broken engagement, and I fear I'll regret anything more. Plus, why not end on a high note, and who knows, maybe I'll actually get to see him again?

"We better not. I had so much fun tonight, though. Good night," I say, giving him one last kiss.

"That's it? You're not going to invite me in?"

"It's late."

"So?"

"And also, I just . . . I'm not ready for anything more."

"Wow, what a fucking tease."

I wait for him to laugh and say he was just joking, but he doesn't. Instead he simply turns around, stomps down the stairs of my stoop, and disappears into the morning fog.

I go to sleep that morning thinking about men in general and the few I've met in New York City. So far, I've met a drunk and high man who flirted with the bartender, a married man who propositioned me for a threesome, and now a pretentious asshole whose only intention was to get laid. Yeah, I don't think this city is one where you meet Mr. Forever. But having my first New York kiss at sunrise on my stoop does make for one hell of a story.

Speaking of stories, I've been avidly writing my book for the past week or so—the first half of my draft was due to my editor—and it turns out writing is much harder than I anticipated. Nobody really tells you how difficult it is to string together three-hundred-some-odd pages. And that whole notion of writer's block? It exists.

You can't just phone it in if you're having an off day. Turns out writing's not just a physical effort but a mental one as well.

And an emotional one. With every page I write, I feel an overwhelming sense of anxiety about the book. *Do I really want to do this? Do I really want to expose my deepest, darkest inner emotions on paper for everyone to judge?* For the first time in my life, I won't be able to combat public judgments with any scapegoats—I won't be able to blame things on a bad edit or a conniving producer or say that the tabloids twisted my words. With this book, I am forgoing every shield I have.

I guess in a way I've already done that. Everyone has already seen me sob over my broken heart on national television, and I've already broken the (brief) streak of successful *Bachelor* couples. But what no one saw was the real torture and pain behind the tears. Nobody saw behind the scenes of the heartbreak show.

It makes me wonder why women, including myself, don't talk more honestly and openly about heartbreak. I mean, yes, it sucks to have to talk about something painful, but it's not like it's an abnormal thing to go through. Every one of us has experienced heartbreak, and yet we hoard the pain, burying it deep inside so outwardly we appear strong, all the while being one broken stiletto heel away from a total meltdown. I wonder, if women shared more about their heartbreak, would it hurt less?

But even if I can get past the hurdle of being ready to talk, I'm left wondering how much is safe to reveal. There were horrible, absolutely horrible, moments in my "fairy tale" relationship that to this day I can't believe happened. Even if I disguise the names, it's not like people won't put the pieces together about which horrible moments belong to what horrible human being. And though my opinions may be harsh, part of me justifies it all as the consequences of fame. The way I see it, when people go on a reality television show, we open the door and willingly expose ourselves to such opinions. And when people subsequently go on *multiple* reality television shows, they aren't just opening the door; they're taking the damn thing off its hinges, and nothing is off limits, right? We all have chosen to do our own things once the show is over; my exes have chosen to go on television shows, I now have chosen to write. All's fair in love and reality television, right? There seems to be no way to be truly raw and still conceal the many truths of my relationship at the same time. I want so badly to air every piece of the dirty laundry that was my engagement. But I don't want to just vent. I want this book to mean something.

So story by story, as I look back through my heartbreak journal, I don't just read them, I feel them. Some entries make me recall the day I got engaged and remind me how genuinely happy I was. People often ask me if I really thought it would last. I want to say no, but I can't lie. Those days bring a smile to my face; they were the highs. But then I turn the page, and I'm dealt a blow when I read about the lows. Moments, like when my fiancé left me at my best friend's wedding, that make me irate, not just at him but at myself for ever tolerating such behavior.

And with another turn of the page, I'm taken back to some of the darkest days of my life, like the day my engagement officially ended. As I read those pages, I cry. But the more pages I turn, the more I write, and the more I feel a sense of purge. And page by page, I find myself crying less and smiling more. With every page, the light at the end of the tunnel feels closer and closer. And then I stop and think about how far I've come from where I was. Months ago, I was wallowing, in pajamas, scarfing down sesame chicken, and now here I am, writing a book and making out on my stoop and building a life here. A life to call my own. A life that's starting to become a routine, in a good way.

I've started to find my go-to spots. There's the small bodega on my corner that carries mundane groceries at extortion-level prices.

It's the type of place that sucks you in because you're so hungry that you'd rather shell out $7.29 for a box of cereal than walk the extra four blocks to the drugstore where it's sold for half the price. I usually try to avoid the cereal and instead go for the breakfast sandwiches. I swear, they make the best goddamn breakfast sandwiches in the city.

Then there's Stan, the fruit man who sets up a few tables under an umbrella on the corner of Seventh Avenue and Greenwich. He's so friendly and sweet but his fruit and veggies aren't. Half of them are usually moldy, but every time I pass him clutching a brown bag from Whole Foods, my guilt subconsciously forces me to dig through my purse and buy the least rotten-looking produce, which is often an apple or two and, rarely, an avocado.

Then there's the homeless guy who sits outside an empty storefront on Seventh, smoking a cigarette in one hand, shaking a paper coffee cup in another hand, as he asks passersby for money. I used to drop a dollar bill or some loose change into his cup, but one day I asked him if he'd like a slice of pizza from the store on the corner, to which he replied, "Nah, bitch, *money*." That was pretty much the end of our relationship. Now, whenever I see him, I do the New York thing and put in my headphones and pretend not to hear him.

I've also found my go-to post office, which is just a few blocks away on Hudson. Despite being in New York City, it still has the archaic charm and small-town feel to it that I love. I like to think of my trips there as a visit to the retirement home, only instead of chatting with my grandparents, I'm chatting with the cashiers. There's Marge, the sweet, fragile grandmother type who is so slow that I have to take deep breaths while counting to ten so I can restrain myself from jumping over the counter and angrily taping the package myself. And there's Carlos, the grumpy grandfather type who never lets me use my American Express card because there's no signature on the back of it. (Marge, on the other hand, couldn't care less.) And lastly, there's Alfred, who might be a robot. Like clockwork, after I pay, he prints my receipt, lays it on the counter, takes out his highlighter, circles the bottom, and says, "Now, please be sure to take our survey online and let us know how your experience was with us today." Either Alfred forgets that I'm there every single week and am therefore well aware of the online survey, or he is, in fact, a robot.

I've even started to volunteer at a charity, Dress for Success, on Tuesday afternoons. It's an organization I got involved with when I first moved to the city—I met the founder at an event. She told me how she was a former prosecutor and that she now runs this charity that gives donated clothes to underprivileged women trying to get jobs and provide for themselves. Having been a career woman and still being a woman who is providing for herself, I couldn't resist the urge to help. So now every week I go in and help women pick out interview outfits, write their résumés, and help prepare them for their interviews. It's good. It's good for them because they get to start fresh and have the tools to make it on their own. And it's good for me because it gives me a sense of purpose. Even if it's just for one day a week, I find myself stepping out of my sheltered world, not caring about who is doing what on social media, and actually doing something that has meaning.

I've even taken up running, something I've never been a fan of. I used to judge people who ran. I'd look at them and think about how they *looked* like they were in pain. Who would put themselves through that? But one day, I was walking along the West Side Highway and saw all these people running, and out of nowhere I decided to start running the next day.

Honestly, I hate it.

I hate every quarter mile of it. But it's a good way to get me out of the house and off the wine. It's actually become a little thing for me. I've got my route down. I start off on Charles Street, always making sure to pass Sarah Jessica Parker's house in hopes of getting a glimpse of her. One time, I actually did. She was standing on her stoop, all dressed up, taking a photo with Andy Cohen. Turns out they were on their way to the Met Gala. I almost died.

So I take Charles down to the West Side Highway. At Washington Street, I stop and say hello to the doormen who work at what appears to be quite a fancy building. I think they must enjoy seeing and talking to commoners like myself. If a few days pass without seeing me, they ask where I've been. Sometimes they joke that I've been slacking. I usually quip back, and off I go across the West Side Highway, headed south. The Freedom Tower is in full view as I run. After I pass the tennis courts on the left, which always seem to have a line of players waiting for the next open court, there's a mall called Brookfield Place. It's one of those high-end malls with designer shops like Burberry, Gucci, Hermès, and so on. Basically, the only people who shop here are the tourists visiting the World Trade Center across the street. But there are a few normal-people stores, like J.Crew and Club Monaco, where I always window-shop. And best of all, there's a lululemon store. I always refill my water bottle here, and I always feel bad about it, so sometimes I'll pretend to shop. Sometimes I actually do shop. Then I peruse the day's offerings at Le District, which is a market slash bunch of little restaurants. I get a cappuccino as I waltz around. Sometimes I wander up to Saks, which never seems to have anything on sale. Again, total tourist trap of a mall. When I finish my coffee, I continue my run down to Pier A, the southernmost part of Manhattan. From there, I can see the Statue of Liberty, and, just like the view of the Freedom Tower, it makes me smile.

At that point, I'm officially halfway done with my run, so I head back. Although sometimes there will be a sale I can't resist. I get so immersed that by the time I walk out of the store with three bags, I realize that I forgot I was on a run and therefore must now cab home. That or a friend will see my Snapchat of the Freedom Tower and tell me to come meet her at Grand Banks, a bar on my route. I usually do, and I usually end up getting drunk and have to cab it home. If I don't get distracted by shopping or rosé, I continue my run, taking the same route north but making a detour to run on top of the Holland Tunnel. I go all the way to the end, where I find myself halfway across the Hudson River in front of a locked gate. I methodically touch the gate, each and every time, before I take a seat on a bench and stare out at the Freedom Tower and the rest of Battery Park City. It's there that I seem to find myself transported into my own therapeutic sanctuary. I do a lot of thinking there for some reason. Some days, I think about whatever is bothering me, whether it's love or where I'm going in life. But most days, the wind hits my face and I breathe the air in, just like I did the very first day I arrived in New York, and I think about how happy I feel. Happy and free. Happy and proud. The skyscrapers have an odd way of making me feel accomplished, almost as if I built them all by myself. But what I've really begun to do is build a life here all by myself.

Whether it's my weekly volunteer job or my weekly visit to the post office, or my running route, I find that all of these little things and people around me are becoming small pieces of my new life. Pieces that finally have me feeling like this city is also *my* city. And even though I may not have a man to call my own, at least I have a neighborhood to call my own.

beach, please

"There's only one place to be come Memorial Day Weekend, and that's the Hamptons," said Michelle.

I've just spent a weekend there, and let me be the first to say, Michelle is wrong. It's not terrible, don't get me wrong. I think I had too high of expectations when she'd invited me to come. I mean I couldn't think of anything that could make a Southerner feel more posh than telling people she's going to the Hamptons for the weekend.

The truth is, I didn't know if the Hamptons was a slew of beach islands off the coast of Manhattan or a cluster of bars or, hell, a hotel in Jersey. All I knew was that this was the perfect way to kick off my first summer as a New Yorker.

Next thing I know, it's Friday afternoon and I'm meeting Michelle at a random block in midtown where we stand in line for fifteen minutes before a green bus labeled THE JITNEY pulls up. We check in with the bus attendant and take our seats. It's a nice bus, one of those luxury liners with air-conditioning and Wi-Fi and even a host who passes around sodas and snacks. Michelle has brought her own rosé that we crack open and start drinking straight from the bottle.

"So, am I even going to know anyone staying with us?" I ask her.

"Well, Pete will be there, some of his friends. A few other girls. And then, Sarah, who you met at my birthday party."

"Oh right, I liked her." I didn't really *like* Sarah, but I didn't mind her. I just remember she wouldn't stop talking about how she was freezing her eggs because she was old and single and hopeless. Eggs, single, sad. That's all I remember about her.

"Good, because you're sharing a room with her." Great, I can't wait to talk about eggs all weekend.

A few hours and a few stops later, we're dropped off in downtown Montauk. We schlep our weekenders half a mile to the house we're staying in, which Michelle had described as a "share house." As with the Hamptons, I had no idea what this meant, but I quickly learned that a share house is a large group of friends who pool their money and rent a house for the summer, offsetting the astronomical costs by alternating weekends. Apparently, it's very common in New York, at least for the commoners like myself who don't own mansions.

There are about a dozen people staying in the five-bedroom house, among them one major hottie. He is the obvious prize of the house, and my eye is immediately on him. Later that evening, we all go out for dinner and drinks as one big, happy share-house family. I try to flirt with the hot guy—it should be the easiest hook-up of my life, considering he's literally sleeping in the room next to me, but he's not even glancing my way. He must have a girlfriend.

The next day, we go to a place called the Surf Lodge, where an epic Memorial Day party is going on. I've heard the Surf Lodge is *the* place to be in Montauk, and when I get there, I instantly see that everything I've heard about it is actually true. People are lined up outside behind barricades, desperate to get in. Our group, having a table reserved, is immediately ushered to the outside deck, where hundreds of people dance to the live band playing on the raised stage. It's as if the New York City club scene has been transported a hundred or so miles to the beach; same people, same vibe, but a better sunset. Sarah sees two of her girlfriends and invites them over to our table. They introduce themselves as Ava and Jess. I instantly take a liking to both of them, because while most of the girls at the party are in bikini tops and stilletos, they are wearing maxi dresses and flats like me.

As the sun begins to set, we make our way to an area off to the side of the bar, where the deck turns into sand and a large fire pit with benches around it becomes the center of the action. We sit around and continue talking and drinking. At some point, a young girl wearing inappropriately short cut-off shorts and a man's oversized sweatshirt lights a cigarette using the fire. She's flirtatious, drunk, and alone, which means her friends have either passed out or ditched her and she is now looking for someone, anyone, to take her home. Some of the staff come over to load more wood onto the dwindling fire pit, which sparks the girl to randomly dare one of them to show the group his balls. In return she offers to show her boobs. Stunned, disturbed, I also find myself intrigued. I'm not sure why she wants to see a man's balls. My guess is she really just wants to show off her boobs, hoping they will land her a ride home and a bed to sleep in, which is fine, to each her own, but does she have to make us suffer through the sight of a man's balls in doing so? Still, I can't help but watch in anticipation as she pleads her case. A young ginger-haired worker looks like he's tempted to take the bait. You can just see it in his eyes. The rest of the staff starts egging him on. Mere seconds later, he pulls up his pleated khaki shorts and there in front of the crowd, whips out one little ball. Making good on her word, the brunette lifts her shirt and whips out one little nipple.

The girls in the crowd, including myself, are a little repulsed by this act of indecency, while it seems to have fascinated most of the men, including one in particular. Yes, the chick who showed the tit accomplished her mission of finding a mate—and it was none other than the hot guy staying in the room next to mine. So much for thinking he had a girlfriend.

The next morning, Michelle, Pete, Sarah, and I pack our bags and head to the Jitney stop.

On the ride home, I can't help but think about men in New York City. I wonder if I'm now in an entire new dating game, or is this how it is everywhere and I've just been too sheltered to notice? I've been in relationships for the majority of my life, including an engagement, and now that I'm back in the game, I wonder if it's passed me by. Once upon a time, I had twenty-five men supposedly vying for me—in hindsight now, I see that half of them were just vying for future television gigs, but nonetheless they seemed to be vying for me. I wouldn't say that I was necessarily in a position of control, but I'd say the odds were definitely in my favor. I was one woman swimming alone in a sea of twenty-five men. Now I'm one in a million women trying to swim the fastest among a giant sea. And though my life might not be as normal as my next-door neighbor's in terms of jobs and red carpets, it most certainly is in terms of dating. Do I even have what it takes to stand out? If I'm not going to invite the guy up, or whip my tit out, am I ever going to survive in the dating world of New York City? And better yet, do I even want to try?

I mean certainly I want to eventually have a boyfriend. I'd like a companion. I'd be lying if I said these past few months of living in New York weren't a little lonely.

My new life as a writer in New York City is obviously quite different from my old life as a prosecutor in Atlanta. I have more flexibility and no boss to report to (other than my editor). And while I wouldn't trade it, I often miss the camaraderie that comes with going to an office. The night times and weekends are fun. Lately I've found myself spending a lot of time with Ava and Jess. And occasionally Sarah, who still talks nonstop about her eggs. It's more the weekdays when I feel the loneliness that comes with being a single woman working from home as a writer. Sometimes I don't see a familiar face, other than Mad Mary's, all day long—who has turned out to be a hell of a good source of entertainment. First of all, she walks around Perry Street barefoot, wearing the same Yankees

T-shirt for three to five days in a row. She calls herself the queen of Perry Street, and she kind of is. Well, more like the Nazi of Perry Street. She questions everyone she sees coming to my apartment, which I have told her on multiple occasions is inappropriately invasive.

One day I was texting while walking up the stoop when I heard a voice say, "Lucy died." I look down to see Mary perched on the stoop crying. I lean down, reaching my hand to her shoulder to console her. She slaps it away. "I'm sure you're happy. Now she won't bark." I politely tell her how sorry I am for her loss and to let me know if she needs anything before frantically digging through my purse for my keys. I wait until I get into the building to mumble, "fucking New Yorkers," under my breath. We've built a love-hate relationship.

As I adjust to life with a crazy super, I find myself having to adjust to life with just myself and all that comes with. When I'm actually writing, I feel great. When I'm not, I feel useless. I feel like I'm just sort of existing instead of actually living. I guess I need to just look at writing more as a job. I have a responsibility, I fulfill that responsibility, I get paid, and then I call it a day.

Maybe I should give myself a little more credit for literally rebuilding my entire life by myself. Which by the way, isn't easy or cheap. Sure, there are advantages to being single, like being able to take baths whenever and for however long I want and usually with a glass—or a bottle—of wine. I love that every day can be a "no pants" day if I want it to be. I walk around wearing anything or nothing, and no one can say anything because no one is here. Sometimes there's no better feeling in the world than that moment you put the key into the door to your apartment and know that nobody is inside.

But this independence comes at a cost. Nobody tells you that living alone is one hell of a tough job. There is no man around to climb onto a ladder and replace a burnt-out lightbulb. No man around to plunge the toilet or help you carry your groceries up the stairs. In fact, I've had to ask my Uber driver to zip my dress for me on several occasions. Do you know how embarrassing that is? And it doesn't end there, the other day, I had to build an IKEA armoire by myself. It took four fucking hours. When I finally finished, I looked it over to admire it, only to realize the door was upside down. A man would have noticed that midway through.

If that's not bad enough, just last week I was in the basement putting my trash in the bin when I turned the corner and saw a giant ass crack on top of the washer. It was Mary. She appeared to be trying to fix the washer or something. Honestly, there is no telling with her. The sound of the trash bag plummeting into the bin alerted her.

"Just so you know, the washers and dryers are temporarily out of order. I'm trying to fix it, but no laundry right now."

"No problem. Do you know when they'll be working again?"

"No."

All righty, then.

I was carefully sorting my recycling so she wouldn't yell at me when I saw her hop off the washer.

"Also, some asshole threw a goddamn air-conditioning unit in the alley."

"Huh?"

"Yeah, some asshole just tossed an AC unit in the alley."

"Well, that's a shame."

"Swear to God, this job is going to kill me," she muttered before climbing back onto the washer.

It wasn't until I was lying in my bed with a pounding headache watching the latest episode of *Orange Is the New Black* that I glanced toward the corner of my living room. There was a box sitting on the hardwood floor below the windowsill. A box that said FRIGIDAIRE. It seemed very out of place. *Oh, shit. That isn't what I think it is, is it?* I got out of bed and walked over to it. As I peered into the box, I saw it was empty. *Fuck. What happened yesterday? Think, Andi. Think.* We had brunch at Chalk Point Kitchen, where we all ordered the unlimited mimosa special, and then we went to Blue Haven, then to another bar across the street, and then I went home and just went to bed. Right?

Oh, fuck.

I did go to sleep, but I woke up in the middle of the night sweating. I opened the window, but it was hot as balls out. *Oh, God, I did.* I tried to install the AC unit. And then it dropped and I ran down in the basement and tried to find a way to access the alley, but I was in the backyard, and there was no gate, no door, no ladder, nothing. And so I said to myself, *There goes two hundred bucks*, and then I guess I just crept back upstairs and into my bed and fell asleep. *I was the asshole who threw the goddamn air-conditioning unit in the alley. Shit! I'm never drinking again. Ever.*

Yeah, add a new AC unit to the long list of costs that come with being a single woman. That's another thing people don't tell you. It's bad enough that you have to build armoires and install chandeliers alone, but you also have to pay more because you are alone. There is no splitting of the rent or utilities or having someone pay for dinners. You don't get gifts for your birthday. Instead, you get bills. Bills that don't pay themselves.

But bitching and moaning aside, I've come to find that there really is no price for the freedom I feel in being single. And I really do love the single life. I'm just a little worried I might love it *too* much. I find myself in my late twenties and feeling as though I'm just coming into my own. On one hand, I embrace this newfound independence, while on the other hand, I'm afraid that I'll become accustomed to it.

What if year after year, I find myself still content with being single only to wake up in twenty years and suddenly realize that because I was so set in my ways, in my own lifestyle, that I didn't bother with relationships and now it's too late? I hate to say this, but what if I'm not far from being the woman who only talks about her eggs, like Sarah? Or even worse, what if I'm not that far from Mad Mary?

i'll have a screwdriver

I've just boarded a plane bound for JFK when the flight attendant comes by and asks me if I'd like anything to drink.

"A screwdriver, please."

She pauses.

Oh, don't give me that look. I know the sun has yet to rise because it's half past six in the morning, and it's a Sunday, and instead of asking for a cocktail, I should either be at church, at brunch (at my church), or at a yoga class like a grown adult woman should be. But as a flight attendant, if you're going to ask me if I'd like anything to drink, you shouldn't be allowed to judge me for responding in the affirmative. Plus, if only you knew just how much I deserve this cocktail.

She brings me my drink, and I take a gulp before closing my eyes. I can't wait to get the fuck out of Canada and be back home. What was supposed to be the weekend I met my potential Mr. Right turned into—well, where do I even start?

I guess I can start at the beginning, where in hindsight it was doomed considering I met him on Twitter. I know, I know. Take away my dignity card now. But here's the thing, it's not like I've had much luck since moving here. I mean I've had the drunk dude who left me for the bartender, the married dude who wanted a threesome, the writer who wanted me to put out, and the Hamptons guy who went for the flasher. So I'm not really in a position to turn down any dating options. Plus, you'd be surprised what an unbelievably great source Twitter can be for finding a date. You see, thanks to my undeserved status as an E-list (maybe D-list if I'm having a really good week) celebrity, I get a cute little blue check mark next to my Twitter handle. Aside from being cute, it also functions as a filter and notifies me when someone else with a cute little check mark follows me, and vice versa.

So one day, out of the blue, I got a notification that someone with a check mark was now following me. Naturally, I clicked on the notification, which directed me to the handle of a guy who, based on his profile picture, seemed to have been or currently was a professional rugby player of some sort. I'd never even met a rugby player, but something about them always made me think they were t-r-o-u-b-l-e, a kind of trouble I was ready, willing, and absolutely able to get into. A quick Google search revealed that he was, in fact, a current professional rugby player. Intrigued, I followed him back, and just like that, the chase was on. Mere minutes later, another notification came across my phone. It was a new message. It was from him.

"Was not expecting a follow back. Thanks! How are you?"

I want to write him back immediately, but I remember the "rule of three." It's a rule I made up that requires me to wait to respond to a guy at least three times the length of time it took for him to respond to me. So if it takes him ten minutes, he'll hear from me in thirty; if he takes one hour, I wait three hours, and so on. I'm not sure when or why I came up with this rule, but it's served me well in the past. I've played enough you-chase-me-first games with men to know that this rule not only keeps me winning, but it puts a hell of a lot of power in my fingertips.

Thirty minutes later, the alarm I'd set to hold me to my own rule went off on my phone. It was time to respond.

"Hi! Ha ha should we pretend it never happened then? I'm good, you?"

So basic, I know, but he took the bait, just like every man does, and next thing I knew, after about one hundred messages over the course of a few days, he finally asked for my phone number. I obliged, giving him the number to my burner phone. Yes, I have a burner phone, which is simply a cool way of saying "second phone." Truth is, a little while back, I'd cracked the screen to my phone, and when I went to get it fixed, the salesperson told me it'd be cheaper to just add a line, and in doing so, I'd actually get a new free phone. In my head, I justified this second line as a business expense, which was only partially bogus. In all honesty, the main purpose of the burner phone has become a way to make me feel like the badass I most certainly am not.

So the Canadian and I began a nice little texting affair, talking all day, every day, before eventually progressing into the FaceTime stage of our "relationship." He might have been an athlete, but he didn't act like one. There was something different about him. He was smart, he was funny, he had plans for life after rugby. And did I mention he was hot? Not just athlete hot, real-life hot. Though I wouldn't call him my boyfriend, clearly he was more than just a friend. Not knowing where it would lead, I figured there was only one way to find out: accept his invitation to come visit him in Canada and embark on my first international booty call, which could very well turn into my first boyfriend since my broken engagement.

Then came the Friday morning of my trip to Canada. A vibration coming from the phone on my nightstand woke me up. I looked over to see it was ten o'clock, which meant my flight from JFK had departed exactly two hours ago. Shit, shit, shit! I knew I shouldn't have taken that Xanax last night, but in my defense, I'd needed it. I'd needed as much sleep as I could get. After all, I couldn't show up to my first international booty call looking like, well, a booty call. In a panic, I jolted out of bed and immediately called the airline.

There were no more direct flights for the day, so I sacrificed and said I'd take the flight with a layover in Minneapolis, which left in two hours. Thank God I was already packed.

After my call to the airline, I texted the Canadian to tell him of my mishap. I expected him to say something to the effect of "Shit, that sucks, but at least you got on the next flight" or "So you'll be a few hours late, but at least I still get to see you." Instead, I was met with "Ugh. K." Maybe it was nerves or anxiety, but whatever it was, it had manifested into sheer agitation. Hoping this agitation would turn into excitement, I endured the flight and the layover before finally landing in Canada, where I cleared customs and skipped my way to baggage claim. Once there, I texted him again.

Me: "I'm heeeeeerrree! Just getting my bags, where are you?"
The Canadian: "Outside at curb. Passenger pickup A."

Uh-oh, looks like someone's still mad. I lugged my suitcase through the baggage claim and outside to find him standing by a black Tahoe. The sight of him was sort of perplexing to me, even though, of course, I'd seen what he looked like during our multiple FaceTime sessions. But in the flesh, he just looked so different. He was kind of an enigma; tall with a long torso and short, thick legs, but then his waist was very lean. It was like someone had taken three different sections of a human body and put them all together with no rhyme or reason. But they were all good sections. With a grin, I jumped on him, wrapping my legs and arms around him in a hug. He stood stiff.

I awkwardly slipped into the passenger seat. The fifteen-minute car ride to his place was filled with one excited front-seat passenger and one still-pissed-off Canadian driver. *He can't still be fucking mad, can he?* I thought to myself. *Maybe it's just nerves.* We'd been talking for weeks now, and not once had I seen this side of him. It had to be nerves. Plus, it had only been one car ride, and though our conversation might not be hot, at least he was.

We arrived at his condo, which was modern, sleek, and undeniably expensive. Hell, the entry hallway was twice as long as my entire apartment. But it wasn't nearly as cozy. It was more like one of those apartments that look like they came straight out of a furniture showroom. Zero warmth, kind of like him actually. He led me through the long hallway that opened up to a spacious kitchen. Pristine, it looked as though it had never been touched. He opened a door to the right, which led to a bedroom, and placed my suitcase at the foot of the bed. I scanned the room. It was quite bare. There was a dresser, one nightstand, one queen bed, one framed photograph of a city skyline, and absolutely zero charm. Attempting to dissolve the discomfort between us, I asked him to show me around the place.

"Hmmmm. Okay. Well, there's the kitchen, living room." He started walking down another hallway. "And over here is the master bedroom."

Holy fuck, he's got me staying in the guest bedroom. On one hand, I saw this as a gentlemanly gesture, but when combined with his salty attitude, I couldn't help but see it as a possible case of buyer's remorse. Maybe it wasn't just nerves.

We made our way back to the kitchen, where he opened a bottle of wine and I took a seat on a barstool. With every gulp we took, the mood lightened. Two glasses in, I found myself having moved from the barstool to sitting on top of the counter. An hour or so and another glass later, we began vigorously making out. Within seconds, my top was off, revealing the La Perla lace bra I'd bought months ago at the outlets in Woodbury. It was ridiculously uncomfortable to wear on the plane, but the moment I revealed it and saw his eyes light up made it so worth it. I pulled off his shirt and stroked my hands down his washboard abs. Wow, even better than I'd imagined. *I want to violate this man.* Soon enough, he was carrying me into the master bedroom and I was flat on my back, down to my bra and the black lace Forever 21 panties (which I cut the tag out of).

An hour later and I was still flat on my back, only this time naked and looking up at the ceiling with a feeling of pure satis-faction. Actually, I was beyond satisfied. In fact, I was thinking I might have just had the best sex of my life. There was something so sophisticated about his touch. It was as if I were an instrument and he was a soloist, every stroke sending a trembling sensation down my body. He was a blend of authoritative and sensual. Something magical had just happened to me. So magical that for a moment, it made me forget about the previous weird hours. I waited for him to start snuggling with me like I was sure he would. And waited and waited. Seconds felt like minutes as our breathing slowed. And then he rolled out of the bed, stood up, rummaged through his dresser drawer, and put on a pair of sweatpants.

"I'm hungry," he muttered as he walked out of the bedroom, leaving me alone in the bed.

What the fuck? Is he back to being mad? Wait a second. What the fuck just happened? Oh. My. God. Did I just get hate-fucked? At that point, I'm just waiting, dreading the moment when he would un-doubtedly walk back in and escort me into the guest bedroom. But I couldn't let that happen. I couldn't bear the humiliation of sleeping in the guest bedroom owned by the guy I think had just hate-fucked me. So I did what any normal woman who'd just been hate-fucked would do: I pretended to fall asleep in his bed.

The following morning, I awoke to the sound of a blender. Re-alizing that all my clothes were in my suitcase in the guest bedroom, I rummaged through his drawer and found a hooded sweatshirt to throw on before meandering my way into the kitchen.

"Want a protein shake?" he said in between pulsing the blender.

I took a seat on the barstool. "No, thanks." *The Canadian is a fucking meathead.* "What are your plans for the day?" he asked.

"Ummm, I'm not really sure. What are yours?"

Why would I have made plans? I'm visiting you in a foreign coun-

try. I knew nothing about this place, nor did I know anyone here. Was I supposed to make an itinerary?

"Well, I told one of my teammates I'd stop by his place. He's having a bunch of wives and girlfriends and people over for a barbeque."

"Nice."

"You can come if you want."

"Ummm, I don't want to intrude."

"I'll just be there a few hours, then. I'll make it quick."

"Okay. I'll just do my thing, maybe walk around and shop."

"There's good shopping about three blocks from here."

"Perfect."

Not perfect. What a fucking ass! First of all, I was not going to any teammate's house with a half-assed invite from a protein-shake-drinking hate-fucker like him. And secondly, my own mother didn't even know I was here, so the last thing I wanted or needed was to be seen in public with this fucking meathead. Hell, at this point, I didn't think I even wanted to be in *private* with him.

Shopping it was. I went to the guest room, aka "my room," hopped into the shower, and got dressed. I'd googled the closest shopping, and he was right, it was only three blocks away. As I headed out the door, he was sitting on the couch on his phone.

"Do you have an extra key I can take?"

He told me there was one in the basket by the door.

"Great. Thanks! So we'll just meet up later?"

"Sounds good."

Asshole. As I was walking down the street, I couldn't help but wonder what the fuck went wrong. I mean, where was the sweet guy I'd been texting and FaceTiming with all these weeks? Did I do something wrong? All this animosity couldn't possibly be due to the minor detail that I'd missed my flight, could it? It took the sight of a lululemon sign to make me stop wondering about what was going wrong and start wondering what I was going to buy. After I'd racked up on yoga pants, I found a Tim Horton's and indulged in a hot chocolate. It was about one o'clock when I got a text from the Canadian meathead telling me he was leaving the barbeque and headed back to the apartment. I'd barely gotten to take advantage of the weak Canadian dollar, and already he was done? Part of me contemplated ignoring his text and carrying on shopping. Hell, part of me contemplated abandoning my suitcase in his apartment and carrying my ass to the airport and home on the next flight out. But I was too much of a wuss to do either. So I headed back to his place.

We went for a late lunch at some empty Mexican restaurant, the kind you take someone to when you don't want to be seen with them, which at this point didn't really bother me because the feeling was mutual. What did bother me, however, was the fact that he spent the majority of the time on his phone. His unease had now turned to complete disengagement.

And just when I thought it couldn't get any worse, he looked up from his phone and, with a chuckle, said, "I told my teammates you were here, and they don't believe me. Can we send them a Snapchat?"

"Huh?"

"Here." He scooted next to me. "Let's send them a snap."

I pushed away. "Ummm. No."

"Whoa. What's *your* problem?"

What's my fucking problem? Where do I start? You've barely said five words to me, hate-fucked me, left me alone for hours, and now you want to brag to your friends that I'm here. "I just don't want to send a snap to a stranger."

"Geeeez. Sorry for even asking."

When lunch was over, he asked what I wanted to do next. I wanted to say, *Anything that doesn't involve talking to you,* but instead I submissively replied, "I don't know. Anything, really."

"We could go see a movie," he suggested.

That would get me out of both having to talk to him and having to be seen in public with him. "Sure," I responded.

"Hmmm, what's playing? Can you look up the AMC 34?"

From the passenger seat, I began listing various movies until I was interrupted.

"Fuck, yes! *Creed!*"

"*Creed?*"

"Yeah, the Rocky movie. It's supposed to be sick."

Fuck my life and this fucking meathead I'm with right now. "Ehhh, let's see what else is playing."

"Nothing sounds good. C'mon, let's see *Creed*. You'll love it. Plus, you owe me for missing that flight yesterday." His smile nauseates me.

"Owe you?"

"Oh, yeah."

And here was where I lost it. "Okay, time out. I'll go see *Creed*, but playing that whole missing-flight card is officially done. I got on the next flight, which involved a two-hour layover. So if you're still pissed about it, then just get it out now, because it's ridiculous, and it's ruining the entire weekend. I've traveled from a different country to be here. I'm happy to be here, so let's just both be happy."

"Geez. If I didn't know better, I'd think you were on your period."

"Well, fortunately, after last night, you *do* know better."

"Whoa."

Dear Lord, please get me the fuck out of here. Actually, please get me to Creed so I can have two hours of not having to talk to this asshole.

After the shitty movie, we decided to go to the grocery store and cook in for my second and final night in Canada. Thank God. At some point on the way home, he asked if we should pick up some weed cookies.

"Are those legal here?"

"Yeah, it's Canada."

I told him we might as well.

The second we got home and unpacked the groceries, I shoved a cookie into my mouth. I figured it was the only way I could bear the remainder of the night. An hour later, the cookie had kicked in and the two of us were in the kitchen, both trying to cook, both laughing hysterically, and both completely stoned. It was the most fun I'd had with him all weekend, which wasn't saying much. Hell, it was the only bearable moment outside the bedroom that I'd had with him all weekend. It was as if our animosity vanished along with our sobriety.

But then at some point, the magic of the cookies had us going from laughing to venting. Shit began to get deep as he started telling me about his childhood, how he grew up poor in a broken home. And that was when I had a hazy epiphany. As he was talking, I looked at him and saw him differently from how I had in the past twenty-four hours. Granted, thanks to the cookie, I was seeing four of him. But for the first time all weekend, I didn't see him as a *douchey*-asshole-meathead. For the first time, I saw him as a *wounded*-asshole-meathead. He spoke of life and his career as a rugby player so resentfully, as if he felt guilty for making it out of his small town and into the fancy world he was living in. His vulnerability made me feel less anger toward him and more sadness. Sad enough to have sex with him yet again. I mean, I figured he had hate-fucked me and now I was going to return the favor by pity-fucking him. And that's exactly what I did. All night long.

I soberly awoke from my high when my phone rang at four the next morning. Fuck, why had I scheduled such an early flight? Oh, right, so if shit went haywire, I'd have an early exit, and if it went well, I could push it back. Though I truly wasn't planning on needing this early flight, I'd never been so thankful for the backup plan.

I looked over at him; he was fast asleep and snoring. I stealthily got out of bed and walked into the guest bathroom. As I was brushing my teeth, I caught a glimpse of my shameful reflection. Why had I felt so bad for him that I pity-fucked him last night? I mean, sure, he grew up poor and his family life sucked, but so what? The guy was living in a multimillion-dollar apartment, was drinking shakes out of a five-hundred-dollar Vitamix, and just flew a chick in from New York City to bang him for the weekend. Joke. Was. On. Me. I debated whether to wake him up or just call myself an Uber and be done with it all. I couldn't help myself. I had to poke the bear one last time.

"Hey," I whispered as I jabbed my finger into his shoulder.

He rolled over and moaned, his eyes shut. "What's up?"

"I need to get to the airport."

"Do you want me to take you, or can I just get you a car?"

Normally, this response would piss me off, but the thought of spending one more second alone with him had me thankful for his lack of chivalry.

"Uber would be great."

"Okay," he said as he grabbed his phone and unlocked it. "It'll be here in seven minutes."

"Thanks."

"Have a safe flight."

Fuck you.

Seven minutes later, I was in the back of an Uber, bound for freedom . . . I mean New York City.

And now, as I sit on the plane, I can't help but wonder how the hell this weekend turned into such a disaster. How did I not realize what a meathead he was? How was I so easily fooled? What has happened to my knack for judging the character of a man? I thought my little mishap of getting engaged to a man I only knew for eight weeks was just a fluke, but now I'm starting to wonder if maybe all this time, these douchebags coming into my life are my own fault. Why am I drawn to such losers? I think I have some soul searching to do, don't I?

Dramatics aside, I guess it could have been worse. I could have fallen deeply in love with the douche and be on a plane sobbing my eyes out right now. But instead, I'm flying home, with no emotional feelings, no regret, and, unfortunately, almost no dignity left. But thanks to this round trip, I have reached Platinum Medallion status. I'd call that a win.

So to answer your question, Ms. Holier-Than-Thou Flight Attendant, I know it's half past six in the morning and the sun hasn't risen, and it's a Sunday, blah, blah, blah, but yes, I would like a drink. I'd like a screwdriver. Better yet, make it a double. Thanks, and have a pleasant flight.

new york slashing week

J ust like that, summer has come and gone. Fall is here, and though I haven't scored in the department of a single woman's desire for love, I have scored in the department of a single woman's desire for fashion, which might be even better. This week, I got to experience my very first New York Fashion Week, a week filled with not only pomp attire but pompous designers.

Apparently, when it comes to New York Fashion Week, and fashion in general, it seems less has to do with fashion and more has to do with popularity. Some designers are cooler than others, and they know it. They make a big fuss about who is and, more important, who isn't invited to their shows. Many of them thumb their noses at "people like me." This year, it's most of the high-end designers, which isn't surprising, but also the two ready-to-wear chicks known as Alice and Olivia. I had my publicist reach out to them because I love their clothes and thought it would be fun to see their newest collection. As it turns out, whoever was in charge of their guest list informed my publicist that, unfortunately for me, they don't really *do* reality television stars at their shows. While this isn't the first time I've heard this, and I know it usually has nothing to do with the designer and everything to do with the PR team, it still has me pissed. Who the fuck are they to look down their noses at reality television? I'm sorry, did

I miss the part where Alice and Olivia became Karl Lagerfeld and started making haute couture, because last time I checked, Alice and her fucking friend Olivia made ready-to-wear clothes that I only buy at the end of the season when they are on sale. Also, you don't *do* reality television stars, but who do you think is buying your shit? People who *watch* reality television. But no, reality stars aren't good enough to wear your clothes. I'm sorry, but people like this, fashion-related or not, piss me off. It's not like I went out and made a porno or went on some racist Twitter rant and offended the world. I went on a television show. Get the fuck over it. You can bet your ass after I heard that, I rifled through my entire closet and tossed every piece of their clothing I owned. Which is sad, because some of it was kind of cute. Maybe next year their team will change their mind.

Anyway, back to the designers who did let me attend their shows. The first was Badgley Mischka. A few outfits were messengered over to my apartment, and I settled on a tweed jacket, something very out of character for me but very in character for Fashion Week.

The day of the show arrives, and I find myself in the back of a car pulling up to a venue on Thirty-Fourth Street. Through the window, I can see lines of women clamoring in the unseasonable heat as they wait behind barricades bearing black tarps and the official NYFW logo. The driver opens the door, and I step out. I'm immediately greeted by two women holding bright orange umbrellas. They aren't shielding me from the nonexistent rain but rather from the very existent sun. And of course ensuring that the large logos on the umbrellas are visible to the mob of surrounding photographers. I'm walking into one very fashionable lion's den. At least I'm dressed well. Plus, I can't deny the exhilaration I feel not only to be at my first New York Fashion Week but also to be getting to sit front row *and* having paparazzi taking my photo before I even get into the building. Moments like this make me pinch myself and say, *Who the fuck am I?*

The show is everything I'd imagined, only much shorter. I swear it must be less than three minutes from the time the lights go down and the models begin walking to the time the lights go on and everyone begins sprinting out of the venue and off to the next show. Me, I'm not off to the next show but rather am being ushered backstage by a woman in all black, who tells me, "The designers would love to meet you." Backstage is less chaotic. The models are changing out of their dresses and into their street clothes. Camera crews are getting interviews from people I don't recognize.

I'm standing in front of a step-and-repeat taking a photo with the designers, when I suddenly see someone I *do* recognize. The last man I dumped before getting engaged, the man who called me out on live television for having sex with him, the man known as Number Twenty-Five! What the fuck is he doing at a fashion show? Isn't this an event reserved only for women and gay men? He's feet away from me, but I don't think he's seen me. I hope he hasn't. I panic. I can't see him. I need to avoid him immediately. Not because I dislike him. I mean, yes, this guy told the entire world on live television that we had sex, but I've been through so much since then, including the ending of my engagement, that I don't care about that anymore. I'm really avoiding him because I don't want to be seen with him. It's terribly shallow of me, but it's true. I'm not playing the role of the mean girl in school who doesn't want to be seen eating lunch with the dork. I'm playing the role of the woman who doesn't want a random meeting to become a story. And trust me, one photo of the two of us together will most certainly become just that. I can only imagine the headlines the tabloids will use despite there being zero truth to any of it. It's the last thing I want and need right now.

So I frantically ditch the designers and run through a set of black curtains and into a random room. The same girl dressed in black who brought me backstage follows me. I tell her what is going on. Telling her makes me feel terrible. I feel like a shitty human being for being so petty and avoiding an ex. She tells me she totally understands and graciously calls a car to come pick me up immediately.

Of course, the next morning, the tabloids run the story that Number Twenty-Five and I were both at the same fashion show and I made a point to avoid him. It makes him come off as a stalker and me as a wuss.

The week continues with a few more fashion shows during the day and parties at night. Some are wild, some are fun, and some, like the Victoria's Secret after-party, are just downright disheartening. Nothing like seeing Gigi Hadid and Kendall Jenner at a table filled with other "Angels" in the flesh to make you feel old and weathered. And to make matters worse, every hot guy in the place is trying to flirt with them while all the old guys in the place are trying to talk to me and Ava, whom I brought as my plus-one.

All the while I'm wondering why the fuck I even bothered getting ready for an event like this. An event where not only did I not stand within a few yards of these six-foot-tall enigmas but where, when it came to finding a man interested in me, I didn't stand a chance. What is it with guys and models anyway? Sure, they're tall and skinny, and most of them are really, *really* pretty. But who gives a shit? Don't they know that ten years, two kids, and a few cheeseburgers from now, those girls are not going to look the way they do now?

With the end of the week nearing, I'm down to my last show, Nicole Miller's. They, too, messengered over some outfits for me. I manage to make my way to the same venue as the first show, where the scene is the same, except that there are no umbrellas waiting for me as I exit the car, but the paparazzi are still there in droves. The show ends up being the best one of the week and it's not over yet.

I've personally been invited to a post-show dinner later hosted by Nicole Miller herself.

I bring Ava along with me since dinner, wine, and fashion are three things I know she'll never turn down, and the two of us make our way to Vynl for dinner.

We arrive a little late, having no idea what to expect as the hostess takes us into the private room. I immediately survey the scene as we find our assigned seats. It's cougar central. There are a few cast members from *The Real Housewives of New York*; Lindsay Lohan is in a corner booth with her posse (she actually looks pretty good). Ava and I are seated across from each other.

I'm next to an older man who introduces himself as Ty-Ron, a stylist. We immediately start talking all things fashion. He tells me how he's Tyra Banks's stylist, how he's styled covers for *Cosmopolitan*, blah, blah, blah. He gets through his list of accolades just in time for the server to arrive and ask if I'd like red or white wine, to which I obviously reply, "Red." This gives me the opportunity to turn and meet the woman to my left. She looks to be in her mid-fifties and the creative hippie type.

"Hi, I'm Andi," I say, reaching out my hand. She doesn't respond. Instead, she just stares at me for a few seconds. "I know you from somewhere." Here we go again. I play dumb, telling her that I'm not sure where she'd know me from. She fires back with a slew of questions, asking my occupation, where I live, where I'm from, etc. But she still can't place me. It's an all-too-familiar game that you'd think I'd have figured out by now. But what am I supposed to say? "I was on reality television"? I leave her dazed and confused as I turn back to talk to Ty-Ron. I'm midsentence when there's a tap on my left shoulder. "I know where I know you from!" she exclaims. "You were on a reality show, weren't you? *The Bachelor*, right?"

"Oh yeah." I say it as if I've forgotten I was ever on it.

"That's it! That's where I know you from! I don't watch that garbage, but my daughter loves that show!" She doesn't realize that she's just offended me by calling a show I was on "garbage." She goes into a rant about how much her daughter just loves, loves, *loves*, the show. As she's telling me this, she takes a hit of a vape pen that I didn't notice lying on the table next to her fork. She continues on about how her daughter has always wanted to go on the show and asks if I think she should. "Yeah, why not?" I say.

"Well . . ." she says with a condescending fuck-you chuckle, "you don't understand, my daughter is a junior studying biomedical engineering. My daughter would only go on it as a joke. She'd just make fun of it the whole time."

"You'd be surprised, producers can usually sniff those kind out pretty easily."

"No, she's smart, she's studying biomedical engineering."

"Yes, a junior? Right?" My sarcasm wizzes by her.

"Wait a second. The attorney. You're the one that guy called out for making love to him if you weren't in love with him, aren't you?"

"That's me!" I say with a smirk.

"Ahhh that was awful. Okay, so tell me how does an attorney end up on television, and I don't mean this to be offensive, I promise." *Too late, lady.*

"I don't know, I just did." I start to turn to my right to save myself, but before I can, she blasts yet another insult. "I mean, geez, were your parents disappointed or *what*, maaaann?"

Oh no, she didn't. I know that I can't make a scene because I'm at a private dinner party and I have no idea who this lady is and what relation she has to Nicole Miller. Hell, she could be her sister. Bitching out the designer's sister would definitely put me on the not-invited list, which would mean I wouldn't be able to go to both Nicole Miller *and* Alice and her friend Olivia's shows ever again. But I also can't hold my tongue any longer. She needs a quick lashing. "I'm twenty-eight years old, I live alone, and pay all my own bills without anyone else's help, I have a great group of friends here, and I call my mother every day. So to answer your question, no they weren't and they aren't disappointed in me. Actually, my parents are quite proud of me."

"Cool," she says as she inhales her vape pen.

I text Ava, who seems to be having a much more pleasant time talking to the woman beside her.

"Let's get the fuck out of here!"

We do, and just like that my first New York Fashion Week has come and gone. It was fun to be able to attend the shows and get sent free clothes, but if I'm being honest, Fashion Week isn't all it's cracked up to be. Everything you imagine—Anna Wintour sitting front row, editors from *Harper's* and *Marie Claire* taking notes—doesn't happen. Instead, the front row is occupied by fashion bloggers and influencers, many of whom dress in ridiculously hideous outfits in order to get noticed. They all live-stream the show through their phones, never getting an actual unfiltered look at the fashions. And while I realize I am one of those "influencers" and only get to sit front row because of it, it makes me a little sad that the glory of Fashion Week isn't what I imagined. I guess I just thought it'd be more glamorous, but instead, it's pretty damn exhausting. You spend all this time getting ready to be seen, and an hour later, you can't wait to take off the heels that are blistering your toes and the lashes that are stinging your eyes.

And you go through all of this fuss just so you can get declined an invite, run into your ex, realize you're never going to look like a Victoria's Secret model, and get asked if your parents are disappointed in you. But hey, at least they let me keep the clothes.

southern guilt

"Pookie, welcome home!"

"Mom, I'm not home, I'm just visiting."

"This is always your home," she says as she wraps her arms around me.

"Then why'd you convert my bedroom into a guest room?"

"It's *your* guest room. Dinner's almost ready. Dad's on the porch, say hi to him."

My mom doesn't need to tell me where my dad is; I can smell the cigar smoke the moment I walk in, even through the closed patio door.

I make my way through the living room, making sure to pet my parents' dog or, as my mom likes to call him, my "brother." God, he's gotten so fat since the last time I saw him.

"Dooley needs to go on a diet, Mom," I tell her, provoking the mother of all eye rolls. "Hey, Dad!" I lean down and give him a kiss on the cheek.

"Hey, dear! How are you? How was your flight?"

"Flight was fine. Delayed, of course, but fine."

I take a seat in the wicker chair next to him. He mutes the flat-screen television that is sitting on top of a matching wicker end table. The cable cords that lead to the back are attached to an orange extension cord that runs across the patio floor. It's the most redneck thing I've ever seen.

My dad takes a swig of his Scotch and looks me up and down. "What'd you dress for a funeral or something?"

"What do you mean?" I look down at my all-black ensemble.

"You look like you're going to a daggone funeral."

He's doing that thing again where he accentuates his Southern accent. It's funny because my dad is really only a pseudo-redneck. He was born in Atlanta but in the city parts, not the rural, and if you're a Southerner, you know that those few miles of separation can make all the difference. But he's a Scotch-drinking, football-loving, avid fisherman and hunter who has all the makings of a redneck. The fact that all he ever wanted in life was to have boys who played sports and instead got stuck with three crazy-ass women in one house I guess entitles him to speak however he wants.

"Dad, this is how we dress in New York."

He takes a puff of his cigar and blows a perfectly shaped ring into the air. "Like you're going to a damn funeral?"

"As if I'd go to a funeral in ripped jeans and Vans," I mumble.

"Vans?"

"Forget it. I see you still enjoy the perks of being a redneck. Couldn't manage to find an extension cord that wasn't bright orange, huh?"

"Oh, this here, this aiiiiiiiin't redneck." His twang has reached a new level of Southernness.

"You know they make wall mounts for televisions and you can hide the cords."

How the fuck did I ever live here?

I head back into the kitchen, where my mom is making dinner, a rarity. Growing up, we used to say the best thing she made was reservations. She's actually not a terrible cook—when she actually cooks. Tonight she's cooking lobsters, a family favorite. Well, I guess

I shouldn't say she's cooking but rather transporting the lobsters from the Styrofoam crate they came in to the pot of boiling water on the stove. But I'll credit her nonetheless. I pour myself a glass of wine and take a seat on top of the granite counter next to the stove.

"So tell me everything. How's the apartment? How's Mad Mary? Is she still giving you shit? You know I'll come kick her ass."

I love when my mom gets protective and aggressive like this. The thought of my mom—at five foot three and no more than a hundred twenty pounds soaking wet—kicking anyone's ass, let alone Mary's, is just comical. But she talks a big game when it comes to protecting her daughters. "Screw with my kids, and you're dead," she always says, and part of me genuinely believes her.

I start to tell her the apartment is great and that I've done some reorganizing of the furniture since she was there and that Mary is as maddening as ever.

"Any boyfriends?"

I knew this was where the conversation was leading. "No, Mom."

"Any dates?"

"No, Mom."

I can't bear to tell my mom the truth, because the truth would be that the last "date" I went on went a little something like this: I flew out of the country to meet a guy, he hate-fucked me, I pity-fucked him back. Not exactly something you say to your mother.

"You know, one of my girlfriends at mah-jongg asked me if you were a lesbian."

"Oh, did she, now? And what did you say?"

"I told her to fuck off."

I spit out my wine out and laugh.

"But . . . are you?"

"A lesbian?"

"It's okay if you are. I'll still love you."

"Mom, we've been through this before. I wasn't a lesbian then, and I'm not a lesbian now."

"I just worry a little about you."

"Why do you worry about me?"

"Well, I just want you to find someone and be happy."

"I'm doing just fine, Mom. Don't you worry."

"But you said you're not dating anyone."

"Doesn't mean I'm not doing okay."

I'm trying to give her an appropriate hint that I'm not having any problem getting action, but this is one of those topics that I just don't have the slightest desire to talk about with my mother, of all people.

"Well, have you made any nice girlfriends? Not girlfriends like relationships, like friends that are girls."

"Yes, Mom, I get what you mean, and yes, I have."

I go on to tell her about all my different friends, mainly Ava and Jess, who have quickly become two of my closest new New Yorker friends. I told her how I met them over the summer in the Hamptons and how we go out once or twice a week for dinner. How each of us brings her own little unique flavors to the group. Ava, a magazine editor, has lived in the city since college. She's barely five feet tall and always up-to-date on the latest trends in beauty. She wears ridiculously hideous gray lipstick, which somehow actually looks good on her. And she rocks blinding bling on her nails, which somehow actually don't look trashy. But other than that, she's pretty reserved. Well, except when you put her on a dance floor and give her a few drinks. She turns into a machine who can shake it like Shakira, twerk it like Beyoncé, and give off those seductive come-get-me eyes like Rihanna. She's really quite the triple threat. But despite her moves and her ample curves, she's the most prudish of our group when it comes to sex. She's also quite the foodie, so she's the best at picking restaurants. I, myself, am the most enthusiastic eater of the group—and drinker, for that matter. I love when we share food and bottles of wine, because I eat more than anyone but pay the same amount.

Then there's Jess. If our group gave out awards, she'd be named most likely to have her shit together. She's an entertainment publicist and a total badass. Jess has a way of offering advice that you automatically assume is right. Being in the entertainment business, she could have sold me out many, many stories ago. But she's just not that type of person. In fact, I often think she's too nice for the industry. She's not a fuck-you-over type of girl, but she's also not a let-you-fuck-over-my-friend type of girl, either. Jess and I call ourselves bury-the-body friends. Basically, if something were to happen and a man ended up dead in one of our apartments, we would call each other, and no one would ever know the asshole went missing.

Then I tell her about Sarah, who is part of our group, especially since she's responsible for introducing us in the first place. But she travels for work a lot, so she's hardly ever around to partake in our weekly dinners. She's still constantly talking about freezing her eggs. We joke about whether or not she talks about them on her dates. I have a handful of other friends, too. There's Emily, who I met at a party, who is also friends with Ava, and a few other girls who sporadically come to our dinners. It's ironic that New Yorkers get such a bad rap for being unfriendly, because I've found them to be just the opposite, especially when it comes to friendships. They're always connecting people with their friends, who then connect other people with other friends, and so on. It's like a friendship game of six degrees of separation, pay-it-forward style, and it's served me well.

My mom seems less worried now that she knows I actually have friends. Over dinner, we talk about my book and my life in New York before my mother hits the red-wine wall at nine and has to go to bed.

Later that night, as I lie awake in bed in the upstairs guest room,

I start to think about what my mom said earlier in the kitchen. The words "Are you a lesbian?" keep echoing in my mind. Does she really think I'm a lesbian just because I'm single? I know *she* doesn't but does everyone else down here think I am? Not that there is anything wrong with being a lesbian, but I'm just not. And I don't understand why people assume that if you are in your late twenties and single, you must be a lesbian. Which then gets me thinking, what is so fucking wrong with being single?

Being a single woman past a certain age has always been the equivalent of a scarlet letter south of the Mason-Dixon Line. And now that I'm the one wearing it, I find it offensive, sexist, and stupid. The way I see it, I'm twenty-eight, and I've been in relationships for the better part of my last decade, including an engagement that ended nastily. Wouldn't now be a logical time to be single? To be on my own and figure out life without the mess of a man?

When did being single become such a thing to worry about? Why do people look at single women with those sad eyes that you know stand for "Oh, poor thing, she's still single." News flash: I'm not miserable being single. I'm actually quite the opposite most of the time. I live in New York City, I have great girlfriends, I pay my own bills, I have no obligations to anyone. If I were a man in the same position, I guarantee you not only would nobody be questioning my choice, but people would probably tell me not to settle down anytime soon.

So why is it so different for a woman to be single from how it is for a man to be single? And don't get me wrong, I'm not mad at my mom for asking the question. I know everyone's thinking it anyway. Is it the fact that I have a uterus and my clock is ticking faster than a man's that makes being single frowned upon? Am I not allowed to sow my wild oats like a man is?

I hate that I get so riled up about this, but I have to be honest and admit that it's one of the main reasons I find myself visiting home less and less often. I just don't like coming back here that much. Once upon a time, it was the bad memories of my breakup that kept me away from here, but now it's the feeling of insecurity I get about a lifestyle that I never question when I'm in New York. It makes me feel lonely, even though I'm generally not. Down here, everyone is married, pregnant, or trying. I come here, and I'm an outcast. People visibly feel bad for me here. Which, in turn, makes me feel bad about who I am: a single woman.

Is it so bad that I am in a place in my life where I actually *want* to be single? I really, genuinely do. For the past year, I've enjoyed living life in New York as a single woman, doing what I please, how I please, when I please. When I decided to move to New York, I did it to look for me, not to look for love. I've embraced the single life and all the glorious independence it has to offer. Is that so wrong? I want to be able to go on vacations with my friends and not have to think about a man. I want to be able to come home to an empty apartment and drink a bottle of wine, or not, by myself. And most of all, I don't want to be responsible for anyone else. I know that sounds selfish, but I don't. I don't want to be responsible for a man's feelings right now. I've been in relationships for almost my entire life. The good ones gave me a sense of security, while the bad ones, particularly the last, were so volatile that I just don't feel like dealing with love right now. Breakups are emotionally taxing, no matter how you slice it. I don't want to be hurt, nor do I want to hurt anyone else. So instead, I find myself in a state of mind where I'm almost rebelling against the entire notion of a relationship. Not in a resentful way but in a liberating way. Sure, there are times when I'd like to have someone romantically in my life, but then I think about my life as a whole and realize I'm genuinely happy being alone.

Plus, I'm not going to lie, I feel better physically than I ever have. My breasts still have some perkiness to them, my metabolism allows me to quickly work off any sesame chicken I consume. All in all, my body has done a good job at not succumbing to the inevitable curse of gravity that every woman faces. The way I see it, I'm in my prime, and I'm not sure I'm ready to waste my body on just one man. Isn't that what marriage is for?

And then I start to wonder, do all things in life revolve around love? And if so, what happens to those who don't find it? What happens to someone like me if I never find a man? Will I not have lived a meaningful life? Will I never be looked at with anything but sad eyes? If the measure of a successful life is a successful relationship, can't that relationship be one with myself? Does being alone necessarily mean being lonely? I swear, there should be a billboard that says, WELCOME TO THE SOUTH, WHERE THE MEASURE OF SUCCESS IS YOUR MARITAL STATUS. And on the back, Y'ALL COME BACK NOW—WHEN YOU'RE MARRIED!

God, I've got to get out of this place and back to New York before I become old and rotten, forever.

once upon a time in mexico

With my first year in New York City coming to an end, it is time to celebrate the beginning of a new one. About a month ago, Ava, Sarah, and I decided to plan a beach vacation for New Year's Eve.

Jess already had plans with her new boyfriend to do something cute and romantic. Gag. I can't wait for her to be single again so she can come back over to the fun side. I don't even remember his name, maybe Mike or Mitch, something that starts with an "M." He lives in Jersey. She actually met him years ago and only recently reconnected when he randomly DM'd her. It's now turned into something halfway serious enough for them to be spending New Year's Eve together. Ava thinks he might be the one, but I'm not so sure about that. From the sound of it, he's more smitten with her, which is a relief. It's never good to see your girlfriend more into a guy than he is into her, because that shit never ends well. I give it a month or two, max.

Anyway, back to our New Year's plans. It all came about because Ava believes the last place you want to be when the clock strikes midnight is in New York City. According to her, locals don't *do* the city on this holiday. Instead, it's a night that caters to tourists and kids in their twenties looking to rage. The tourists will brave the freezing-cold weather and pack themselves into Times Square with hundreds of thousands of other tourists just to watch a ball drop, despite the fact that they could watch the same ball drop on television from the comfort of their warm hotel rooms. The kids will brave the other kids and pack themselves into whatever bar they can get into without a cover charge. They will do the same thing they do every other night out: get wasted before filling the streets in their scanty outfits, some of them vomiting on themselves as they stumble around trying to catch a cab, which will be impossible. Hearing this, you can imagine how quickly I was sold when Ava brought up the idea of a beach vacation.

Fast-forward to a cheap flight and a reasonably priced two-bedroom suite in Playa del Carmen, Mexico, and the three single amigas are bound for some fun, sun, and whatever trouble we can get ourselves into.

We arrive at the hotel early Friday morning, just in time to catch a few rays at the rooftop pool. It is eerily quiet. One older couple is reading as they sunbathe, two small kids are playing tamely in the pool as their parents watch from the side, and then there are the three of us. Not quite the party scene I was expecting, in all honesty. I can tell we all feel the same sense of disappointment, but none of us wants to be the bitch who starts whining the very first day we're in Mexico.

Within twenty minutes or so, however, out of nowhere, a group of guys comes barreling into the pool area. It doesn't take long for them to make their way over to us and introduce themselves. They are from Brazil. I physically eye each one of them up while mentally making notes about their hotness. Most of them fall into the never category, a couple fall into the if-I'm-drunk category, and one falls into the I-want-to-marry-that-guy category. My eye goes immediately toward him.

He's not just vacation hot, or pick-of-the-bad-Brazilian-litter hot, but real-life hot. And not in a pretty-boy kind of way. Just under six feet tall, he has a semi-ripped body. The kind that says, *I don't drink protein shakes and water, but I don't only drink beer.* His brown hair is thick, and I can tell it naturally styles itself. His light brown eyes stand out against his tan complexion. And the scruff. God, I love a man with scruff. And he has the perfect scruff.

We spend the day partying with the Brazilians. Everyone is drinking, dancing to music, and having a blast. Except Sarah, who is sitting on a lounge chair, texting on her phone. She's not drinking today because she is trying to curb her alcohol intake so she can start her egg-freezing process, so I give her a pass.

At some point, I notice two random girls in the hot tub. I haven't seen them before; they must have casually come in unnoticed. But there they were in the hot tub, both kind of oddly bouncing up and down. Strange, I thought. It's not until one tilts her head to the left that I catch sight of what they are bouncing up and down on that my jaw hits the ground. Two of the Brazilians have also managed to slip into the hot tub, and each now has a woman atop of him.

"Holy shit! Are they fucking?" I say aloud.

"They probably are." The hot one has magically appeared and is now sitting in the chair next to me. "Brazilians love their women." He rolls his eyes.

"Gross! Do they even know them?"

"I think they met them last night. I know. Don't hold it against *me*, though."

I'd like to hold a whole lot of stuff against you.

"I'm a little out of my element with these guys, if you couldn't tell."

"I could. And your English . . . no offense, but where did you learn to speak so well?"

"My father is American, so even though we were raised in Brazil, we learned both cultures."

"We?"

"Yeah, me and my brother, Rodrigo, over there, and we have a sister."

"That's your brother?"

He nods.

"You two look nothing alike. But at least he's not one of the guys in the hot tub."

This makes him laugh, and when he laughs, he goes from a ten to a fucking twelve, and I go from enamored to completely smitten. "My dad says he's the milkman's son, but no one really gets that joke in Brazil."

"Oh, well, don't worry, I get it."

"What about you? Do you have any brothers or sisters?"

And just like that, thanks to two guys banging two girls in the hot tub, the conversation with one fine-ass Brazilian has officially begun. We somehow figure out that we both grew up playing competitive tennis. Not exactly the sexiest conversation, especially considering sex and alcohol are all around us, but at least it is a conversation. At some point, we shift from family life to talking about Brazilian life. Mainly the life of Brazilian women and their enviable asses.

"Yeah, we American girls weren't blessed with that." I chuckle.

"Aww, but you have a cute little pooch," he replies as he pinches my belly.

I swear to God, he actually leans over and with a thumb and an index finger pinches my pooch. Normally, my reaction to such a degrading move would be to take whatever glass I have near and smash it over the asshole's head. But I don't. Something about the way he says it is so adoring and charming that I can't bear the thought of smashing his pretty face with a bottle, so instead, I lean over and pinch his gut right back. Mind you, there isn't much to pinch, but it gives me a valid excuse to stroke my hand over his washboard abs. He laughs in an impressed way, almost as if it was a test, and I (and my pooch) passed with flying colors. And just like that, we've gone from officially talking to officially flirting.

A few hours of flirting later, someone has the brilliant suggestion of taking this pool party to some swanky beach bar everyone is "dying" to check out. Having yet to see the Mexican sand, we all agree. Plus, at this point, I am going anywhere the Brazilian is going. We all stroll down the beach, the two of us walking side by side and exchanging flirtatious looks. At one point, his hand casually brushes mine.

We arrive at the beach club, where a DJ is behind a sound board playing EDM music. Girls in G-string bikinis are dancing on tables, grinding up on average-looking men in T-shirts who are spraying bottles of champagne into the crowd. Basically, not exactly the type of place you want to be wearing a one-piece trying to impress a guy. But there I am, one-piece and all.

"Want to go to the ocean?" he whispers in my ear.

I don't hesitate for a second. "Yup!"

He reaches out his hand to me before leading me outside the club. We weave through kids building sandcastles before reaching the shoreline. The brown water is freezing cold, filled with seaweed, and choppy. I have no desire to let it touch any more than my toes. But the Brazilian dives right in. He emerges from under the water and shouts for me to come in. I play damsel in distress as I stand on the shoreline, whining about how cold it is.

"Oh, c'mon, you little cock."

"Excuse me? Cock?"

"Cock-a-doodle, like you little chicken."

I laugh in relief.

He's standing up, his abs somehow looking even better now that they are wet. Fuck, he's so hot. How can I waste a chance to get pummeled by waves with him? The things I'm willing to do for hot men, I swear.

I slowly make my way into the water inch by inch. I'm about waist deep when he starts splashing me. I rev up my damsel-in-distress game. He likes it. He likes it enough to pull me toward him. He likes it enough to take both his hands, place them on my cheeks . . . and kiss me. Right there in the middle of the ocean. The perfect amount of romantic but sexy but publicly appropriate kind of kiss. The I-don't-know-if-these-chills-are-because-the-water-is-cold-or-I-am-sold type of kiss. The kind of kiss that takes a massive wave slamming against us to make us stop. If not for the salty taste of the dirty ocean water, it might go down as one of the best first kisses I've ever had. Because it isn't just the kiss. It's the feeling the kiss brings with it. A feeling of confusion. Did I just fall in love because of a kiss? I've only known him for a day, I've only talked to him for a few hours, but that one kiss somehow said so much more than words can say. But it can't be love. Can it?

I'm freezing as we head back to the beach bar. We are now hand in hand. The seal has been broken, and we can't stop kissing. Everyone takes notice.

At one point, Sarah moans, "Why do you always get the hot one?"

I want to downplay it and tell her he's not the hot one, but she and I both know that would be a lie. So instead, I smile and say, "Don't worry, we'll find you a hottie tonight."

She rolls her eyes.

Later that night, we get dolled up for the New Year's Eve party the guys have invited us to. The party is swanky and fun, but I'm not noticing much of anything or anyone except my Brazilian. Before I know it, the crowd is counting down from ten when I realize I've lost sight of him.

"Nine, eight, seven."

Shit, where is he?

"Six, five."

An arm wraps around my waist from behind.

"Four, three."

I turn around. There he is.

"Two, one" . . . and we kiss.

Fast-forward to four in the morning, and my white mini-dress now looks like graffiti art with different colors of alcohol splattered across it along with a twelve-digit number. It's the Brazilian's phone number, which he wrote with a Sharpie borrowed from the bartender. Swoon. The club is closing, and the partyers are all going their separate ways. I have an eight a.m. flight back to New York, which means that at this point, my night is going one of two ways: to bed or into the morning. The Brazilian wants to go to the beach. Hmmmm. Beach, stranger, four in the morning? It sounds like one of those situations that your mother always told you to avoid, but my mother isn't here right now, and one sexy Brazilian sure is. Fuck it.

"Let's go."

I'm pleasantly surprised to see that the beach is actually packed with people. It doesn't look or feel like four in the morning. We lie on the sand and make out before deciding to walk back to the hotel. The streets are still littered with people, and music continues blaring from the bars we pass as we walk along the cobblestone strip. It's nearly five o'clock now, and though the sun has yet to rise, the energy is as vibrant as it was hours ago.

And then out of nowhere, I hear a crack of thunder. It begins to rain. Pouring rain. There I am, in my high heels, wearing a white dress (hoping the phone number doesn't smear), hand in hand with a hot Brazilian. We run to the corner and stand underneath an awning in an attempt to stay dry. He asks if we should get a taxi, but I say no. Instead, in an act of sheer spontaneity, I take off my shoes, walk into the street, hold my hands to the sky, and lift my head, letting the rain drench me.

"You are loco!" he shouts from under the awning.

"Come be loco with me," I respond.

And he does. It is the best line I've ever used to get a man to dance in the rain with me. Granted, it's the first time I've ever tried to get a man to dance in the rain with me. With a giant grin, he takes off his shoes, wraps one arm around my waist, takes his other hand, and grabs mine. And we begin to dance. It's the most romantic scene I've ever seen, let alone been a part of. I begin to twirl around. He kisses me. I twirl again. We kiss and twirl . . . all the way home.

When we arrive back at the hotel, it's around six in the morning, which means I must be on my way to the airport if I have any shot of making the flight. We're standing in the lobby, my shoes still in my hand. He's begging me to stay in his sexy Brazilian accent. I want to. I want to stay and go to his room and top off this seductive story with some seductive sex. I know I could, and it wouldn't be the first flight I missed. I'm standing in the lobby with two paths in front of me. The path to the right leads me to my room, where my suitcase waits to be packed. The path to the left leads me to his room, where his hot body waits to be touched. The path to the right has me going out on top, taking the weekend for what it is, an unbelievably romantic time with an unbelievably hot Brazilian, and nothing more. The path to the left has me going out on bottom, literally, capping off the weekend with a bang or two. I have no reason not to go left. In fact, I have every reason to. I take one last look in his eyes. Damn, they are tempting.

"Good night." I kiss him on the lips and walk away.

I don't turn around, because I know one more glimpse of him will lead to me being in his arms again. Instead, I walk with dignity into my hotel room, pack my belongings, and get a cab to the airport, still smitten but in control. I may have had my fairy tale and my prince, but we all know that once the clock strikes midnight, or, in this case, six, the princess has to disappear. And so did I. Maybe it was love, maybe it was just another kiss of a frog. I think I'll never know. All I know is I've just had one hell of a weekend with one hell of a guy. And it is one hell of a way to start a new year.

And though it may have been nothing more than a midnight kiss and a weekend fling, it's managed to get me over the hump of dating life in New York City. It's almost as if this romantic weekend is my reward for a year filled with anything but romance.

one wedding and my funeral

I've succumbed to the world of dating apps. I blame Chris Harrison. Him and the *Bachelor* franchise as a whole.

    It all started on a Friday night, when Chris was in town to do some promotions for one of the franchise's upcoming shows. We meet for dinner like we do anytime he's in New York and has a spare night. While it might sound weird to go to dinner with the host of a show I got engaged on, it's not in the least. It's merely two friends shooting the shit, and I love it. I love it for so many reasons. First, thanks to our similar senses of humor, there is never a dull moment. We joke about anything and everything that is politically incorrect and it's goddamn hilarious if you ask me. I usually walk away from our dinners having broken even in regards to calories consumed versus abdominal calories burned. Second, Chris has a taste for good food and good wine. Which leads me to the last reason I love dinners with him: he's rich and pays for meals that would have me otherwise unable to afford my rent. That's really just the icing on top of the cake. Basically, a night with Chris is a night of good food, expensive wine, rich conversation, and a drama-free evening. I wish he were gay so I could claim him as my "gubby." I know that sooner or later, when he settles down and starts dating someone, our dinners will probably stop. Because, let's be honest, no woman lets her man wine and dine a twenty-eight-year-old single girl, just friends or not. The tabloids always have a field day whenever either of us posts something on social media. Sometimes I'll post a photo just to get a rise out of the weeklies. It's vain and childish but oh, I'll take any entertainment I can get these days, especially at the expense of a rag mag.

There we are eating at one of my favorite restaurants in the city, the Polo Bar. I've actually only been here once, because it's another one of those new trendy restaurants that is impossible to get a reservation at unless you are somebody. Luckily, Chris is somebody. The restaurant is so country-club chic it should just be known as a golf clubhouse. The rich green walls are adorned with framed oil paintings of horses and portraits of wealthy-looking white men. The ceiling is wood-paneled with detailed crown moldings. Modest chandeliers hang over the plush leather-tufted booths. As stuffy as the decor sounds, the vibe is far from that. Once you get inside (if you get inside), you find there's something opulent yet cozy about this place. The waiters aren't pretentious assholes like they are at other hot spots, there is no doorman eyeing you up and down to see if you are hot enough to be granted entry, and the food, though very simple all-American fare, is orgasmic.

Somewhere between ordering the entrée-sized corned beef sandwich as an appetizer and the salad, we find ourselves on the topic of dating. Chris tells me about a friend of his who has just created and launched a new dating app. I roll my eyes at him. He tells me it's different. Basically, it's more exclusive than the other dating apps that are out there. You don't just sign up and get on; you have to be vetted and approved. It sounds pretentious as fuck, if you ask me.

As he's going on and on about it, I interject, "Wait, is this like Tinder for celebrities?"

"Basically."

"Kill me now. And if you tell me you're on it, I'll kill you, too."

He laughs in a hell-no-are-you-kidding-me way. "Nope, but you should do it."

This prompts a feministic rant from me about how I am happily single, and not only do I not need a man to make me happy, but I don't need a goddamn dating app to help me find a man who won't make me happy. Chris sits silently, desperately trying not to laugh at me. Instead, he pours me more wine without saying another word about the app. The night ends with me going home and packing for my trip to California the following day.

I'm off to attend a wedding. Gag. And not just any wedding, either, but a wedding spawned from the same reality television show I once got engaged on. I feel bad considering I've never even met the couple. Basically, they got engaged on a spinoff of the *Bachelor* franchise, on a show called *Bachelor in Paradise*, and are actually going ahead with it, unlike most of us. Thus, they get the pleasure of a televised wedding while I get the pleasure of a free trip to California in the dead of winter and a chance to see friends. I did buy them a gift, at least.

But what I thought was going to be a "blissful" weekend celebrating the love of two strangers turns out to be a complete nightmare. Surprise. Surprise. I arrive at the pre-ceremony cocktail hour where there is a mix of people I know and some I've never met but have heard of. Of course, in true *Bachelor* form, the cameras are rolling, capturing every moment. It's annoying at first, but then I realize the cameras aren't there for me, but rather there for the most recent contestants, who have decided to take this wedding cocktail hour and turn it into their own reality show. I watch with horror as they take shots off each other's chest, shotgun beers, and make out with one another. It's as if they've forgotten they are wearing suits and gowns and are at someone's wedding, a wedding that hasn't even started. That or they just don't really care. I won't lie, though—I'm also kind of glad they are creating the drama, because it means I can happily mingle and get as drunk as I want to without fear of exposure. I never knew being irrelevant could be such a relief.

The cocktail hour ends, and we are ushered into the ceremony, which is beautiful. Even though I don't know the bride and groom, I'll admit, I'm buying it. You can tell that neither of them is the attention-seeking type. They seem simply happy, but not in a juvenile way; and two quick "I do's," later, they are also the latest couple to beat the *Bachelor* curse and emerge as husband and wife.

It's not until we all head into the reception that everything really begins to unravel for me. I make my way to my assigned table, where there are eight chairs. Three are occupied by other former Bachelorettes, Ali, Deanna, and Kaitlyn, along with their significant others. I take my seat next to Kaitlyn and wait for the eighth chair to be filled by someone. And wait and wait.

The DJ comes on the microphone and begins introducing the newlyweds. I look at the empty seat beside me, and surrender to the fact that my biggest fear has come to fruition. I am the single chick with an empty chair beside her at a wedding. A wedding that is being filmed from every angle for the world to see. A wedding in which I am seated at a table with two pregnant women and one engaged woman who is challenging herself to a month of sobriety, making me the lone alcoholic. Kill. Me. Now.

The embarrassment I feel has me not just sad but physically nauseated. But I know that even the slightest hint of sadness will bring a load of unwanted attention from the camera crew and the producers, who are bouncing around from table to table, pretending to say hi but really sniffing out everyone's level of drunkenness and weakness. I'm trying to hold it together, but as the minutes pass, speech by speech, toast by toast, my eyes begin to tear up. My jaw is clenching harder and harder. And then a slow song comes on. I can't take it. I make a beeline for the bathroom. It's empty, thank God. I go into the handicapped stall, sit on the toilet, and cry.

Within minutes, I hear two girls come into the bathroom. I stifle my tears and hold my breath. I can hear them talking about someone's ugly dress, a hot groomsman, and then . . . me.

"Oh, my God, did you see Andi with that empty chair next to her?"

"God, yes, poor thing. I'd totally be dying if I were her right now!"

A few minutes later, I can hear them washing their hands before the sound of a door closing restores the silence. I resume crying. I'm blotting the tears as fast as I can, but no amount of toilet paper seems to dry them up. I've been in the bathroom for a solid ten minutes now, though I doubt anyone has noticed. I'm sure they're all way too busy frolicking and flaunting for the cameras.

The only thing worse than being the single girl sitting next to an empty chair at a wedding is being the single girl sitting on a toilet in an empty bathroom crying at a wedding. I need to get it together at least for the next hour or so. I cannot let these people see me like this.

I take a deep breath and reapply some concealer and blush before I stand and straighten my dress. I make my way back into the reception hall, where, just as I suspected, no one has noticed my absence. A few hours later, I see some people heading out, and I follow suit.

Back in my hotel room, I lie in bed with my gown still on and cry yet again. I feel so alone. I'm beginning to wonder if I really am happy being single after all. Why is it that being alone feels so liberating at times but so debilitating at other times, like weddings? Note to self: never attend a wedding alone again. Never.

With the wedding over, my pride shattered, and my insecurity at being single in rare form, I'm off to the airport and bound for home. I'm reading through my emails on my phone when I come across one saying I've been approved for a dating app. Fuck, I must have applied when I got back to my room after the wedding. I seriously need to make a rule that I am not allowed to use my phone after a certain number of drinks. The shit I do when I'm drunk just . . . well, it just lands me in even more shit.

The sadness of being alone at the wedding has me feeling the need to concede. I figure I've already been approved so it can't hurt to download it, check it out, make fun of it, and then delete it. Nobody has to know. Plus, let's be honest, I am in no position to thumb my nose at anything dating-related, even an app. Who knows? Maybe thanks to the Brazilian, this year could be *my* year. But I'll never know unless I try, right?

I arrive at LAX with time to spare, which means time to create a login and follow the tutorial on how the world of app dating works. I've played on enough of my friends' other dating apps to realize quickly that this one really is different, at least in terms of logistics. Instead of swiping right or left, you click on either an X or a heart. This is genius, because I've never understood how someone could remember which swipe direction meant yes and which meant no. Also, there is a link on each profile that takes you directly to the person's Instagram page. Another genius move. There is no better way to stalk a man than on Instagram. You can tell what kind of guy he is just based on whom he follows and how many posts he has. If he follows a bunch of "models," he's a douche. If he posts more than one selfie a week, he's a super-douche.

Now it's time for me to create a profile of my own. There's an option to add photos from Instagram to your profile. I select this. Wow, I'm lazy. I select my age range as twenty-four to thirty-four. I probably shouldn't be looking at twenty-four-year-olds, and I probably should be open to looking at men older than thirty-four, but then again, I probably shouldn't even be on this app, so screw it. Last, it prompts me to "Upload a song that best describes you. This will play alongside your slideshow." A song that describes me? I mean, what

the fuck, I don't know. My first instinct is just to go for my favorite
song, R. Kelly's "Bump n' Grind." But then again, I'm not sure this
is appropriate. Actually, I *know* it's not appropriate. Nothing says
skank like the lyrics "I don't see nothing wrong with a little bump
and grind." Scratch that one. Hmmmm. Taylor Swift would probably come off as juvenile, even if the twenty-four-year-olds would
appreciate it. Hmmm. Several thoughts later and I finally decide to
play it safe with "Concrete Jungle" by Alicia Keys. I click the button
labeled NEXT, and just like that, I have a dating profile.

I wait as the app searches for my potential husband, I mean
matches. Twenty minutes later, I'm hooked like a teenager on
Candy Crush. And not because there is anyone hot or promising on
it—quite the opposite, actually.

First up is Lars, age thirty-four, lives in New York City. Who
the fuck names their child Lars? I mean, poor guy, I guess it's not his
fault and I guess I don't really have much room to talk, considering
my parents gave me a boy's name, but come the fuck on, Lars? *Hi,
Dad, this is my boyfriend, Lars.* No way. X.

Next is Geoff, age twenty-eight, Los Angeles. Geoff's profile
picture is him with the gold-leaf crown filter from Snapchat that
gives you a bronzed glow that makes you look the most like J.Lo you
ever will. And while *I'm* a fan of this filter, I'm not a fan of a *man*
using this filter. X.

Next is Steven, twenty-nine, New York City. "Steven is just
here for friends." I'm confused. What the fuck does that mean?
Dude, you're on a dating app. Why the fuck would you be on a dating app looking for friends? You want some friends, join a goddamn
fraternity. X.

I continue with my countless Xs. Neil's profile picture shows
him wearing sunglasses—not a good sign. Jake's profile picture is
a silhouette of his back. Again, not a good sign. I want to see your
face. I want to indulge for a moment and be shallow and judge you

based on your looks alone. Come on, this is a dating app! David, thirty-four, from Orange County, is posed next to a red Lamborghini, which deserves not just an automatic X but a slap in the face with an actual bag of douche. In all likelihood, David does not own this Lamborghini, let alone lease it. I would bet a pair of Jimmy Choos that either (a) he rented it for the day, (b) he saw it in a parking lot, or (c) it belongs to a friend or family member. If he does happen to own it, then he is still a douche for flaunting it. Whatever the case . . . X!

In terms of potential mates, this app is quite disappointing thus far. However, in terms of entertainment value it's magnificent, dare I say addictive. And just when I'm starting to think I'm on the brink of yet another profile to poke fun at, a new screen pops up alerting me that those are all the profiles I get to see for today. What the fuck? I've been cut off! I have to wait until tomorrow? Shit. This chase is only making me more intrigued . . .

matchmaker, matchmaker . . .

I'm not sure if it's that I'm fresh off attending a wedding alone or the new snow on the ground, but I've had a bout of single woman depression this past week. It doesn't help that Valentine's Day is approaching and this will mark the second year in a row I've been without a boyfriend on the most nauseating holiday of the year. It also doesn't help that it's the dead of winter in New York City. And by dead, I mean, the city literally dies for a few months. Everyone bitches and moans about it being too cold to go outside, let alone go to a bar, and instead just goes into hibernation. If you're lucky, you have someone to stay in with. If you aren't lucky, you find yourself going an entire twenty-four hours without having so much as left the house—or put on pants, for that matter.

One person not afraid to brave the cold this week was Michelle. She'd asked me to go to dinner and even offered to trek from uptown to the West Village. I knew there had to be some hidden motive behind this move, and the second I walked into the restaurant where she was waiting for me in the corner booth, I could see I was right. A giant pear-shaped diamond on her ring finger was blinding me. Yup, another one had bitten the dust. Though, if anyone is deserving of such a statement ring, it's Michelle. I mean, the woman freaking sets the dinner table with real napkins, for crying out loud! We gab on and on about the proposal details before she wipes her newly-engaged-woman smile off her face and replaces it with a let's-get-serious smirk. "So . . . I have a question for you," she says. I'm all but certain she is about to ask me to help her do something for the wedding. "Pete and I were thinking . . . don't get mad, but . . ." Oh shit, they are going to want me to do a toast aren't they? "We were wondering if you'd be open to letting us try just just oooonneee more time to set you up with a guy."

"Fuck no!" I blurt out.

"Geez, you don't have to say it like that."

"Sorry, that just came out wrong. I just—I'm—I'm good."

"But I want you to have a date for my wedding."

"Which is when?"

"Well, hopefully by this fall."

"It's February—that's like six, seven, maybe even eight months from now."

"Okay . . . well, this isn't going how I thought it would."

Now I feel bad. And so does Michelle, and the last thing I want to do is ruin this moment for her. "We can figure that out later, okay? Ahhh, this is really exciting. So tell me what you're thinking, what color scheme, what is the dress going to look like?"

She starts describing different hemlines, but I can't hear the words that are coming out of her mouth. My mind is occupied wondering when and how she and Pete hatched this plan to set me up again. Was it over a candlelit dinner as they basked in their newly engaged lovey-dovey bliss? Did they suddenly feel sorry for all their single friends and out of guilt decided to start pairing them up together? Also, what makes Michelle think she's more capable of finding a date for me than I am? Is she totally delusional about how shitty the last guy she set me up with was? Yeah, real fucking winner there, Michelle. I'd rather die alone than have to spend one more second with that dick. Oh shit, I hope he's not invited to the wedding.

I leave dinner that night seeing Michelle in a different light, and not the sparkling kind that was coming from her hand. As I lie in bed I wonder if I've become that pity project for all my engaged and married friends. And once again, I begin to question my relationship status. So I'm back to hiding under my newfound security blanket, my dating app.

I spend the better part of the week hearting and X'ing nonstop. Sometimes I find myself clicking the heart button simply out of boredom, but other times I click out of attraction. Some guys I match with will message me with a cheesy line, like "So, when am I taking you out on the best first date of your life?" I don't respond to those. Some I do respond to, but after a few messages back and forth, the conversation tends to die down. Lately, though, there's been one that hasn't been cheesy, hasn't died down, and has me crushing . . . hard.

I think he was someone I'd originally hearted out of boredom, because he's not significantly good-looking. But we matched, and since then, we've been texting back and forth a good bit. He's smart and kind, which makes him more attractive to me.

The only problem is—well, there are two problems. First, he's an athlete, and second, he's young. *Very* young. Well, I shouldn't say very, because that makes me sound like a pedophile, but he's twenty-five. I'm twenty-eight, so it's not *that* bad, right? I guess I've just always thought that when it comes to men and maturity, you have to subtract about five years from their actual age. But this one seems different. There's a depth in our conversations that I haven't found with anyone else. He responds quickly but not so quickly that it comes off as desperate. He's thoughtful. He'll send me messages saying good morning and good night. We talk about our days and make random jokes that we then text about until we've beaten them to death. There's an ease in our conversations that isn't boring but rather exciting. And though he may be young, there's a mature vibe to him that makes him seem older than half the men I've dated.

Now on to the second problem, the fact that he's an athlete. A baseball player. A baseball player who lives in Seattle. I couldn't find a guy any further away from my house and any closer to my type. And though I doubt it will lead anywhere, right now, he's all I've got in the man department.

Our texts finally lead to our very first FaceTime, when I find myself in the back of a car on my way to JFK, already running late for my flight. I am bound for San Francisco for my very first Super Bowl. I'm going solely for the thrill of it while Jess, whose hotel room I'm crashing in, has to go there for work. Sitting in bumper-to-bumper traffic I find myself bored in the back of a cab, so I do what any bored woman would do: I whip out my phone and text my latest crush, my Seattle baseball boy.

Five minutes after my text, my phone rings with an unfamiliar tone. Shit! He is FaceTiming me. Why is he FaceTiming me? I decline it, because obviously I need to check the mirror and make sure I look halfway decent before I allow him to see my face. A few minutes and a dab of concealer later, I decide to FaceTime him back. He answers on the second ring. It's the first time I've actually seen his face in real time. He's just gotten done with a workout and is sitting on the couch. I should be giddy and blushing, but I'm not. I don't know, his face isn't as cute as his texts are. There isn't that instant chemistry that I expected. Then again, I wasn't expecting this random call, either. I hang up in disappointment. But being in no position to turn down attention from the male species, especially when they make the effort to FaceTime me, I decide I won't completely cut the cord just yet. Instead, I'll just keep him on the bench. He is a baseball player, after all. And while he may not be a starter just yet, I might need him to come close out a game for me in the near future.

I arrive at JFK, check my bags, and make my way to the Sky Club, where I immediately see Jess at a table by the bar.

"Umm . . . Hi! I thought you were on an earlier flight," I say as I hug her.

"I was, but I forgot my license at home, and I had to go back, and long story short, I missed my damn flight, so now I'm on yours."

"Well, that blows, but I'm not gonna lie. I'm selfishly happy."

"What seat are you?"

I look at my boarding pass. "Three C. You?"

"Hell, yes, three E."

We've got about forty-five minutes until boarding starts, so I order a drink and sit with her. Mr. Seattle and I are texting, which must have induced me to smile, because Jess immediately says, "Okay, spill, who is he?"

I look up guiltily before telling her everything about him. I'm gushing but then clarifying that I don't think I'm into him, then gushing, and then downplaying it. I'm beginning to nauseate myself with my back-and-forth rant. I can only imagine how Jess is feeling.

"Wait, how is *your* new guy? What's his name again?"

"Mike. He's really good."

"Okay, now *you're* gushing."

"It's early. We'll see."

I haven't met Mike yet, considering they've only been together a short time now, but from all that she's told me, he seems to be more into her than she is him, so I'm not worried. Plus, she seems happy, so despite seeing her less because of him, I guess I'm happy for her.

"Well, cheers to us!" We clink our glasses before heading to the gate.

Fast-forward through a plane ride filled with bottles of red wine followed by a night of partying, and it's Saturday night. We're tipsy in San Francisco, and we've managed to persuade the Uber driver to let us cram ten people, most of whom work with Jess, into one Suburban. We're on our way to another party, and this one has me amped up, not because it's more free booze but because the Red Hot Chili Peppers are performing. To be honest, I don't think I could name a single song of theirs, but everyone else is so excited that I'd feel uncool if I'm not.

I'm sitting on Jess's lap when I feel my phone vibrate. I have a new text, and it's from a number I don't recognize. I swipe my screen to view it.

"Hey! Jess gave me your number. How r u?"

I turn around and glare at Jess behind me. She knows she's in trouble, because without having to say anything, she blushes with guilt and says, "Whaaat?"

My eyes shift from my phone back to her guilty face. "Did you give someone my number?"

"Ummmm, maybe." Her nose crinkles as she shrugs.

I shoot her the visual what-the-fuck glare.

"What? He asked for it. Asked about the brunette in the photo I posted of us yesterday. He's my friend. He's hot. What did he say?"

I pass her my phone. "Who is he?"

"A baseball player."

"No! Absolutely not. I've already got one baseball player on the roster. I'm good."

"I doubt they know each other, plus this one lives in New York during the off-season. Much more feasible. Just say hi."

Begrudgingly, I do as ordered and type an H followed by an i. Three dots immediately come up. He's typing already. Shit!

"How r u?"

Does this dude not know how to fucking spell *are* and *you*? What is it with men nowadays that they abbreviate words that have no business being abbreviated? It's obnoxious. I wait a few minutes before responding with "Great. Actually out in San Francisco right now. How *are you*?" I'm hoping my appropriate grammar will lead him into the land of appropriately formed sentences.

"Ha. Nice. R u having fun?"

Nope. "Yeah, it's great!" I reply.

We arrive at the entrance to the party and file out of the Suburban. I tuck my phone into my clutch and reapply some lip gloss before checking in at a table with a sign that says VIP. A woman asks if I would like to walk the red carpet.

Jess answers yes for me immediately. "This is a good one to walk," she whispers in my ear.

The rest of our group decides to go into the party, and Jess offers to stay with me. I walk the red carpet like usual. Flashes of light blind me while photographers shouting "Over here!" "This way!" and "Over the shoulder!" deafen me. I've gotten so used to this that it kind of freaks me out. Like, who the hell am I, and why am I still relevant enough to be walking a red carpet? I shouldn't question it, though, because sooner or later, everyone is going to catch on and start asking the same thing, and I'll never be able to score tickets to parties like this again. So, instead, I just smile and pose.

After the photo snapping ends, a line of reporters waits to get a sound bite, which is really just an industry term for a quote I will say and then later regret. Some of them ignore me because their outlets are too good for reality television people like myself. But most of them are nice. Aggressive but nice. They ask generic questions like "How is New York?" and "What are you doing now that the show has ended?" And without fail, the final question is always, "Are you dating anyone?" Sometimes I get creative in my answers and say coyly "Maybe" or "You're making me blush." Tonight I keep it pretty basic, since the rest of our group is waiting inside for us.

It isn't until the Chili Peppers actually take the stage that I remember I was in the middle of a texting conversation when we arrived. Certain there are a barrage of texts waiting for me from Jess's friend, I pull my phone out of my clutch, and sure enough there's an unread text. It's from Mr. Seattle.

"You make it okay?"

Disappointed, I tuck my phone back into my clutch.

It isn't until the next morning that Jess's friend texts, "Sorry, went 2 bed early. How long r u in San Fran for?"

Fucking abbreviations. "Just the weekend!"

"Nice, well when you get back, maybe we can grab dinner?"

"Yeah, sounds good."

"Great. Have fun!"

And just like that, I've managed to score at the Super Bowl without ever so much as stepping foot on the field.

the yankee

The day after I return from San Francisco, I'm greeted with a text from the baseball player Jess is trying to set me up with. A quick Google search of him reveals that not only is he a baseball player, but he plays for the most famous baseball team in America, the Yankees. Go big or go home, I guess.

He asks me what my schedule looks like this week. I tell him the only night I'm free is Thursday, which turns out to be the only night he's free as well.

"So dinner Thursday?" he asks.

"Let's do drinks," I respond.

"Okay. Drinks and maybe dinner Thursday?"

"Perfect. Maybe."

He's intrigued, and I know it. To be honest, I wasn't suggesting we do only drinks as a smooth move. I really wasn't trying to play games. I just didn't want to commit to a full dinner with someone I knew nothing about. "Drinks" could mean just drinks. You could have one, maybe two, and then call it a night because you only agreed to drinks and nothing more. Or "drinks" could mean drinks followed by dinner, followed by more drinks, followed by who knows what else. Anything can happen with "drinks."

I call Jess to whine about being set up on a date. I go on and on about how I am dreading having to go on a first date with a stranger because I hate first dates because they're awkward and they never lead anywhere—and she cuts me off. "Shut the fuck up and go on the date with the Yankee." She's right. I'm bitching about "having" to go on a date with a professional athlete, a Yankee no less.

Thursday afternoon rolls around, and he texts me.

The Yankee: "Still good for drinks?"

Me: "Yeah! Are you bringing any friends or is it just you?"

The Yankee: "Just me. U killing me."

Me: "Sorry ha ha, why? Was that bad for me to ask?"

The Yankee: "I'm trying to ask you on a date. U already downgraded me from dinner to drinks ha ha."

Me: "Shit. I did, didn't I? Okay so drinks, just us. Good?"

The Yankee: "Yes. Anywhere you've been dying to go?"

I tell him not really. The conversation continues with him asking what neighborhood I live in and what my address is. He tells me he'll pick me up at eight and we can walk somewhere in my neighborhood. I agree.

Five minutes before eight fifteen, I get a text from the Yankee telling me he's downstairs. I quickly grab my clutch and throw on a coat before locking my apartment door behind me. I can see him standing at the bottom of my stoop as I push the door open. And just like in the movies, when I emerge, he turns around with a smile on his face. Damn, he's hot! Everything about him is hot. His athletic build, his salty-blond hair, the perfect amount of scruff on his chin and cheeks that says *I care about hygiene, but I'm still a man.* Even his peacoat is hot. It's not a feminine-looking peacoat, it's a sophisticated, simple but expensive-looking one.

He gives me a hug and a small peck on the cheek. I've got the chills, and it's not just from the cold air. We start walking down Seventh Avenue before turning left on West Tenth Street. I'm really just following his lead. We arrive at a black door with steps leading down to it.

"This good?"

I nod in disbelief. It's Bell Book & Candle, the same damn place where I went on my first New York date with the guy who was coked-out and drunk and flirting with the bartender. Oh, my God! What if that skanky bartender who flirted with my date is working tonight? Oh, my God! What if she remembers me? Oh, my God! What if that douchebag is here? I don't even dare glance toward the bar. Instead, I hide my head behind the Yankee's back as he talks to the hostess. We're immediately ushered into the dining room. Crisis averted. I think.

We sit down, me in the booth, him in the uncomfortable wooden chair, and both order drinks, me a glass of wine, him a vodka and soda. He tells me he's hungry and asks if it's okay if he orders some food. I smirk at him in an I-know-what-you're-doing-but-okay kind of way. He chuckles. He's hot. He's even hotter when he chuckles. He orders a few different appetizers that, of course, being unable to resist food in front of me, I pick off of. We're talking and laughing and actually having a good time. Good enough for me to forget about the asshole I was here with not so long ago and the fact that I hate first dates.

By the end of the night, he has moved from the wooden chair across the table next to me in the booth. Our body language has reached beyond the level of flirtation; now it's just straight-up sexual. He grabs my hand at one point in the conversation. Next thing I know, it's one in the morning, and the restaurant is closing. The waitress drops off the check. I look around to see that we are the only people left. The chairs are now upside down on tables. I didn't even notice.

Like a gentleman, he offers to walk me back home. It's only been a few hours, but the walk home is completely different from the walk there. I now have my arm linked in his when we arrive at my stoop, where I'm certain he will either kiss me or ask to come up. But in a surprisingly chivalrous move, he does neither. Instead, he gives me a hug and a peck on the cheek. But it's a little warmer than the first one. We say goodbye.

I'm lying in bed with a grin when my phone chimes. It's a text.

The Yankee: "Tonight was fun. Thanks. Can we do it again tomorrow?"

Wow. He actually formed a complete sentence.

Me: "Yes. And yes."

The Yankee: "Good night."

Me: "Good night."

Ahhhh . . . I love this part of dating. I love lying here in bed with butterflies in my stomach. I love the anticipation of what the next week will bring; the excitement of something that could, possibly, maybe, just very well turn into *something*.

The next day, he texts me to see if I want to grab dinner. Two dates in a row? I am on fire! I coyly say sure, and next thing I know, it is eight o'clock yet again and he's texting me from my stoop. I make him wait a few minutes just for good measure before making my way out the front door. I greet him with a hug and a kiss on the cheek.

"Where are we eating?" I ask.

"I figured we'd just walk and find somewhere."

I'm a little annoyed that he didn't bother to make reservations anywhere. It's Friday night in the West Village, and every restaurant is bound to be full. Why do men ask women on dates and not bother to plan? I decide to hold my tongue. It is, after all, only our second date. I can't be a bitch this early on. We start walking down West Fourth Street, only to find that every restaurant is, just like I predicted, packed. He suggests we go to the Soho Grand. With no other options, I agree, and we hop into a cab.

Twenty minutes later, we are sitting side by side on a velvet couch in the lounge area of the hotel. It's quite posh, I must admit. There's a piano player in the corner playing sultry songs. The patrons at the other tables are pretty eclectic. Some tables are filled with suit-clad men, clearly enjoying the few precious hours they have between getting off work and having to go home to their families in the suburbs. There are the typical New York models who take notice of each man walking by. They laugh in a fake candid way like someone is taking an Instagram photo of them. The other tables are filled with groups of martini-drinking chic locals.

We order a few drinks and some appetizers. Drink by drink, we become more engaged with each other, just like we had on our first date last night. Only this time, the occasional hand holding and thigh grabbing happen more often. At one point, he takes his hand and brushes a strand of hair off my face, tucking it behind my ear. I'm giving him my best flirty eyes.

Somewhere between rounds three and four, I find myself in the middle of conversation and gazing into his eyes, when out of absolutely nowhere . . . he kisses me. Not a full make-out but not just a peck. A real, publicly appropriate (by New York standards) kiss. We're both a little taken aback by his boldness. I didn't take him for a public-display-of-affection type, and from the look on his face, this spontaneity isn't something he's used to, either. But it's a pleasant surprise, one that has me yearning for him more than I ever expected. I want the full kiss. And so does he.

As we both finish our drinks in unison, he whispers in my ear, "Want to get out of here?"

"Absolutely." I grin.

"My place is around the corner. We can have a drink there."

"Works for me."

His place *is* right around the corner—well, two blocks away, to be exact. I follow him through the lobby and up the elevator to his apartment. The door flies open, revealing floor-to-ceiling windows that overlook all of Soho. It is an exquisite, modern, and very expensive New York apartment. The couch has an unfolded blanket on it. The dining-room table looks to have never been used. Come to think of it, there aren't even any chairs around it. The kitchen countertop is made of pristine white marble. A few Coors Light cans and some old takeout food sit atop the island. Such a bachelor pad. There's a bottle of red wine on the counter, which he opens and pours into two tumblers.

"No wineglasses, I see."

"Don't judge."

I smile, but inside I am judging a little.

I take my glass of wine with me as I strut over toward the couch, passing the windows and taking in the view. It really is an incredible view. I'm gazing out at all of Soho below when he comes up behind me and brushes my hair to one side, kissing my neck, sending tingles down my spine. He removes my jacket, leaving my silk camisole and bare shoulder to be kissed. I turn around. He kisses my lips. The kissing starts slow but quickly escalates. His hands move from my cheeks down my arms before making their way around my waist. Everything about it is steamy. He lifts me up. I wrap my legs around his waist. My back is against the living-room wall, my legs wrapped tightly around him. We can't stop kissing. My silk camisole is now halfway off, my black lace bralette teasing him. I'm tempted to take it off, and so is he. He starts to lower one of the straps, but I pull it back up. He tries again, and I pull it back up again.

I love this part of a make-out session, the part when you know the guy wants more, and you know you have the option to give him more, but you tease him instead. I am more than satisfied with his kisses, but they are so good I do, in fact, want more. But I don't want to be the woman who gives more this easily. And then I remember I am on my period. Never have I ever been so thankful to be on my period. It is as if my worst enemy has suddenly become my greatest ally, keeping me from taking this too far, too quickly. I need to remain strong, and I can't do it alone. I abruptly end the make-out session and tell him I have an early morning and need to get home. He begs me to stay. I don't. Instead, I play the power card only a tease of a woman can have and go proudly home.

The next day, I awake to a text from him saying good morning. I type back, "Good morning." He asks what my plans for the day are, and I tell him I have no real plans. Then he asks if I want to come hang out. The player side of me wants to make him chase, but the infatuated side has me saying yes. It isn't long before I'm back on the couch in his apartment, only this time, I'm clothed and sober. We spend the afternoon cuddling and making out. We spend the next day doing the same thing. And the next and the next.

And just like that, what started out as a favor to Jess has turned into the beginning of a relationship, I think.

all men should go to hell

The Yankee and I have been inseparable over the past two weeks. Pretty much whenever he's in town, I'm over at his place. Well, that's how it started, at least. In the meantime, I've been completely ignoring my Mr. Seattle. I'm sure he's taken the hint, because his texts have ceased completely. In hindsight, I probably shouldn't have blown him off so quickly. Despite having spent so much time together, I know the Yankee and are aren't going to last much longer, let alone forever.

Our downfall began shortly after we had sex for the first time. Surprise, surprise. Sex always seems to change relationships; it makes them either sink or swim, and there's not a lot in between. I waited about four dates before finally giving up the goods. I couldn't resist any longer. I was out drinking with Ava, Jess, and Emily when the Yankee texted me asking if I wanted to come over. I say yes, of course. And then I do what any drunk, horny woman would do: log on to my Amazon Now account, which is basically like Amazon Prime on steroids. Instead of waiting two days for shipping, this version can have things delivered within the hour. I type in "condoms." And what do you know, there on my screen for sale is a box of condoms available for delivery within one hour. I add it to my cart. I go to check out, only to realize there is a twenty-five-dollar minimum. So I add another box.

Fuck it, twenty-five dollars is a hell of a lot cheaper than the cost of having a child.

Shortly afterward, I drunkenly make my way to his apartment, stumbling through the lobby and up to the doorman who regularly works the night shift, who now recognizes me, and ask if there was a delivery for me. He goes in the back and brings out a brown paper sack. He's got a smile on his face. He definitely peeked inside. I thank him and head to the elevator. I take a peek in the bag. Two orange boxes of condoms. I can't help but feel like a fucking badass as I knock on the door. The Yankee opens it to see me standing proudly holding up the brown bag of condoms.

The sex ends up being pretty good. Nothing mind-blowing, but then again, I'm not exactly in the clearest state of mind when it happens. I'm a firm believer that the first time you have sex with a man shouldn't dictate your future sex. You've got to give it a couple of tries before giving up. Plus, I've learned from firsthand experience that sex isn't everything in a relationship. Hell, look at the Canadian—best sex of my life and also biggest asshole in my life.

It's not until the next morning that the Yankee gets his first strike. With a pounding headache, I look over to my left to see something peculiar: a U-Haul box turned upside down being used as a nightstand. I look around the room. Is this the first time I've been in this room? Now that I think about it, we've always just hung out in the living room. It's so bare. There is a bed that we are sleeping in and a television on top of another, bigger upside-down U-Haul box. Is this the new wave of modern decor? It can't be, right?

I get out of bed and quietly make my way to the kitchen to get a glass of water and then tiptoe around the apartment to do some investigating. I open one door to find a bathroom. I move on to the next door, where I find a completely empty room, a large one. There is a closet off to the side that has men's clothes strewn on the floor along with some boxes of Ferragamo dress shoes, Gucci shopping bags, and a hanging Burberry garment bag. Wait a second, this has to be the master bedroom. But there's no bed in it. No furniture. No artwork. Nothing. If there's a master bedroom, why in the hell are we sleeping in the guest bedroom? I remember him telling me that he's been living here for six months, so how the hell is this place not furnished? It's not like he doesn't have the money. So what the fuck is going on?

My head is pounding as I gulp the water. I'm hungover and confused as hell. I'm so turned off that I've been seeing, and just had sex with, a grown man who has money but who can't bother to even pay someone to furnish his house. It's one thing if the guy doesn't have taste in decorating. In fact, I actually find that kind of endearing, and it allows me the chance to decorate on someone else's dime. But seeing his half-empty apartment reveals a laziness about him that has me not even wanting to wake him up but instead calling an Uber to take me and my pounding headache home. I get dressed, leave him a note that says "Didn't want to wake you, have a good day," grab the remaining condoms, and head back home.

I hadn't seen the Yankee for a day or two when we find ourselves hanging out again. I ask him about the furniture situation, and he gets a little defensive, so I decide to just pretend that living in a guest bedroom despite having a spacious master bedroom is perfectly normal.

Each hangout seems to be as monotonous as the last. Eventually we get into a routine where we spend our days doing our own thing, then I come over at night, we hook up, and then I leave either in the middle of the night or first thing in the morning. I will say the hooking-up part has gone from decent to pretty damn good. Not Canadian good but certainly good enough to keep me coming back each night. But the more time we spend together, the more I realize this "relationship" will never be anything more than a physical one. We never talk about being exclusive or calling each other girlfriend and boyfriend. Hell, we hardly talk at all. Which is fine for now. I feel bad saying this, but I'm kind of just buying time until the next man comes along, and I think he is too.

The physical touch of a man has a way of fulfilling me right now. Hell, the other day I texted him while I'm out on a run to see if he's home. He is. I tell him I'm going to come by and get some water. I walk in the door, don't get any water, but do get him. I leave and continue on my run without feeling even the slightest ounce of guilt. I figure, it's a win-win, he gets laid and I get my run done, leaving both my body and my libido satisfied.

The truth is, even though I know he isn't the one I will spend the rest of my life with, he's all I have right now. Maybe sometimes you can just date without needing love, date for companionship, for passionate make-outs, for snuggling. At least, until you meet the real thing, right? Whatever was happening, as shallow as it was, seemed to be fine.

Until strike two comes. The Yankee has just returned from being out of town yet again and asks if I want to come over. I'm at a bar so I ask if he can just swing by and pick me up on his way. He tells me just to meet him at his place and he will even send a car for me. We go back and forth a little bit. I want him to come get me; he wants me just to come over. He's being lazy and I'm being stubborn. We are in a stalemate. Part of me wants to abandon him for the night, but I know that will only bring more drama come tomorrow. I want to win this transportation war, but eventually I cave when he tells me that he told the doorman to give me a key to his apartment.

I'm tipsy and irked when I arrive at his building. I check in with the doorman and wait for him to hand me a key. He doesn't. Fuck, this is awkward.

"I think there was supposed to be a key left for me." I'm definitely slurring.

"Oh, right, follow me."

I follow the doorman to a room filled with silver mailboxes. They aren't labeled like the ones in my building, but they are much shinier. Rich people. The doorman takes out his ring of keys and opens one of the mailboxes. He reaches in and grabs another ring of keys. He slides one off and hands it to me.

"I'm not even going to ask how many times you've done this." I try making light of the awkwardness of it all, but it blows right over his head. But really, how many times has he given out a key? I wonder as I ride up the elevator.

Now, with an even saltier attitude, I make my way down the hall and toward the Yankee's apartment. I take the key, turn the lock, and burst through the door. I'm determined to curse him out and then withhold my body from him. The first happens, but after one apology, the second doesn't. Whoops.

The following day, I think everything is fine, but I don't hear from him. Two more days go by, and still nothing. I'm at happy hour when I finally get the liquid courage I need to text him.

Me: "Hey stranger."

The Yankee: "Hey, what's up?"

Me: "Not much, u?"

The Yankee: "Going to dinner."

Me: "Nice!"

An hour passes . . .

Me: "Everything okay?"

The Yankee: "It's fine but not gonna lie, didn't appreciate your attitude the other night."

Me: "Well I didn't appreciate you not making an effort to come get me. Why do I always have to be the one to come over?"

The Yankee: "I told you I'd send a car."

Me: "It's not about sending the car. You could have just picked me up on your way."

The Yankee: "And you could have just taken a car."

Me: "That's not fair."

The Yankee: "Your attitude wasn't fair. I'm not looking for some-one with that kind of attitude."

Me: "What does that mean?"

The Yankee: "Just what I said."

Me: "Well, I'm not looking for someone who can't even bother to pick me up."

The Yankee: "I'm out to dinner, you're clearly out, so let's just let this blow over and we will talk about it tomorrow."

Me: "K."

Four days pass, and we haven't said a word to each other. Part of me thinks it's probably over for good, even though it's only been two strikes, but the other part of me thinks we are both just being stubborn and any day now we will be reunited and ready for strike three.

Three more days go by, and just as I expected, we have our strike three. He texts me to say that he is sorry for getting upset with me and that he wants to go to dinner. I tell him I'm sorry, too, and that I think dinner would be nice. We make a date for Sun-day evening. The morning of our date, I go to my cousin's house in Brooklyn to visit with her and her newborn baby. A few hours pass, and no word from the Yankee. I make my way back into the city at around five and start to get ready for our date. Seven o'clock rolls around, and still no word. By eight, I'm pissed enough to fire off a text.

Me: "What's up?"

One hour later . . .

The Yankee: "Out to dinner with my parents, u?"

Me: "Huh? I thought we were doing dinner."

The Yankee: "My parents are in town tho."

Me: "Then why'd you schedule dinner with me?"

The Yankee: "I forgot."

Motherfucker!

I decide not to respond. I am done. So done. And the thing is, I'm not really angry that it's over, I'm more just annoyed that I did my makeup for nothing. I guess the fact that I'm more upset that I put on fake lashes for no reason than I am at being stood up tells me that the Yankee is far from "the one." I know that I was never emotionally invested in him. I never saw us really working out. There was a major void in our conversations, there was a difference in our maturity levels, and it was a relationship that was fun but nothing more than that. I have zero regrets about it, nor do I despise him. He is what he is, and he served his purpose until he could no longer serve. And that's what happens when the only thing you really enjoy about a man is his penis.

Looks like I'm headed back to the land of the Single Ladies. But I probably won't be alone for long. Turns out my relationship isn't the only one headed out of style. Jess's is, too.

Jess had invited me and Sarah to her parents' house in the suburbs for Sunday dinner. I love Jess's parents because they remind me of my own family. They're outgoing, funny, and warm, and they like to drink wine. And given the fact that the oven in my apartment is currently housing my sweaters, I wasn't about to miss an opportunity for a home-cooked meal. But *this* Sunday dinner was going to be different. This was going to be the night Jess introduced her boyfriend to her family. I couldn't wait. The only thing better than a home-cooked meal is a front-row seat to the awkward introduction of a new boyfriend to a girl's parents.

We get to Jess's parents' house, with one notable absentee, Mike. Jess doesn't so much as mention his absence, though I can see the disappointment written across her face. I don't dare bring it up. I know Jess well enough to know you can't push her to talk; when she's ready, she will, and now is not the time. We have a typically lovely evening with Jess's parents, sharing tidbits of New

York gossip while making sure we all stay just on the right side of parent-appropriate.

After dinner, Jess rides the train back with us. As we settle into our seats, Sarah can't hold her tongue any longer. "Okay, so what the fuck happened with Mike?"

Jess takes a deep breath. "I don't really know. He said he woke up and the dog was vomiting blood and he had to take her to the vet. I guess that's what happened."

Sarah and I stay silent for a moment. I mean, what can we really say? If we call him a liar and the story turns out to be true, then *we're* the assholes.

"I know it sounds like an excuse, but maybe it's true. And I'm sure he'll make it up to you."

I sound unusually optimistic. So much so that Jess is looking at me like I am a stranger.

"Or he's a total asshole!" I quickly revert back to my usual man-hating demeanor.

Jess's face fills with relief.

"Everything else going okay with him?" I ask.

"He's just been weird lately. I get the dog situation, but then last Friday, he was supposed to go to the Knicks game and come over after, but I didn't hear from him all night. Not a word. He texted me the next morning saying his phone had died."

"Ummmmm, that's sketchy as fuck, not gonna lie." I suck at playing the optimist friend.

"I know, right?"

The three of us begin a heated debate about whether or not Madison Square Garden has cell-phone chargers. I put my lawyer hat on and argue that if he was sitting courtside, he obviously had access to some sort of suite, which undoubtedly had a cell-phone charger. Sarah makes a solid point that even if there wasn't a charger in the suite, certainly at least one of his friends had a portable charger. We all come to the conclusion that the "dead phone" excuse just isn't going to cut it. I want to say, his phone died and so did his relationship along with it, but I resist the urge.

Instead, I just reserve an extra chair for Jess for when she's ready to come back in the Land of the Single Ladies.

twenty-nine calls for a good time

With the Yankee officially off my roster, I am more single than ever. I am also on the brink of twenty-nine and looking for a good time. If that good time happens to be with a man, then so be it. But it's going to take more than good sex and a good job to tame this soon-to-be-twenty-nine-year-old woman!

What started out as a casual get-together with some of my girl-friends like Ava, Jess, Michelle, Sarah, Emily, and even Kelly, who had flown up from Atlanta, to celebrate my birthday turns out to be nothing short of yet another epic night. I decide to go casual, since I figure reaching the milestone of twenty-nine isn't something to go all out for. I mean, twenty-one, yes. Thirty, hell, yes. Twenty-nine, not so much. Plus, I'm not one of those chicks who celebrate their birthdays for an entire month. I can't stand those girls. I don't get why birthday celebrations are a big deal to begin with. It's like, congratu-lations, your mother endured hours of pain while you just popped out and then got to do absolutely nothing but eat, sleep, and poop in your own pants for a year while your parents cleaned up after you. Birthday celebrations really should be reserved for the women who give birth. And then to be the type to celebrate that for an entire month? Plus, with no man to shower me with gifts or plan a party in my honor, I was good with just a girls' dinner.

We are eating at a trendy place in the Meatpacking District when I notice the somber mood Jess is in. I can tell the Mike situation is weighing on her, but I don't know who else knows about it, so I keep quiet. It isn't until Jess and I go to the bathroom that she breaks her silence and breaks down. The instant the door shuts, tears start streaming down her face.

I immediately wrap my arms around her as she sobs. "What happened?"

"He cheated. It's over."

"Did we find out for sure?"

"Yes."

She whips out her phone and shows me a photo. It's her boyfriend. At the Knicks game, on the night his phone supposedly died. He's sitting courtside. He's sitting courtside next to a woman. He's sitting courtside next to a woman with his hand on her thigh. I'm in disbelief. I'm less shocked at what a dick he is and more at what an *idiot* he is. Did he really think he was going to get away with sitting courtside at a Knicks game with a chick and not get caught? People who sit courtside at a Knicks game sit there for one reason and one reason only, and it's not to enjoy the game. It's to get photographed "getting their PDA on."

"Who is she?"

"A fucking cocktail waitress from Miami."

"You're lying."

"I wish I was."

Apparently, when Jess confronted him with this evidence, he told her that while he was at the game, he was "randomly" given courtside seats. And a "random" girl who was with them just happened to sit next to him.

She starts to wipe away her tears. "I'm sorry. I don't want to ruin your birthday night."

"Are you fucking kidding? You're not ruining my birthday night.

Who gives a shit? It's just a birthday. Who wants to be twenty-nine anyway?"

"Me." She laughs. "I just knew it. And the thing is, *he* was the one chasing *me*. And then for him to be cheating on me, it's, like, I don't get it."

"He's a fucking tool. There is nothing more to say. He's a tool who doesn't deserve someone like you."

Jess continues wiping away her tears. It breaks my heart to see her this way. In fact, I've *never* seen her this way. She's usually the rock of our group, the one lending out the shoulder for *us* to cry on. But on my birthday, there, in the bathroom stall, Jess is the one in need of a shoulder, and I'm just glad I'm able to give it to her.

"Fuck men! They're all fucking bastards!"

This causes her to giggle as she sniffles and wipes away the rest of her tears. "I look like shit, don't I?"

She does have mascara running down her face, but I can't bring myself to tell her she looks like shit. Instead, I dig through my purse and find my emergency concealer. I pat it underneath her eyes. "Not anymore."

"Let's keep this between us for right now?"

"You got it. Bury the body?" I say.

"Bury the body."

We return to the table just in time for me to blow out the candles on a Momofuku cake one of the girls brought. Just when I think the night is over, I see a tall guy in a smoking-hot leather jacket approach our table and start talking to Ava. It is clear they know each other as they exchange pleasantries and chat. I look at him curiously. I don't find him particularly attractive, yet I am drawn to him.

"This is the birthday girl, Andi. Andi, meet my friend!" Ava shouts from across the table.

He walks over and reaches out his hand to introduce himself. "Nice to meet you, and happy birthday."

"Thanks. Sick jacket."

"Really? You like?"

"Yeah, I actually do," I say as I pet the sleeve.

Next thing I know, I'm stroking the sleeve of his leather jacket and he's inviting us to go to the rooftop bar next door after.

"Oh, yeah? Maybe we will."

As he walks away, I can't help but feel even more perplexed by my fascination with him. Maybe it's because I realize he never told me his name. We're just getting up to leave when from across the room he shouts, "You ladies ready to go?"

"Yeah, we're going to head out. Nice to meet you." I'm trying to hint to him that he's yet to tell me his name. The next thing I know, I'm starring in a joke: ten girls and one dude wearing a sick leather jacket walk into a bar. He shakes hands with the doorman, who lowers the red velvet rope as we file in. Another doorman opens a large door, revealing the bar. It's dimly lit with neon strobe lights, and music blares from the DJ booth as bandage-dress-wearing chicks dance atop tables that line the walls of the room. Led by the nameless man wearing a sick leather jacket, we make our way to a large booth where two waitresses clad in thigh-high stockings and corsets ask us what we'd like to drink.

"Let's do some champagne, a few bottles of vodka, and some mixers. You like vodka?" He's even sexier when he takes charge.

"Sure," I say.

"Ehhhh, that doesn't sound too convincing. Hold on," he says to the waitress. "What do *you* want, birthday girl?"

"Kind of craving an old-fashioned."

"Done. Do the champagne and vodka, and then can we get her an old-fashioned, please?" His sexy meter continues to climb.

"All right, jig's up. Who are you?" I ask, hoping third time's the charm and maybe he'll actually tell me his name.

"I'm a nobody. But I do own the bar."

I laugh in defeat. Of course he does. Mr. Leather Jacket stays with us as we dance and drink in our private booth for the next few hours. Everyone's dancing on the table and having fun, even Jess, which makes me happy to see.

"Let's go to the Box!" he says.

"The Box?" I scream over the music. "What the hell is the Box?"

"You've never been? It's a New York City staple."

"Do any of you girls want to go to some place called the Box?" I shout across the table.

"Can we get in?" Jess asks.

"Can we get in?" I ask Mr. Leather Jacket.

"I got us." Just like that.

"He says yes."

"Then *hell*, yes!" shouts Jess. I nod.

"Great. I'll order a car."

A short drive across town, and ten girls and one guy in a sick leather jacket arrive at another club. Yet again, our fearless leader is greeted by the bouncers, who lower the velvet rope as we file into a small foyer. A hostess in burlesque attire talks to him as she looks at the computer on her podium. She offers us a table upstairs.

"Right this way," says another burlesque-clad hostess. She pulls back two thick purple crushed-velvet curtains to reveal a massive room filled with lively clubbers. A spotlight shines on a large stage with the words THE BOX on the closed curtains. The hostess leads us up a staircase to a private booth overlooking the crowd and stage below. We have what can only be described as the Lincoln booth, hopefully sans any assassination. Two more waitresses wearing sequined booty shorts, fishnet stockings, feathered headpieces, and nipple tassels—and nothing else—come over and tell us the show will be starting in about fifteen minutes.

"She'll have an old-fashioned, please" he says without even asking me.

"Good memory."

"Birthday girl gets whatever birthday girl wants."

"*Whatever* I want?"

"Within reason."

By now, a few of the girls have invited their boyfriends, so there's a nice mix of drunk girls and guys. And I've got a date of my own, though I still don't know his name, and at this point it's way too late in the evening, or probably morning, to ask. Instead I whisper in his ear, "Thanks for doing this."

"You're very welcome." He squeezes my thigh.

Suddenly there's a voice coming over the entire club shouting, "Ladies and gentlemen . . . welcome to the Box."

Applause and "woo-hoos" erupt. The red curtains draw back. A spotlight turns on. And there in the middle of the stage is a woman. She's not wearing fishnets. She's not wearing feathers or nipple tassels. She is completely naked. She doesn't say a word. She just stands there for what feels like a minute or two. What the fuck. Sultry music begins to play. The spotlight shifts to reveal a four-poster bed with a woman in lingerie lying on it seductively. A naked man walks out and makes his way to her. He begins kissing her. They roll around on the bed in coordination with the music. Is he penetrating her? Or is this just weird soft-core porn? Is this the same woman who was narrating? I'm so confused but so enraptured by the entire scene. I'm in disbelief that this is happening but more so that it's *allowed* to be happening. Only in New York City. The curtains close. My jaw is on the floor. I cringe, wondering what is next. I can feel Mr. Leather Jacket staring at my face. I turn to him.

"What the fuck?"

He's dying with laughter.

"Oh, you haven't seen anything yet."

I laugh. He places his hands on my shoulders and gives a squeeze.

The next act is a woman doing some rendition of a striptease that involves a red boa. She takes off her sequined G-string only to reveal that she is really a he.

"Just check your judgments at the door," he says over my gasp.

He's right. There are about ten more acts. Some of them are hilarious, some are artistic, and others are just straight up vulgar.

As the night goes on, my friends begin to fade, one by one calling it a night. It's down to me, Kelly, Jess, Ava, and the man in the sick leather jacket when the lights come on.

"Y'all ready to go?" I ask the girls.

"You should stay," Kelly whispers.

"Stay?"

"With *him*."

"But you're staying in my apartment."

"Umm, so what?"

"I can't leave you for a guy."

"It's your fucking birthday, Andi. Have some fun. Live a little. Make out. Do what single New York City girls do on their birthdays."

Ava overhears us and offers to drop Kelly off on her way home.

"Are you sure you won't be mad?"

"Give me your keys. I'll only be mad if you don't. But you have to tell me everything tomorrow morning. Deal?"

I hand her the keys. "Deal. Love you! Love you all!"

Now it was just the two of us, alone in the Lincoln booth, as everyone below files out of the club. It takes about three and a half seconds before we start making out. Honestly, I can't believe it's taken this long. I must have lost track of time because the next thing I know he's called an Uber and we're walking down the stairs. I follow behind him as we exit the club when suddenly I'm blinded. Holy shit, it's morning. We climb into the awaiting sedan.

"I should just go home."

"No, come to my place, you can just stay and lay with me."

"Ehhhh, not really a stay-and-lay kind of girl."

"Wait, did I just get used for some birthday fun?"

"No, no, no. Well, maybe. Depends. How does it feel to get used by a birthday girl?"

"Different. Sexy. Intriguing."

"Then yes, you sure did."

I tell the driver my address. It's now seven in the morning and I'm holding my stilettos because my feet are killing me, pressing the button on the call box buzzing my own apartment, praying Kelly won't be pissed off to be awakened so early. She lets me in and immediately shuffles back to bed.

"How was it?" she mumbles.

"Amazing!"

"That's my girl!"

I crawl into bed myself. Best. Birthday. Ever.

The next morning, I'm lying in bed next to Kelly, nursing both a physical and a moral hangover when my phone buzzes.

"Hey. Wishing you a Happy Birthday."

My heart sinks. Unlike the rest of the birthday texts I received, this one isn't from a friend or family member. It's from my past. It's from . . . Seattle. And it's got the wheels in my head working overtime. One generic text has me thinking deeply about the Jess ordeal. I start to wonder, if Jess, the woman who has her shit together the most, can get cheated on, are any of us safe? Is it possible that she, or I, or any of us, for that matter, will ever find a man who is sweet and loving and faithful? A man who maybe isn't the most attractive but *is* the most loyal?

What is it with these New York men? It's like in order to be a resident here, you have to be a douchebag. And as I reread the six-word text, it hits me. Maybe I have found that man. Maybe I have found a guy who I let slip away because he isn't the hottest, isn't the head turner, isn't the dreamy stud. Maybe he's been under my nose the entire time, but I just haven't been ready to sniff him out. I start to type.

"Thank you. How are you, I've missed you lately." I press "Send."

And just like that, the brief romance I once had with the average-looking but sweet Mr. Seattle has officially been rekindled. I ignored him for so long because I was too busy hooking up with the Yankee, and yet, even after all that time, here he is still responding to my text. The thing is, I really did enjoy our conversations before I met the Yankee, but I think I got wrapped up in the Yankee because he was hotter and, well, it was all just so much more convenient. But with that over, I'm hoping that just maybe Mr. Seattle might be willing to give me a second chance. After all, it is my birthday . . . and birthday girls get whatever they want, right?

the dark horse and a bestseller

Two things have been made official since my twenty-ninth birthday. The first, I'm a published author. The second, I'm in a relationship, well sort of. Ironic given the fact that my book is about heartbreak.

I'll start with the second. I say sort of because it's still in the early stages, but since that random birthday text, Mr. Seattle and I have spent practically every morning on the phone with each other. What used to be casual texting has escalated to distracting in the best way. One night we FaceTimed for seven hours straight. I called him when I got into bed to say good night, and the next thing I know, the sun is coming up outside my window. Mind you, this is the same guy whom, not long ago, I couldn't FaceTime for more than five minutes while in the back of a cab on the way to JFK. And now here I am, FaceTiming with him for seven hours.

He's still not the hottest guy I've ever met (or, technically, seen on a screen). But his personality makes him attractive to me. There's something about him that I just can't seem to get enough of. We talk about things without any tone of judgment in our voices, without any condescension, without anything but acceptance. That's what it is, I think; there is an acceptance for each other that I've never experienced before. He doesn't care about my past as a reality television contestant. He doesn't care that I've been engaged. He doesn't see me in that light; he just sees me as a woman he likes. He doesn't just accept me, but he admires me. He tells me how proud he is that I'm writing a book and that I am making my own living in New York City. He says that my independence is "sexy." And I believe him. And beyond the pride and acceptance, there is this overall feeling of sweetness and ease between the two of us. He's the first man in a long time who makes me not want to play games just to stir up drama or fish for compliments; instead I just want to be nice. Who the fuck have I become? A woman smitten, that's who. A woman who has finally realized that I don't want to be in the same kind of relationship I've had in the past. I don't want to be on a roller coaster ride anymore.

Don't get me wrong, I think we all have to experience those roller coaster relationships at least once in our lives. They give us the unhealthy dose of highs and lows that satisfies our craving for drama. And I did that kind of relationship. I did it for far too long. But now that I've indulged in the roller coaster, gotten my thrill, I'm happy riding on the merry-go-round, slowly, peacefully, and eas-ily. I think I've finally reached the point in my life where steady is more intriguing and exciting than anything else.

And in just two short weeks from now, this long-distance thing we've got going on is going to become face-to-face. Oh, yeah, I am heading to Seattle! It was a no-brainer that I'd visit him, but I was waiting for the invitation. And just last week, it came, along with a first-class ticket purchased by him. I haven't told too many people about him yet, especially not my family. Jess, Ava, and Kelly know, but that's about it. I think I'm keeping my guard up a little when it comes to him. I don't know, I've just been through this before, where I get into a relationship and it doesn't work and then every-one knows about it and it haunts me forever. Of course, that was in part due to the fact that millions of people knew about my last breakup. But that's the other thing: this is the first time I've had feelings for a man since my engagement. I don't want any outside sources to ruin that. I don't want to worry about the backlash if this doesn't work out. I just want to bask in my secret right now. Plus, it's kind of hard to tell the world I've met a new man when I'm busy promoting my new book.

Oh yes, the week has finally arrived! *It's Not Okay* has made its way onto bookstore shelves and into the hands of anyone willing to read it. My publicists and agents have scheduled a week-long, jam-packed, full-court press junket with every major media outlet you could imagine. My parents have come up to New York to support me; my mom even brought smudge-proof pens and markers to sign books with. Kelly and my friend Christy have flown up from Atlanta. My most valued core of friends and family are here.

I should be panicked. I should be in an ultimate tailspin considering this is to be the biggest week of my life, the week I've spent a year waiting for. I am about to have to face the criticism of fans, book reviewers, and God knows who else. But I'm not. I'm not because for the first time in a long time, thanks to my family, my friends, my new life, and most of all my upcoming trip to Seattle, I am able to see beyond the book, beyond the heartbreak, and beyond the reality television show I once appeared on. I am able to see beyond what the critics will say and how I will be judged. And instead, I just see what is around me right now, in the present. It almost feels as if releasing this book is also releasing me from my past.

We kick things off with my very own launch party, thrown by my publisher. All my New York friends, like Jess, Ava, Michelle, and Sarah, come out to support me, along with plenty of my acquaintances and kind-of-friends. At one point, I look around and wonder, is this the first event in my life that is in honor of me?

Sure, I got plenty of attention being the *Bachelorette*, but this isn't about attention. It's about a celebration. When I think about it, I've never had a wedding or an engagement party. I've never had a baby or a bridal shower. Is this book both, my child and my lover?

The week continues with interviews with *Good Morning America* followed by *Entertainment Tonight*, *Extra*, *The Insider*, AOL's *Build*, and a dozen more.

I am on my way to my very own book signing when my agent calls to tell me that my book has made the *New York Times* Best Sellers list. Upon hearing the news, I immediately begin to tear up. My mom is in the backseat and asks what's wrong.

"Nothing."

"Then why are you tearing up?"

"I have some good news."

"Whaaaaaaat?"

"I made the *New York Times* Best Sellers list."

"What the faaaaack!" my mom squeals. The use of the f-bomb makes it undeniable that she is both ecstatic and surprised. "Seriously, though?"

"Yeah!"

She leans across the backseat to give me a hug and a kiss on the cheek. "Oh, my God, I am so proud of you."

My dad leans back from the front seat. "Wow, that is so awesome. I am so proud—" His voice starts to crack. "So proud of you."

"You have to call Shishy," my mom says as she is already dialing my sister's number. "Shishy, how are you?" my mom shouts into the phone. "Oh, good . . . Hang on, I'm with Pookie, and she has something to tell you." She hands me the phone.

"Hi, Shishy! How are you?"

"Hi, Shishy! Good! How are you? Have you killed Mom yet?"

I laugh. "Not yet. But I have some good news." I pause as my mom nudges me and mouths *tell her*. My mom knows I hate boasting, even if it is to my own sister.

"I made the Best Sellers list."

"Wow, that's amazing! Congratulations. Holy shit, you are a bestselling author, and you aren't even thirty."

For some reason, hearing her say this takes my high to a new level. It takes her putting it into context for me to realize that I have actually accomplished something in my life. I did it. I wrote a book, I got it published, and it made it to the Best Sellers list. It is one of the rare times where I actually take a second and give myself some credit.

I think since moving away from my old job as a lawyer, I've struggled to find substance in my life. I've found that a job is the single most tangible and obvious measure of success. Whether it's winning a case, getting a raise, or landing a promotion, most jobs allow you to visibly see your progress. But having quit my legal career, I don't have a job that allows me to see my progress. My day-to-day life often feels like it lacks a certain substantive value that it once had. It feels stagnant at times. I don't get promotions. I don't get raises. In fact, I've never gotten either in my life. I have no boss to buy me a holiday gift or coworkers to celebrate my birthday. I've never had a wedding or a baby shower, and I know those things are trivial, but the point is that I just haven't felt proud or celebrated in a long time. Until now. My sister's words replay in my mind. I am a bestselling author, I am a bestselling author. I. Am. A. Best. Selling. Author. It is the single greatest accomplishment of my life. And even if it is the last, I will always have that. No show, no ex, no one can take that away from me.

Someone equally excited for my accomplishment is Kelly, who is also in the backseat. She immediately asks, "Now that you're a bestseller, what are you going to buy?"

"I haven't thought about it."

"*How* have you not thought about it? That's the best part of being a *New York Times* Best Seller."

"That I have to buy myself a gift?"

She rolls her eyes.

She's right. I haven't thought about the fact that I need to celebrate my accomplishment. "I don't even know what I'd buy."

"Well, is there anything you've been eyeing?"

"Yeah, that watch!" I point to her wrist. When the fuck did she get a Cartier watch?

She laughs and tells me it's just on loan until the one her husband custom-ordered for her anniversary comes in.

"Great. Then I can get it." I'm half joking, half serious.

Kelly takes it off her wrist and hands it to me. "Try it on."

I do, and it's perfect. "I can't, though."

"Why not?"

"Cartier? How many dollar signs do I need to explain why not?"

"You can, and you will."

That night, I share the news with Mr. Seattle. He's overcome with pride. He can't stop saying how proud of me he is. There's not a shred of jealousy or the desire to knock me off a pedestal like I've experienced in past relationships. My success makes him happy, and that in turn makes me happy for my success.

The following morning, Kelly and I head north to Madison Avenue. It's the first time I've ever walked through the doors of a Cartier store. Kelly takes the lead as if it were just her regular neighborhood bodega, while I follow behind, eyeing the pristine glass cases. Before I know it, Kelly has flagged down a woman in a black suit behind the counter.

"Hi. She'd like to see the Tank Solo, please, all three sizes."

The woman returns moments later with a tray of three silver watches on a red velvet pillow. There in the middle is the most perfect Cartier Tank Solo I've ever laid eyes on. The woman places it on my wrist. I look down, admiring it. It's the second time I've ever felt love at first sight. But it is the first time I am feeling love at first sight over something that I know won't end up being a crazy asshole.

"She'll take it," Kelly barks.

"I will?"

"*Yes*, you will."

"It's a lot."

"You can afford it. Plus, when is the last time you bought yourself something?"

"I buy clothes and shoes all the time."

"No, the last time you bought something really special. Something to celebrate an accomplishment."

She's right. The last time I bought myself something to celebrate anything was . . . well, I guess the Burberry coat, but that was a year ago. Since then, I haven't really had anything to celebrate.

"You just wrote your first book, and it became a *New York Times* Best Seller. And you did it by yourself. You didn't just slap your name on it, *you* wrote it. *You.* And now *you* are going to celebrate that by buying this watch."

She's right, again. Expensively right.

A small tear wells up in my eye as I realize how hard I am on myself. I get caught up in this world where everyone expects perfection, and thus I, too, expect perfection. My feats nowadays may not be the same as winning a court case, but they are still feats. And perhaps I need something as simple and as materialistic as a piece of jewelry to remind me of that.

I look down, admiring my wrist. It really is great. "I'll take it," I say to the woman, handing her my credit card.

She starts to place the watch in a red leather box but I tell her I'd like to wear it now. She places the empty box in a bag and hands me back my card and the receipt. I make Kelly sign my name, because I can't bear to look at how many zeros might be on there. I walk out, red bag in hand, feeling a little poorer yet again. But this time, a feeling of pride drowns it all away. I smile knowing that the title of my book might be *It's Not Okay*, but the jewelry around my wrist is straight-up Cartier.

smitten in seattle

I've just returned home from visiting Seattle, and what a ten days it was. For starters, I think we were both a little overambitious in making the first time we ever met each other in person a ten-day trip. Note to self: ten days with one man in a city you've never been to . . . is a long time.

I'd be lying if I said I wasn't a nervous wreck as the plane took off from New York. First off, if anyone knows that phone relationships don't always translate into real relationships, it's me. And despite feeling as though I knew him better than any man I've ever met, including my own ex-fiancé, there was still a fear that everything would change once we finally met face-to-face. Second, I lied to my own mother about why I was going across the country. I told her it was for a book signing. (Sorry, Mom.) I doubt she even believed me, but I just didn't want to tell her. I didn't want her asking a zillion questions and googling the guy like any normal mother would. And I didn't want to let her down if this didn't work out. She's had to endure my relationship mishaps too many times, and something inside me needs to protect her from that now. I know she's not going to grow emotionally attached to someone I've never met and who lives thousands of miles away, but still I feel the need to shield her. Plus, it was kind of too late to tell her now, considering this thing had been going on for so long.

What was I going to say, *Hey, Mom, I've kept this secret from you for six weeks, but I've been talking to this guy, and now I'm going to visit him?* I guess that's the perk of being independent. I get to do me, how I want, when I want, and I don't have to tell anyone if I don't want to, not even my own mother.

After a six-hour flight, I exited the plane and nervously walked through the terminal, making a pit stop in the bathroom to freshen up. As I walked toward the baggage claim, there he was, holding a bouquet of flowers. My heart sank. The first thing I thought was *Awww, how sweet.* The second thing I thought was *Wow, he's a lot shorter than I imagined.* Like really short. I mean, I knew he wasn't huge, considering when I googled him, his height came up as five-eleven, but there was no way he was even close to that. And his hunched-over posture wasn't doing him any favors. *Thank God I brought flats.* We hugged each other with relief and excitement before making our way to his car, a sleek Mercedes G Wagon. As we drove away from the airport, I couldn't help but feel his undeniable nervousness and wonder if this was going to be a repeat of the Canadian, who turned out to be a hate-fucking meathead.

We decided to grab some lunch on the way to his house, and a few drinks later, he began to relax. We both did. After lunch, we drove through town a little bit before he pulled over on the side of a gravel road and told me he wanted to show me a cool view. We got out of the car and peered over the guardrails at the beautiful sight of downtown Seattle and snowcapped Mount Rainier in the background.

"It's stunning," I said.

"It really is, isn't it?"

And then he pulled me toward him and kissed me. It was a tender kiss that felt like a ribbon being tied on a present. The final touch to make all of this the perfect gift.

We drove to his house, which sat atop a hill overlooking the neighborhood below. It was big and expensive-looking. Sleek and modern, it was the home of a grown man, not a twenty-five-year-old boy. I suppose that's what you get when you are a professional baseball player with a fat paycheck.

As we walked in the front door, I could immediately hear a woman talking on the phone coming from upstairs.

"Mom?" he shouted.

"I'll be right down!"

I shot him a what-the-fuck look.

"She's in town visiting our family, helping me decorate the house. I didn't think she'd be here today, sorry," he whispered.

"No problem." I bit my top lip.

I must say, I've seen a lot in my days of dating, but the mother at the house on the first day was new.

Within seconds, she emerged into the kitchen. She looked quite young, but then again, he was young, so that made sense. She introduced herself, and we started talking. She was actually really great—very outspoken and very outgoing. The kind of woman you can tell likes to kick back with a few bottles of wine and have a good time. She was the kind of woman I like. And now she was the kind of woman who was on her way out.

"Okay, you kids have fun! If it's okay, I was going to stop by in a few days because the tile people are coming. But if you want some privacy, I can totally cancel them."

"No, no, no. It's not a problem at all. Please don't let me intrude," I said.

"No, I would be the one intruding. Okay, so I'll keep the appointment, but I'll call before I come, I promise." She hugged both of us and told me how nice it was to meet me, and then out the door she went.

Mr. Seattle wheeled my suitcase into a massive bedroom, which couldn't possibly have been the guest bedroom. But then again, I could never be sure. I asked him to take me on a tour of the house to confirm. We walked upstairs, where he showed me a small office, a laundry room, and another bedroom.

"And . . . well, yeah, this is the guest bedroom." He said it in a way that was like *Why am I telling you where the guest bedroom is?* Little did he know how relieved I felt.

We hung out a little bit before we decided we were hungry again and ordered Thai food. We cracked open a bottle of wine and sat on the terrace listening to music. We were both getting buzzed, not off the wine but off each other as I eventually found myself sitting on his lap. He was the same man in the flesh that he was on the phone but better. There was a comfort about him that was almost paralyzing. Silent pauses felt peaceful instead of awkward. There was a chemistry with him that wasn't off-the-charts intense, but steady and calm. It was the type of chemistry that doesn't fizzle after a few weeks. It was the type of chemistry that I think is the type that lasts forever.

The sun had set, and we decided to lie in bed and watch a movie, where I ended up falling asleep. I awoke the next morning still wrapped in his arms and thought to myself how nice it feels to wake up next to a man. It wasn't until the second night I was there that we finally had sex. I wanted to try to hold out until the third or fourth night, like I usually do, but I couldn't resist. I usually don't get intimate this early with someone I like, but I didn't feel like it was early with him. Sure, I'd only ever really met him over the phone before this, but in those six weeks of phone dates, I felt like I *really* met him. They were quality weeks, not weeks occupied by grandiose dates or fabulous vacations. That's the thing that I think gets taken for granted when it comes to long-distance relationships. Everyone complains about how hard it is to not be able to see each other every day. But I think it's a blessing in disguise. You don't realize how much you can get to know somebody when the physical factor isn't involved. I'm not saying I'm going celibate (clearly), but it's true. Distance makes you actually talk. And in doing so you get to know a man, who he really is. You get to know beyond the annoying things about him, like how little he brushes his teeth and washes his hands or how messy he is, but instead for his jokes, his opinions, his communication habits. Yes, long-distance courting is like dating without the pressure of intimacy. And let me tell you something, intimacy has a way of blinding you to someone's personality.

Speaking of intimacy, the sex was pretty good. Nothing unreal like it was with the Canadian, but then again, being that he was an asshole, his magic fingers were useless the other twenty-three hours of the day. It was good enough with Mr. Seattle for me to remain smitten as the week went on. One day we played golf, another day we went on a hike. Both were pretty uneventful, but it didn't matter. Neither of us cared what we were doing, we were both content just being together. We were lost in a world that consisted of nobody but the two of us.

Later that week, he invited his friends to come over, and we cooked for them. We played house like a little married couple; me inside making sides and drinking wine, he manning the grill with a beer in his hand. Everyone was getting along and having a great time, until the evening escalated into one of those nights where everyone had drunk too much, too quickly. The case of wine we'd bought was gone and with it most of my memory. I do remember a few key moments, though.

First, I remember having a full bottle of expensive wine in one hand and a full bottle of cheap wine in the other as I stood on the patio asking Mr. Seattle which one I should open. Before he could even respond, I dropped the expensive one and it completely shattered. Then one of his friends stepped on the glass with his bare feet and tracked red footprints through the house. I examined them and determined they were not blood, but rather wine. Everyone else examined them and decided I was wrong. Granted, I'd just dropped a hundred-dollar bottle of Cabernet while saving the twelve-dollar bottle, so I was hardly in a condition to play *CSI*. I admitted defeat. We all laughed about it. The time had come though for everyone to leave. I was happy to make my way to bed.

Then I remember washing my face and brushing my teeth and talking and laughing with Mr. Seattle, who was laying in bed, about the shitshow that had just occurred. I climbed into bed and was just about to give him a kiss good night when I saw a weird look in his eyes.

"What's wrong?" I asked.

He paused for what felt like a decade before shaking his head and saying, "I just can't do this."

"Do what? Go to sleep?"

"No, I can't do *this*."

"Huh?"

"This. Me and you. I can't get feelings like this."

What the fuck? I sobered up instantly and started asking him why. All he could say was that he was scared and he just couldn't do it. At first, I was trying to talk him off the ledge, because he was being ridiculous and probably had just had too much to drink. As I attempted to calm him down, I realized what strange behavior I was exhibiting. Usually, if a man told me he couldn't "do this" with me, I'd say fuck it and walk out the door. But with him, I was unusually composed. Until fifteen minutes of him repeating that he couldn't do this began to wear on me. The fighter in me had no choice but to surrender. I said "Fine" and walked into the closet and began packing my bags. I didn't think I was actually going to leave, but then again, I didn't think we'd be having this conversation after such a great night, either. He came into the closet, and at the sight of me sitting on the floor packing, dropped to his knees beside me. He gently grabbed my hand and tried to pull me up from the floor.

"Stop," he said.

"You told me you don't want to do this."

"I know. Just stop and talk to me, please."

I stopped packing but remained seated on the floor.

"I don't want you to leave."

"You just said you did."

"I know. I panicked. How could I want you to leave?" He paused. "I'm in love with you."

This jolted me. Did he just say *love*? I looked up at him to see that he was serious. Not in a psychotic or drunk way but in a genuine, vulnerable way. I stood up and put my head against his chest. He wrapped his arms around me. And in that moment, I went from feeling abandoned to feeling the safest I ever had. In that moment, I realized that the takeaway from the conversation wasn't the fact that he'd just professed his love to me but that I was in a situation where a man was being irrational but was able to pause, collect himself, and rectify a situation before it got out of control. Drunk or not, panicked or not, he was the first guy in a long time who was able to own up to his ridiculousness and better yet, fix it. It was our first fight and it wasn't a good one, but I had to take a step back and realize the situation we were in. We'd been spending every waking moment together, we'd been having this intense relationship, we'd been drinking. And when it all came down to it, perhaps we were just two people caught in the midst of this vulnerable thing called . . . falling in love.

The next morning, we went to play golf, yet again, nursing our hangovers with mimosas on the course. We made light of the previous night's debacle, joking around about the bloody footprints. I'd make comments like "But remember you love me," and he'd laugh. He wouldn't deny that he said it, but he wouldn't repeat it, either. Everything was back to normal. Over the next two days, we hung out, went shopping, went to the market, and so on. All very couple-y.

It wasn't until a few nights later that another shitstorm touched down. Somehow, on our way home from dinner, the topic of exes came up. It's a subject I don't care about shying away from. I believe that you can tell a lot about a man you're dating when you discuss past romances with each other. If he flies off the handle, he's got jealousy issues, which will undoubtedly lead to control issues in the future. (Trust me, I know.) If he bitches and moans about how terrible his ex was, he has resentment issues. If he doesn't really care that much or says whatever, it's in the past, he just might be sane.

He knew I'd been engaged, so we didn't have to talk about that, luckily. But it did surprise me when he asked me if I'd ever dated any other baseball players. Shit, the Yankee. I told him "just one" and "very briefly." When he asked who it was, I told him his name and how nothing ever came of it, that it was the kind of situation where we were never going to date long-term. He asked me if I had sex with him, and I told him the truth. I'd learned from my ex-fiancé that lying about sex is not a good idea. I also learned from my ex that if a man can't handle the fact that you've had sex before him, then he needs to go find a fucking virgin. I could see worry flash across his face as we pulled up to his house and walked inside.

I was brushing my teeth and getting ready for bed when he asked again, "So you dated and slept with another baseball player?" *Damn, what is it about me brushing my teeth that starts trouble?*

I crawled into bed beside him, and in an effort to comfort him yet again, I began telling him that it was a part of my past and that it wasn't even worth spending another second on.

"I just feel weird."

"Why?"

"I'm not mad or anything, just kind of surprised." I could see in his eyes that he wasn't angry, he was disappointed. "What if I play against him? Am I going to think, damn, he had sex with my girlfriend?"

"Who cares?"

"I do, that's super embarrassing."

"So you're embarrassed by me?"

"I'm not saying that but you don't understand how locker rooms work, Andi."

Now I was the one starting to get upset. He continued explaining his feelings and as he did I tried really hard to listen and understand and show a sense of empathy. And I did. In fact, I empathized with him so much that I took his insecurity and manifested it into my own. I started to feel unworthy of him. I started to feel like something no woman wants to feel like: damaged goods. My past was coming back to haunt me once again, and there was nothing I could do about it.

The next morning, there was a coldness to him. It wasn't anger; but he was still clearly bothered about my past. I only had one more day left in Seattle, but it was clear that we both needed a little break from each other. So, I went shopping downtown while he went to play golf with his friends. I came back to his house early in the evening to find him sitting on the couch watching television. As soon as I walked in the room, he stood up and gave me a huge hug and a kiss. I don't know what had made him change his demeanor. Maybe it was the time off. Maybe the same way I sit on a bench above the Holland Tunnel and sort out the shit in my head, he sits on the golf course and works out his. I don't know, but I didn't want to question it. I didn't want to call attention to a fight that felt over. And so, I just hugged him back. It was that easy with him. I didn't need to be the winner of the fight. I didn't need him to grovel. I just needed *us* to be okay. With our embrace, it was as if we had made a silent agreement to leave our pasts behind and were seeing each other for the very first time. The smile I adored was back on his face. It was so dramatic but yet so very real. So real that he told me I couldn't leave tomorrow.

"But I have to get back."

"One more day, please."

"Are there even any flights on Monday?"

He whipped out his phone and logged onto Delta. "Yes, same time, just one day later. Please."

I agreed.

That night, we went to an early dinner and acted like those obnoxious lovebirds who couldn't get enough of each other. Afterward, we sat on the patio and watched the sunset.

On Monday morning, he drove me to the airport. It was a somber ride until he suggested we take a vacation to Hawaii next month. This was music to my ears, considering I've never been to Hawaii and that he was basically asking me out on a second date. It made me feel better about leaving him, because now I knew that wherever this went, at least there was hope that it could go somewhere.

On the plane ride home, I analyzed the situation like I always do. It was kind of a mixed bag of emotions for me. Overall, the trip was incredible. Really, some of the greatest moments of the trip were just being wrapped in the arms of someone who accepted me. There was an underlying sense of companionship with us. We enjoyed being together, doing things together, things like golfing, hiking, drinking. There was a compatibility factor that was undeniable.

But there were issues that were undeniable, too. His insecurity about my past concerned me then and still does now. Despite his seemingly having moved on, I couldn't help but fear that perhaps he wasn't really as over it as he led on. I was less bothered by him being upset and more bothered by how it made me feel. Maybe that was selfish of me. I hated the fact that my past seemed to continuously haunt me no matter how far I traveled. I couldn't get away from it. First it was my ex-fiancé getting mad that I slept with someone else, and now it was the fact that I had moved on from my ex-fiancé with a baseball player. I couldn't win, and I couldn't get rid of the skeletons.

And then, of course, I analyzed the night he panicked. To be honest, I was trying to erase that night from my memory forever. It hurt too bad to think about it and the fear of it happening again terrified me. I knew I was ignoring a red flag on purpose, I just didn't know why. Maybe it was because I was trying to see the upside. It was, after all, a great week. Sure, it had its hiccups, but that's life. I've dealt with way more shit from a man in the past.

The truth was, a few nights aside, Mr. Seattle was pretty damn great. And I thought I was finally ready to accept a relationship that might not be perfect but had a foundation. A relationship that wasn't based on looks but was based on mutual respect. A relationship that was based on intellect, emotion, chemistry, admiration. And to be honest, foundation aside, it was good to know that I had found something I thought had been taken away from me: something I thought might have been lost forever. I had found that feeling again. I had finally found what it feels like to love and be loved.

something is off

I can just feel it. The same way that men have a sixth sense about when to swoop in and fuck shit up for us, women have a sixth sense about when something just isn't right.

It's been exactly five days since I returned home from visiting Mr. Seattle. Though the number of times we've talked and FaceTimed has subsided gradually over the course of this week, that isn't what has me feeling this way. *That* I expected. I know that it's impossible to sustain talking that much that often. What has me concerned isn't the quantity of conversations, it's their quality. They don't seem to pack the same punch they once did; they're shorter, colder. I try to chalk it up to being an overanalyzing woman, but deep down, my gut knows differently. It knows he's getting ready to dump me. Well, we're not officially dating, so I can't technically get dumped, but he did say he loved me, so it's more than casual. I guess it would be classified as a "semi-dump."

And as much as I'd like to wait and let things play out until I get semi-dumped, I can't. I'm out to dinner with Ava and Jess at Tartine, this tiny BYOB restaurant in my neighborhood. My wine shop is on the way, so it makes for the perfect cheap Friday night. Ava, Jess, and I each bring a bottle of wine to share. By the time we open our third bottle, they've heard all about my trip, even though I kept them updated throughout so there wasn't much new to say. But with the coming of the third bottle I'm feeling loose—loose enough to admit my concerns about how I feel like he is pulling away.

"You don't know that. Maybe he's just really busy." Ava is playing the optimist of the group, like usual.

I am playing the pessimist. "He's not busy, he's dumping me."

"You don't know that for sure," says Jess, even though I can tell by her tone that she agrees with me. She's trying to look on the bright side, which is impressive, considering she's still reeling over Douchebag Mike, whom she hasn't heard from at all.

Ava is sweet but delusional. Jess doesn't have the heart to be the I-told-you-so type of asshole friend. They, too, know he's about to dump me, right?

"Why don't you just text him and say something like, 'Hey, everything all right?'" Jess says.

Of course, I listen to her, because she's Jess and I always listen to her. I whip out my phone and start crafting a text.

"Hey, babe—"

Delete! I cannot call him babe right now.

I retype, "Hey! Everything okay?" That's better. Send.

Immediately, there are three dots coming from his end. Shit, he's typing! "Yeah kind of."

Three dots. He's typing more. Double shit. "I don't know how to say this."

Here we go. "Say what?" I reply.

"I want to be single."

I turn the phone facedown on the table, pretending not to have seen what I most definitely did just see. My entire body, from my ears to my brain to the tips of my fingers, is pulsing with numbness. My face is burning with shame and fury.

"What did he say?" Ava asks.

"Exactly what I thought."

"Wait, what?" Jess asks.

I slide the phone across the table. They take turns reading the text. Their eyes are lit with shock.

"Aww, honey, are you okay?" Ava asks.

"Yeah. I knew it. I just had a feeling." Tears are welling up in my eyes. My jaw is clenched, and I'm trying to hold back the merciless tears that are on the verge of pouring out.

Ava reaches her arm and rubs my shoulder.

"What a fucking asshole. To say that in a text! I swear to God, men these days." Jess is pissed. She starts ranting about what a tool he is and that I am going to be better off without him, blah, blah, blah.

I know she's right, and I'll eventually agree with her. But right now, I'm in complete disbelief. Despite knowing it was coming, I feel like I've just been hit by a freight train. Like I was standing in the middle of the track watching the train come at me, and when it did, I was stunned. I'm an idiot!

There's nothing any of us can really say at this point. Just like that, two texts have changed not only the mood of our girls' dinner but also the status of my relationship. Several minutes pass before we ask for the bill.

My phone rings, and it's him. What the fuck? He has the fucking nerve to be calling me right now? I am in even more disbelief than before. I decline his call. He calls again. I decline again. Jess and Ava watch incredulously.

I text him: "Can't talk right now. At dinner."

Three dots. He's typing. "Please, can we talk?"

I don't respond. Instead, I finish my wine and say goodbye to Jess and Ava, promising to fill them in on all the juicy details tomorrow morning.

I walk the two blocks home. It feels like two miles. I'm still numb. The moment I walk in the door, I open some wine and start drinking straight from the bottle. I sit on the couch and pull out my phone.

Wiggling my fingers like a pianist, I'm trying to craft the perfect response. "You are single."

He responds: "I know. I think it would be unfair to you right now because I really don't know if I'm ready for anything. I know you are at dinner, though, so we can chat later."

Oh, *now* he wants to leave me be? Fuck that, we will talk when I say we'll talk. "Okay. No worries. Nothing to explain later. Not going to lie and pretend not to be disappointed after such a fun week. But I clearly read it all wrong. You should do your thing right now and not let anyone hold you back."

"I know. You know how I feel about you. It's tough because this is great but I know if I'm feeling like this now then I'm not ready. That's not fair to you because you are awesome and shouldn't be with someone who only has one foot in."

I take a few more swigs from the bottle before responding, "It's just bizarre. Something had to have happened in the last two days to make you do such a 180."

"Nothing happened. I promise. Maybe just time to think."

"If you weren't ready to begin with, then why fly me out? Was I just a hookup?"

"Not at all! I swear to God this was real. I thought I was ready and I'm just not."

Bullshit. It's all fucking bullshit, and I know it. "K. Well, you feel the way you feel, and there is nothing I can do but respect your feelings. Not sure what suddenly changed your mind, but all I can do is say okay and accept it." Wow, why am I being so fucking understanding? Is there some kind of sedative in this wine?

"It's like that night when I freaked out. I'm still feeling that in a way and I don't want to get into something serious because it will only make it harder."

God, this guy is even more of a self-sabotager than I am. "I get it. I don't want to be someone's second best. You are justified in being scared. We both are. I guess better for you to back out now. Might keep us from something great but might keep us from both getting hurt, too."

"What do you mean?"

"It's the second time you've given up. Sure, I've thought about walking away from it all, too, but you've actually done it twice now. I'm not going to fight for someone who operates out of fear. I'm just not."

"I know you're right. I'm just trying to be honest."

"What is it exactly you are scared of?"

"Having a girlfriend. I had one for eight years and I'm not sure I'm ready to get into something again. That's the truth."

"Fair enough. Nothing I can say to that. It's hard for me to comprehend someone walking away from something that was going well, especially when there hasn't been any pressure to label or define it, but again, nothing I can do about it. Thanks for being honest, I guess."

"I'm sorry. I hate this feeling. I really hope you don't hate me."

Of course I fucking hate you. "Not at all. Take care."

"This sucks. I honestly want the best for you and for you to be happy. Hopefully you know that."

I can't even bear to respond. I'm too dejected and too angry right now, and I know that if I respond, I'm going to say something I will regret. I just know it. I need to put the phone down and put myself out of my own misery and just go to sleep, but I can't. Not before sending one last text.

"Are you drinking, or is this for real? Because if this is for real, then fine, you will never hear from me again. My mind is just blown. Everything was fine, and now here we are having this conversation." I cringe with embarrassment as I send the message.

"I'm not drinking. This is for real. I feel like I'm going to cry but I know this was going to happen eventually and it would only be harder the longer we do this. I'm not ready for a girlfriend."

I can only muster up a one-letter response. "K." With that, I turn my phone on silent, put the wine away, and slip into bed.

But I can't sleep. I can't stop thinking about how quickly this escalated. I can't stop thinking about what the fuck happened. There has got to be something more. There just has to be. You don't spend that much time courting someone and physically being with her if there isn't something there. And then to just turn it off in an instant? Someone must have said something. He must have found out something about me that he didn't like. Maybe I'm delusional, but with every fiber in my body, I just can't believe that it's as simple as not being ready. What *really* happened?

The entire weekend passes with no word from him. Not a single text, nothing. Just like that, it is over. It isn't until Monday night that he has the balls to reach out to me on FaceTime. I shit you not. The same guy who dumped me in a text is now FaceTiming me. What, did he have a bender this past weekend and now suddenly wants to come crawling back? Did he realize that dumping someone in a text is a cowardly move? What could he possibly want? I don't know, I don't care, and I sure as fuck am not answering. I decline twice in a row before receiving a text from him.

"Please pick up."

"I'm at dinner," I lie. I'm really sitting at home without any makeup on. I know that no matter what I tell myself, I'm eventually going to answer him, but I sure as hell am not going to do it with no makeup on. "Can you give me an hour?"

"Of course."

Exactly one hour later, he calls again. This time, I can't fight the urge, and I answer. He's lying in bed despite it being daylight there. He looks like shit, with dark circles around his eyes. His hair is a mess. He looks like someone who has just had a major bender. The conversation starts with him asking what's up and how I'm doing. I reply with one-word answers, which triggers him to get to the meat of exactly why he's calling.

"Well, I guess I'll get to it. I didn't want to end this over text."

"Well, it's a little late for that."

He starts apologizing for texting. I tell him what a cowardly move it was. He agrees and says he did it because it was such a hard thing to say and he didn't know how to say it.

"I'm sure it was hard, but did you ever stop for a minute and think of how getting a text like that would make *me* feel?"

He apologizes a few more times, and I realize I can't beat a dead horse.

Then he starts in about how he just needs to be single right now. Blah, blah, blah.

I interrupt him. "I know, you said that already."

He apologizes for repeating himself.

I'm looking at him, and it's as if I don't even recognize him. I spent six weeks talking to him every day, followed by ten days frolicking around Seattle with him, and now it's as if he's a stranger. I don't see the same sweet, smart guy I once saw. Instead, I see the face of a cowardly little boy. He has tears in his eyes, and so do I. He just keeps repeating that he needs to be single right now, and I just keep repeating that I understand. I'm being way nicer than I should be, considering he dumped me over a fucking text, on a Friday night, no less.

The conversation has gone on for thirty minutes, and it's as if we are talking in gut-wrenching, painful circles. Nothing is getting accomplished, because there is nothing to accomplish. The guy has made up his mind, and there is nothing I can do to change it.

I'm to the point of annoyance when he says, "I'm just not where you are at right now."

And instead of agreeing, something inside me unleashes. "Do you even *know* where I'm at right now?" I say in a bitchy tone.

"What do you mean?"

"I mean, in all of this talk about *you* wanting and needing to be single, have you ever once stopped and actually asked me what *I* felt about all of this?"

"I'm not sure I'm following you."

I roll my eyes.

"Sorry. Please explain to me what you mean. I really want to know."

I take a moment to collect the scattered thoughts that have me on the verge of releasing all my pent-up anger and going psycho ex-girlfriend on him. *Deep breath, Andi. Do not make a fool of yourself.* "Well, since we are being honest. When I got home from Seattle, I had dinner with my girlfriends, and of course, they were asking me about the trip, which I told them was great. Then one of them asked me if I was ready to really date you. I told them the truth, which was that I wasn't sure. I wasn't sure if I was ready to give up the single life, but luckily, neither of us had put any pressure on each other to label us as anything. So I was just going to see what this turned into."

He looks confused. "Okay . . ."

"So you didn't even stop to think maybe I want to be single, too. You've just assumed this entire thing was all about how *you* feel. I haven't mentioned us being exclusive, because I'm not sure that's what *I* want. But instead of seeing where it goes, you've made it clear that you see things as black-and-white. There is no gray with you. And there's also a self-centered side to you that I've never seen until now. I don't mean that to be harsh, but you never even thought that maybe I wanted to be single, too. You just assumed I was madly into you."

"I guess I never thought about it that way."

"Of course, you didn't."

"What is *that* supposed to mean?"

"Nothing. I think we've both made our points. I don't want to get angry, so let's just be done with it."

Before he can even say goodbye, I hang up the phone. I just can't take it anymore. I can't take seeing his face. Not because he dumped me but because I wasn't seeing *his* face. I was seeing the face of someone I didn't know. Someone I never knew.

karma has no deadline

I should be in Atlanta at my friend's wedding right now, but I'm not. Instead, I'm having a glass of wine on a terrace overlooking the Aegean Sea. I'm in Santorini, Greece.

I struggled over whether or not I should do the right thing and go to my friend's wedding. I even made a list of reasons why I should and shouldn't attend and then compared them. It didn't take much for me to realize the cons won by a landslide. I hadn't seen this friend of mine in years, hadn't even met her fiancé, and ultimately I just couldn't bear the thought of attending another wedding alone right now. Yes, this was one of those weddings with a "no ring, no bring" policy. And since I've just recently been dumped by a twenty-something-year-old baseball player and have exactly zero diamonds to my name, I would fall into the "No" category. So, I decided, fuck that. Here's a new policy for you: "No plus-one, no come!"

I'm sorry, but I'm so over all of this single shaming when it comes to weddings. I think once you reach a certain age, such as your midtwenties, if you are single and invited to a wedding, you should be allowed to bring a date. I understand if the bride is trying to cut costs; that's fine, don't invite me. I understand that the bride doesn't want to look out into the audience and see an unfamiliar face, but who's to say you'll ever even see a familiar face again? I've brought plenty of legitimate boyfriends to weddings, and the bride has never seen them again. Brides just don't seem to see it from the single woman's perspective. Here we are shelling out a shitload of money to celebrate your overpriced love fest of a day, and while we are happy to do so, we do so alone. Alone at an event in which love is everywhere, which obviously will make us feel depressed and defeated by life. Every slow song that comes on will have us awkwardly hiding in the restroom, but we will show up, because we care about you. So if you care about us, throw us a fucking bone, and give us a plus-one. Not that I'd even have a plus-one anyway, of course. Fucking Mr. Seattle, I swear.

So instead of going to the wedding, I sent a gift, scrounged up all of my SkyMiles, and booked a trip to Greece with Kelly. I've spent most of the trip trying desperately to leave my worries behind and not think about anything related to Seattle, with little success. I just can't seem to get him off my mind. I think about him all hours of the day; hell, I even have dreams about him. Somewhere out there, he's probably screwing chicks left and right, hamming it up with his guy friends and laughing about how he played me like a fool, while I'm still thinking that maybe he'll come crawling back to me. They say if you let someone go and they come back, it's meant to be. But no one tells you how crazy you look clinging on to something that is long gone.

And cling I do. Like when he sent me my burner phone. Turns out, not only did I leave my pride in Seattle, I also accidentally left my burner phone at his place. I couldn't help but wonder if perhaps he had snooped on it and found something on there and that's why he dumped me out of the blue. Maybe he was turned off that the screen was cracked? Nothing says *I've got my shit together and you should reconsider me* like a left-behind cracked burner phone. Upon realizing that I left it, I decided to just call it a wash, considering I wasn't about to text him asking him to send the thing back. I figured like him, it was long gone. So you can imagine my surprise when I saw a package from Seattle, Washington, in my mailbox.

I ripped it open to find my phone. It looked different. "Awww," I sighed aloud. He got the screen fixed for me. Maybe he was a nice guy after all. I sent him a text.

Me: "Got my phone. Did you fix the screen?"

I'm not sure why I asked that; it wasn't as if the screen was going to magically get fixed while bubble-wrapped in a FedEx envelope sent from his address.

Mr. Seattle: "Yeah, ha ha, I did."

Me: "Thank you! You did not have to do that."

Mr. Seattle: "I wanted to. It's why it took me so long to send it, ha ha ha."

Me: "Ha ha. When did you do it?"

Mr. Seattle: "Found a guy out by me who dropped it off Sunday. I'm in Dallas playing golf, it's smoldering hot, ha ha."

Me: "Ha ha. Well, thanks for doing that, very sweet of you."

Mr. Seattle: "Don't mention it. Have a nice weekend!"

Me: "You, too."

Ugh, just thinking about that makes me want to text him so badly. I want to be the confident girl who says "Fuck it" and puts her heart on the line. But deep down, I know that right now, even with the most killer proclamation of love, nothing will change. But what if he was the one to reach out? Oh, my God, did I just say that? What the fuck is wrong with me? Of all the guys I've dated in the past year, none of them has had this post-relationship effect on me. Why is this one different?

I feel this odd sensation. It's not pain, it's more like an achy feeling. It's as if my heart isn't quite broken, it's just sprained. Oh, fuck, my heart is going to really break when it hits me that this is over, isn't it?

It's not until another ex resurfaces that my mind finally gets a much-needed rest from thinking about Mr. Seattle. It's my ex-fiancé and based on my Twitter feed that is blowing up, he's back!

"Oh shit, looks like my exes are causing a shitstorm right now on *Bachelor in Paradise*," I tell Kelly.

"Oh that's right, I forgot that's been airing. You know he's engaged again, right?"

"Is he?"

"Yeah."

"Gross. Like, really, dude, on a television show again?"

"Seriously. But do you expect anything more from him?"

She's right. I was actually surprised when I heard he was even doing the show, considering all of the bitching and moaning he used to do about how much he hated everything about "what it stood for." Then again, he's the quintessential type to preach, not practice. And now he's the kind who apparently is being ripped apart right now on the internet. Talk about karma being a bitch!

Turns out he isn't the only ex who went on a paradise vacation this summer. Only he wasn't in Greece, he was in Mexico. And he wasn't sipping wine in Santorini, he was eating pizza while cameras captured his every move.

He was a contestant on yet another reality show, *Bachelor in Paradise*. They take all the craziest contestants from seasons past, send them to a tropical beach, and sit back and watch the ridiculousness unfold.

Since I refuse to watch, I ask Kelly to give me a recap. Apparently, it all started with Number Twenty-Five, the runner-up for my affections back on my season of *The Bachelorette*, arriving on the show first. He took a girl out on a date, and everything looked to be on the up for him, finally. Until my ex-fiancé, Number Twenty-Six, arrived. With no love lost between the two of them, Number Twenty-Six promptly flashed his pearly whites and stole the girl from Number Twenty-Five. Sounds familiar. But that wasn't going to be the end of it. He wasn't going to go down so easily this time. With tensions soaring, the cast began to take sides. All of them chose Number Twenty-Five. They began questioning Number Twenty-Six's intentions. Enter my book . . .

Turns out *It's Not Okay* must have been on everyone's reading list, because they were all very well versed in the way I'd described the assholeness of my ex-fiancé. And now they were seeing it firsthand. Week after week on the show, the book kept coming up in conversations. Week after week, Number Twenty-Six would dismiss it as fictional and ludicrous or say that he had never even read it. (Which makes no sense, because if he hadn't read it, how would he know if it was fictional or not?) Nonetheless, his controlling, condescending behavior toward his new girl and the other contestants spoke louder than his denials over my book did. And in the most ironic plot twist ever, it was none other than Number Twenty-Five who made the most compelling case for the veracity of my book. In a heated face-to-face encounter, he said something to the effect of "Well, everything she said about me was true, so I find it pretty hard to believe that everything she said about you wasn't, and so does everyone else." It was clear that no one was buying Twenty-Six's facade, including the internet.

Part of me feels bad for him. I know that sounds crazy. I never thought I'd feel bad for Number Twenty-Six, but I don't take any pleasure in seeing him be the villain. Okay, maybe I take a *little* pleasure. Or maybe the right word is vindication. Yes, that's it, I feel vindicated. He's reaping what he sowed, and his true colors are finally showing. Did he really think he was going to waltz back onto the show a mere month after my book came out and nobody would say a word about it? But that's the thing with Number Twenty-Six. He is far from normal. He can call my book fictitious all he wants, I honestly don't give a shit, because I know what is true, and I think now the rest of the world does, too.

Truth be told, the drama is doing wonders for my book sales. With press requests flooding in and a new run on the *New York Times* list, all this had become the greatest publicity platform my publisher could ask for. I'd practically gone on the show without ever having stepped foot on the Mexican sand. All because two of my exes were once again fighting for the same woman.

What does bother me a little bit, however, is that I'm so out of the loop. Even though it's been filmed and is now airing, I still have to hear about all of this through Kelly or Twitter, which just doesn't sit right with me. You'd think that having been a lead and having developed close relationships with the producers, there would be some show of courtesy when your ex-fiancé goes on the spin-off of your own show. But no. Not a word. I guess I shouldn't be surprised. The truth is, when it comes to everyone associated with the show, every contestant is disposable. The day your season is over, the producers are on to the next.

I noticed this shortly after my season ended. Some of the producers had gone from texting me daily or weekly, to monthly, to eventually never at all. I watched as they slowly trickled out of my life. And it made me start to think about relationships in real life. The bottom line is, people come and go. Some relationships are just business, pure and simple. Did I think these producers were my friends at one point? Sure. But at the end of the day, they all had jobs to do and livings to earn. I was a project, and, like any worker, once you complete a project, you move on to the next. I'd be lying if I said it didn't sadden me a little to feel like I was nothing more than work to them.

But maybe I should just start getting used to that. Being taken in only to be disposed of when I'm no longer needed. Then again, I am sitting here sipping wine watching the sun set in Greece, so I'd say the joke is kind of on everyone else right now, isn't it? Cheers, from paradise!

game, set, engaged

I'm back in New York with a nice Grecian tan. Jess, Ava, and I are out to dinner when I find my phone blowing up. It's Twitter again. Jess's is blowing up, too, which means something big must be happening in the *Bachelor* world.

"Holy fuck, did you see who they just announced as the next Bachelor?" Jess looks up from her phone.

"No, who?"

She hands her phone over to me.

"No shit. Didn't see that one coming."

It's Number Twenty-Five. Somehow he's gone from being the villain, not once but twice, to becoming the hero of the summer and crowned the fucking *Bachelor*. Though I've felt betrayed by him ever since he called me out on live television for having sex, I can't help but laugh about the irony of it all. Plus, that was years ago and since then he's apologized, and though I'll never truly forgive him, I don't have the space in my heart to hate him. I hurt him, and in return, he hurt me back. Simple as that. Jess warns me to get ready to give a statement because every media outlet is going to want one. I can't say "Cool" or "It is what it is." But I also can't be disingenuous and gush about how he's my best friend and I'm just so over-the-moon with excitement for him and his new journey to find love. I mean, once upon a time, I compared this guy to herpes and said his sex was a ladyboner killer. I may be a psycho, but I'm not a fake psycho.

I know I'll have to craft a statement tomorrow, but tonight, I need to do what's right. I take out my phone and send a text.

Me: "Hey! Just want to say all bullshit aside, congrats. I think you'll be great, and I hope you find a good woman and finally get your own love story. You deserve it, and you know I mean that."

Twenty-Five: "Thanks, Andi. I know you do, and I appreciate it. I'm glad we buried the hatchet."

I give myself a mental pat on the back for taking the high road and put my phone away.

"Okay, enough *Bachelor* talk. How was Greece?" Ava is much more a fan of vacations than she is of reality television. I start telling the girls about Greece, but somehow find myself talking about how Mr. Seattle had been viewing all of my snaps lately.

"You still think about him?" Jess asks.

"Yeah."

"Wow, I didn't realize it was that deep."

"I know. I think I kind of downplayed it because I was afraid of getting hurt, but the truth is, I've thought about him every single day."

"What do you think about?" Ava asks.

"What the fuck really happened, how he's doing, is he thinking of me, all of it."

I go on to tell them that something inside me is telling me that I need to fight for him. They're even more shocked. They've never seen me fight for a man. In fact, me fighting for a man is so not the me they know. But then I start to tear up, and then I start to cry. And now they know the pain is real.

Jess suggests I write him an email. I look at her like she's crazier than I am. But then Ava agrees. They tell me I have nothing to lose.

I tell them I still have my dignity, thank you very much. Somehow they persuade me to just lay it all on the line in an email.

The next day, I go for a run. I take my usual route to my bench above the Holland Tunnel, gazing out as the sun sets over the Freedom Tower, and I think. Today I think about Jess and Ava's pleas for me to just lay it on the line. I think and think until I remember the look he had in his eyes the night he told me he was in love with me. I abruptly get up, sprint home, and head straight to my computer, where I begin feverishly typing up a letter. I start typing and typing and typing, and before I know it, it's midnight, and I have three different drafts of an email to a guy who isn't even my fucking boyfriend. Someone call the closest looney bin, please.

I text Jess and Ava at midnight that I wrote an email, and I send them all three drafts. If anyone can help me edit this thing, it's the girl who works for a magazine and the girl who won't let me look like an idiot.

The next morning, I read the drafts again. The first one is a little too gushy. The second one is kind of bitchy. The third one is pretty damn good, I must admit. But I'll let my girls decide.

Me: "Check your mail. Ahhhh."

Ava: "Reading now."

Jess: "Same."

A few minutes go by.

Jess: "I like the third."

Ava: "Agreed."

Jess: "Also, I'm sorry I didn't realize how sad you've been."

Me: "No, it's my own fault. I was embarrassed."

Ava: "You should never be embarrassed. We are your friends."

Jess: "I'm also really proud of you for putting yourself out there like this."

Ava: "I agree. Win or lose, it takes guts that I definitely don't have to do this. Super proud of you."

Me: "Aww, love y'all. Thanks."

Ava: "Love you."

Jess: "Love you. Now send it!"

I decide to read it one last time before I send it. Fuck. As I re-read the email, I'm getting chills. I don't know if they stem from being nervous, being delusional, or being on the brink of the most humiliating email I've ever sent. But the words are true.

"I hope all is well with you. Before you read this, please know that I've debated whether or not to say what I'm about to say, considering that, as you know, I'm not the greatest at being vulnerable. After having some time to think, I've realized everything between us got so much more complicated than it ever needed to be. I understand how *you* feel about it all, and I know it's unlikely that anything will change that. But in pushing aside my pride, I know that I owe it to myself to honestly and simply tell you how *I* feel.

"Despite everything that's happened, I can't help but still believe that there was something between us that is still worth fighting for. What exactly that something was, I'll be honest, I don't know. Part of me feels disappointed and duped, but another part of me still believes that whatever we had was real. I've been in my share of relationships enough to know whether there's something there or when it's time to move on. I've never looked back and wondered 'What if?' But with you, and us, I do.

"I replay in my mind the trip and the weeks of phone calls leading up to it, and I'm reminded of how happy and easy everything felt. Was it sudden? Yes. Intense? Yes. Scary? Absolutely. But above all, it felt *different*. At this point, I'm not even sure if you ever felt the same way. But whatever it was, it has made me not want to do what I normally do, which is run away at the first sign of trouble. And if you felt the same way, I don't want you to run away, either.

"The last time we talked, I couldn't help but feel absolutely shocked and helpless. I understand your reasons for walking away were not because you were unhappy but because you were scared, the timing sucked, and you wanted to be single. All valid reasons. I get being scared, because I am, too. Logically, it's easier for me to get out unscathed than to risk getting hurt. But emotionally, what I've realized is that the only thing that scares me more than getting hurt is being too scared to fight for a chance at something with someone I truly believe in. Maybe it works out, or maybe it was just a onetime thing and nothing deeper. I don't know. I just know that I'd rather have the answer to that than always wonder what if.

"If, on the other hand, this *genuinely* comes down to you not being scared but simply wanting to be single, and I was nothing more than a fun fling for you, then so be it. But if there is a part of you that felt something more and still wonders what could have been, then now is the time to say so.

"Though it might not be the best timing, I guess sometimes we don't get to choose when things and people come into our lives. I'll admit, I wasn't exactly looking for you or to have these feelings, nor do I know if I'm even ready for them, but they happened. So this is me, for whatever it's worth, telling you I haven't let go and wanting to say I did everything I could to fight for someone I care for.

"I know this is all probably a little unexpected and a lot to take in. It is for me, too. Please know that this isn't any sort of ultimatum. It's just me, as out of character as it may be, needing to tell you how I feel. I needed to swallow my pride. Because at the end of the day, I've realized that no matter how hard I try to fight it, I still miss how things were. I miss talking to you and having you in my life. Most of all, I just miss *you*."

I may have taken this whole new career as an author a little too far. But fuck it. My hands are visibly shaking when I press "Send."

I'll wait for his response in angst for what I'm guessing will be either about a week or forever. In the meantime, it's summer in New York and between traveling and getting dumped, I've hardly been able to take advantage of it. Luckily, Jess has invited me to attend an event tonight that not only will take my mind off Mr. Seattle, but will make up for my lack of summer fun this year . . . the U.S. Open! We arrive at the Emirates Suite, where there is no shortage of men in suits talking to other men in suits as they all sip out of green Heineken beer bottles. What is it with men and Heineken? Maybe it's their version of our Cosmopolitan. Scattered among the Heineken-drinking men are women holding silver trays of champagne, dressed in red flight-attendant uniforms. From their red berets securely fastened onto their gel-slicked buns, to the name badges, down to their nude hosiery and their shiny black stilettos, every inch of them looks pristine. Pristine but extremely uncomfortable. I wonder if they're actual flight attendants or just servers dressed as flight attendants.

We make our way past the dessert buffet and to the bar, where I order us two Honey Deuces. I have no idea what is in the drink, I just know that it's *the* drink of the U.S. Open. And that it's strong as fuck. I'm on my third, which has me feeling as electric as the crowd. There's just something about a summer night at the U.S. Open. Maybe it has to do with my love of tennis, which I grew up playing, or the roar of the crowd that will cheer a player on one point only to boo them on the next. Maybe it's just the fact that it's oh, so New York-y. It doesn't hurt that we happen to be sitting in the best seats, in the best suite, and all for free. As the bartender mixes us another round of drinks, I see a mass of people gathering in the far corner of the suite. I look over to see a ginormous black man with a bald head towering over everyone.

"Holy shit! It's Shaq," I whisper to Jess.

"Good God, he's huge!"

"I'm completely star struck right now."

"Over Shaq?" She crinkles her nose.

"You don't understand, he's LSU."

"You Southerners and your alma matters. Want me to intro-duce you?"

"*You* know Shaq?"

"No, but when has that ever stopped me?"

She's right. Jess has the balls of a thoroughbred stallion. I'm sure her bravery is due to her years in the industry and the fact that she's met everyone from reality television stars like myself to Madonna. Yet I have a feeling even if she weren't in the industry, she'd be the same.

"I'd legit die."

"Well then, come on!" she says, dragging me behind her as she maneuvers through the crowd. Next thing I know, we're standing inches away from Shaq, and Jess is nudging me to talk to him. One final push.

Here goes nothing. "Hi!"

I reach my hand out and place it in his massively large palm. He's enormous. My entire body is the size of his left thigh. Damn, I picked the wrong day to wear my flats.

"Wait a second, I know you," he says.

What the fuck?

"My girl watches that show, with the roses. You're LSU."

"I am! Geaux Tigahs!"

"Shaq, can we get a picture?" a man interjects.

"Yeah, man, one second," Shaq says. "LSU, huh? What year?"

"Do you *really* want to know?"

He laughs.

"Okay, 2009."

"Damn. I'm getting old. I was there until '92."

There's an awkward few seconds of silence, because I don't want to be *that* girl and ask for a photo (plus, I can see out of the corner of my eye that Jess is standing two feet away with her phone held at eye level, capturing every second of this encounter), but I'm at a loss for any more words. So I awkwardly tell him it was nice to meet him, and he awkwardly gives me a fist bump. No big deal, just a casual fist bump between two old friends.

"Holy shit, that was amazing," I whisper to Jess as we walk away.

We meander through the crowd toward the doors that lead back out to the stadium seats. As I pull the door handle, I hear, "Later, LSU!" shouted from across the room. I turn around. It's Shaq.

"Peace out, LSUUUU!" I yell back with as little swag as a white girl could have.

I'm on a high as we take our seats. Jess hands me her phone, and I start scrolling through the burst of photos she took. Midway through, a notification pops up on her phone, so I hand it back to her.

She looks at it. "Ummm . . . I think your ex just got engaged again."

"Oh, shit, that's right! The finale of *Bachelor in Paradise*, huh?"

"Yeah, my Twitter feed is blowing up." She scrolls with her thumb. "Yup, officially engaged."

"Gag." And just like that, my Shaq high comes crashing down.

Later that night, as I lie in bed, I can't help but think about the man I swore I'd never think about again. Goddammit, Number Twenty-Six. Not only did he beat me to the punch by getting re-engaged first, but he just had to do it in the most public way possible, on reality television. And not just any show. No, that would be too easy. It had to be on the spin-off of the show we got engaged on barely a year before. Thank God I knew months ago back when I was in Greece with Kelly. I check my email, like I do every night before I go to bed, and see that just like after the announcement of the new Bachelor, my inbox is once again flooded with requests for a comment. I don't know what I'll say, because I don't think I've thoroughly worked out how I really feel about the whole situation.

When I first heard the news back in Greece, I was too distracted with missing Mr. Seattle to really digest the fact that my ex-fiancé was engaged. But now that I've poured my heart and soul into an email, which Mr. Seattle still hasn't responded to, I know there is nothing more I can do, I'm starting to think about how I really feel.

It's not as simple as caring versus not caring; there's so much more to it than that. There is the way he got engaged: on a beach, with cameras and a Neil Lane ring. When your ex-fiancé gets engaged, this ranks among the worst in terms of ways to rub it in. It all makes me feel recycled. I think every woman wants to feel unique, especially when it comes to a proposal. It feels strange knowing that another woman has been proposed to by the man I thought I'd spend the rest of my life with. When we get engaged or married, we think it'll only happen once. It becomes a sacred moment that you share with only one other person. But when it doesn't work out and that moment happens again, well, it's weird.

But that's just the *act* of him getting engaged. How do I feel about the *fact* that my ex, whom I did once love, is now in love with someone else and engaged? I keep repeating the question in my mind, hoping to get some sort of powerful, thought-provoking answer. But, honestly, when it comes down to it, I don't really care. I'm not happy for him, I'm not mad at him, I'm simply . . . indifferent. The truth is, I look at him and all that he's done since the show and since we broke up and I don't even see the man I was engaged to. I see a guy who is just, well . . . kind of a loser. Honestly, if I hadn't had genuine, honest feelings for him, I'd probably be mortified that he will forever be a stain on my romantic résumé. At the end of the day, when it comes down to it, my ex, like many other men out there, was a controlling asshole. And just like many other men out there, he is a closed chapter of my past that I have no desire to reopen.

Who knows, maybe I'm masking pain that I'm unaware of with the pain of Mr. Seattle that I am very much aware of, I don't know. Maybe I've simply replaced one heartbreak with another. Maybe

I've realized that what I felt was love years ago doesn't come close to comparing to what I feel is love now. All I really know is that when I dig deep and think about how I feel now that my ex is engaged again, I can sum it all up in four words: Not. My. Problem. Anymore.

it's three in the morning and i'm . . .

Drunk. Not hungover, drunk. It's all Mr. Seattle's fault. Fuck him. Fuck every man on this Earth actually. He really is the reason I'm drunk. It'd been days since I'd emailed him and I'd yet to get a response. Then, yesterday I woke up and checked my email for the seventy-fifth time and there it is. His response. I don't want to look. I can't look. I have to look. I take a deep breath and start reading. It doesn't take long to finish, considering it's only a paragraph long. It's a paragraph saying exactly what I thought he would say. He's telling me how much he appreciated my letter and how hard it must have been for me to send it but that the way he feels hasn't changed, and even though he cared about me and still does, he's in a different place from where I am. He ends with "I hope you don't resent me."

I feel like such an idiot. Why did I email him? What the fuck was I thinking? I mean, I was fully expecting this type of response, so if I knew deep down that this was how it was going to be, why did I do it? Why do I still believe that love can happen for me? Don't I get it by now? Love is just not in my deck of cards. Failure after failure, and yet I still can't seem to come to grips with it. What more will it take for me to see that I will never find love? Ever.

It's not just that I poured my heart out, it's that I actually believed in what I was saying. I believed that what I felt for him was different and real. I believed in him. I believed that I made him happy. So much so that I was willing to put it all out there, to open my heart to someone, to dive deep into shark-infested waters with no cage. I was willing to fight for what I believed in. And everything I believed in was wrong.

Now there was only one thing I could do. Round up the girls and get wasted. I group-text Jess and Ava to tell them about the email and they agree that a Sunday brunch is to take place immediately. I text Sarah, who is probably off somewhere getting her eggs frozen, as well as Emily, who hasn't been around much lately because she has a new boyfriend. But he's out of town this weekend so she's all about a boozy brunch in honor of my broken heart. Not that Sunday Funday needs justification, but it's a well-known secret that every woman slightly enjoys it when one of her girlfriends is irate at a man and wants to take it out on some alcohol. And boy, do we.

I arrive at Chalk Point Kitchen around two fifteen, and Emily is the only one there. Come to think of it, that's probably why she's the only one of our friends with a boyfriend.

"Fiiiiinally," she says as she greets me with a hug. She's clearly annoyed at everyone's tardiness.

"Well, you didn't actually expect anyone to be on time, did you?"

I help myself to the bottle of champagne and the orange puree in the middle of the table. This is why I love this restaurant. They offer bottomless mimosas, but unlike at other places, you get to make them yourself, which means none of that premade, watered-down bullshit. By two thirty, Jess and Ava have arrived. Sarah gets there about forty minutes later, as usual.

I'm now on my third mimosa, aka champagne with a splash of orange juice, when Jess takes notice of my pace.

"Someone planning on going hard today?"

"Planning on seeing how many of these I can put down in one sitting."

We all know that I am drinking at such a rapid pace today in order to numb myself from all things Seattle, but none of us are actually talking about him, the email, or what the fuck went wrong. I think the girls are probably waiting for me to bring it up, but I honestly don't know what to say. I'm still in some sort of post-traumatic shock, and even though I know that it's definitely over, I'm not so sure I'm ready to believe it is.

"Four?" guesses Jess.

"That's offensive!"

"Six?"

"Better. Maybe seven, maybe eight. Who knows? It's Sunday Funday, right?"

I'd be lying if I said I'm not a little tipsier than I anticipated when I stand up. We all are, but the day is far from over. There is a storm brewing. Literally. As we walk out of the restaurant, the dark clouds roll in over Sixth Avenue, and it begins to pour. We run across the street to a dingy bar, where we randomly spot a group of our guy friends sitting at a high-top table, enthralled in some "big game." They are our party friends, the type you never see during the daylight unless you're drinking. Seeing them always guarantees a shitshow, and unsurprisingly, it isn't long before shots of Fireball line the table, vodkas are being passed around like water, and I have officially gone from tipsy to straight-up drunk.

"Let's go to Bounce!" shouts one of the guys.

The word jolts me. I look at Jess and whisper, "If I go to Bounce, I'm going to pull an Elizabeth. I can't." I shake my head.

Jess laughs.

Elizabeth is Jess's twenty-three-year-old sister who has recently graduated from some smart school, either Columbia or NYU, I always forget. One Sunday night a while back, I was over at Jess's watching the Emmys on her couch when Elizabeth burst through the door and stumbled into the living room. She was slurring in between chugging a bottle of water. I noticed her eyes were blood-shot, her hair was a mess, and she was nothing short of absolutely hammered.

"Where have *you* been?" Jess asked.

"On a date, kind of," Elizabeth said with that mischievous drunk giggle every woman has when she's done something semi-bad. "I thought we were just going to do brunch, but then we went to a bar, and I met a guy, and he asked me to dinner, so I went."

"Seriously?" Jess isn't disappointed, she's impressed.

Elizabeth shrugs her shoulders in admission.

"So . . . who is he? Did y'all hook up? Is he hot? What happened?"

"Umm, well, we may have made out . . ." More mischievous drunk giggles. "He's actually really hot."

I can't help but interject. "Hold up! You just casually went to brunch and ended up getting asked out on a date with a guy who's actually hot?"

"Guilty!"

"And you were wearing *that* shirt?"

Elizabeth looks down at her loose-fitting white cotton V-neck.

"With your hair like *that*?"

She drunkenly takes out her ponytail and whips her hair around.

"And . . . no makeup on?"

She closes her eyes, tilts her head up, and smiles with pride.

I look to Jess. "What the fuck? What the fuck is wrong with us? I mean, no offense, Elizabeth, you know I love you, but you've got to be kidding. She goes to brunch wearing that and no makeup and gets a date *and* a make-out?"

Ever since then, it's been a secret goal of mine to, as I termed it, pull an Elizabeth, and I'm thinking that today might be the perfect day for it.

Before I know it, we've all gone from the dive bar to a table at Bounce. It's hard to describe Bounce. I guess you could say it's a mix of a club and a sports bar, but really it's just a club disguised as a sports bar. Probably so patrons don't feel like alcoholics for being at a club during the daytime. It's one of those places you talk shit about and pretend you're too cool for but yet you secretly love. The women there can be like myself and my friends, who come as an afterthought. This is reflected in our attire: jeans, flats, maybe a wedge or two, and absolutely zero false eyelashes. Then there are the women who come here not as an afterthought but as a plan of attack. This is also reflected in their attire: platforms, bandage dresses, red lipstick, and cleavage that stops just short of their chins. The waitresses wear fishnet stockings, booty shorts, and matching bustiers as they bring out bottles of Veuve Cliquot (not Dom) while waving sparklers in the air. Basically, within minutes of being at Bounce, you realize you've officially entered the Twilight Zone. The time passes quickly here. Your vision becomes blurry, and your memory, well, if you're lucky, you'll find it to be fuzzy at best. And today is no different. Today, just as I expected, the place is filled with thirsty girls. You know the type, the ones with bodies made for swimsuit ads, faces made for radio, and shamelessness made for sex tapes.

Looking back, I can't say I remember much about the hours after we walked in. I *do* remember at some point a cute guy coming over to our table to say hi to some of our guy friends. I think I found him cute and funny, and I may or may not have made out with him at the bar. Then he told me he was hungry and asked if I wanted to grab dinner. Apparently, I said yes, because I do vaguely remember sitting across the table from him at an Italian restaurant and guzzling red wine and water at an equal rate. And then I think we either walked or took a cab to a hotel.

The rest is crystal-clear to me. We were rolling around on the bed, indulging in what I think is the greatest pastime known to woman: a steamy make-out session. I love make-out sessions, I really do. I could literally be completely content with a steamy make-out session and nothing more. I don't know why. There's just something so innocent yet also so sexy about a passionate hour of kissing and maybe a little groping. My plan was to just do that, but next thing I knew, he was naked. Naked and erect. *Very* erect. There he was, just standing tall, in front of the floor-to-ceiling windows that showed off the Empire State Building. I don't know which was bigger, him or the Empire State. Nevertheless, it was quite the view. I was in the midst of debating what to do with such an enormous view when, with a stern face, he looked me dead in the eye and asked, "What's your rate?"

Huh? "You mean, like, umm, what I make for appearances or whatever?" At this point, I was giving him the benefit of the doubt. Perhaps he knew I was on television and thought I did appearances. Maybe he was in public relations or marketing.

"No, no, like, what is your rate?"

He couldn't possibly be saying what I thought he was saying. I looked around the hotel room; it was stunning. The door to the large bathroom was ajar, and I could see the marbled countertops and a Jacuzzi that—oh, my God! The Jacuzzi was filled with bath bubbles and had flowers floating on the top. There was a candle lit. I glanced back to the bedroom, where for the first time I noticed a table in the corner with an opened bottle of champagne in a silver tub. The entire suite had been set up . . . for sex. Oh, my God! Does he think I'm a hooker? Oh, my fucking—wait, what part of me re-sembled a hooker? I got it, I was in his hotel room, but we met at a sports bar. Who picks up hookers at a sports bar? Not to mention the fact that I was in jeans. What kind of hooker wears jeans? Part of me wanted to ask what he thought I was worth, but I was too terrified to hear the answer. Instead, I just tried to ease my way out of this epic blunder.

"I think you got the wrong impression."

"Ummmm, okay. I mean, you can just give me a rate, and we can go from there."

Oh, my God. Oh, my God. Oh, my God! "No, there is no fucking rate. I am not for sale! I am not for rent! I am not a hooker!"

I looked at him like he was the biggest piece of shit I'd ever seen in my life, hoping he'd be absolutely mortified and begin profusely apologizing, but he wasn't. Instead, he was defensive.

"Whoa! Simmer down. I never said you were a hooker. I just asked your rate."

I can't. I just fucking can't right now.

Instead of apologizing for such an obvious error, he rolled his eyes. "So dramatic. Jesus, normally New York girls are cool."

I stayed silent, knowing that if I responded, there was a likely chance that I would leave here and have to call Jess to help me bury the body of one erect hooker-seeking prick. I don't even bother calling a car; I just scurry to find my bra and shirt, grab my purse, and Usain Bolt the fuck out of there. It wasn't until the elevator door closed and I saw my reflection that I noticed my shirt was inside out, but I didn't even care. The door opened to the lobby; I lowered my head and covered as much of my face as I could with my hair before power walking through the revolving doors, bypassing the bellmen. My hand was raised to hail a cab before I even reached the curb.

There I was, alone in the back of a taxi at nine o'clock on a Sunday night. It was the first time I'd ever felt dirtier than the grimy leather seat of a yellow cab. I gazed out the window as one word flooded my mind. Hooker! He thought I was a fucking *hooker*!

i left my dignity in kansas city . . .

Along with my suitcase, my shoes, my earrings, and my nipple covers. Oh, yeah, and something I've managed to hold on to for twenty-nine years: my one-night-stand card. Yup, what was supposed to be the weekend of Nikki's wedding, where I was to serve as a bridesmaid, ended up being the weekend I had my very first one-night stand. I blame it on Mr. Seattle and the guy who thought I was a fucking hooker. Both have me feeling less like a depressed woman scorned and more like a vengeful one. And there is no telling what can happen when you mix scorn and a wedding.

It was the night before the big day when I found myself in Kansas City, in a barn, sitting with the rest of the bridal party, all of whom worked alongside Nikki as pediatric nurses. Out of nowhere, Nikki decided to make a confession.

"So don't hate me, but . . ."

I clenched my jaw and glared at her.

"I may or may not have invited a date for you tomorrow," she says in her sweet kiddie nurse voice.

"Why?"

"Well, I wanted you to have a date."

"Why?"

"Well . . . I don't know." Yes, she did.

"Because everyone else in the bridal party is married or engaged?" I offered her the answer.

"Well, I wasn't going to say it like *that*."

I rolled my eyes as I asked who he was.

"Don't hate me. Actually, you can't hate me, I'm the bride."

Another eye roll, but she was right.

She flagged down her maid of honor. "Meg, come here. Tell Andi about Hot Rob."

I scowled in disgust.

"Ahhhhh, he is hot as a motherfucker," squealed Meg. "That's your date tomorrow, right?"

"How did you know?"

"Girl, we *all* know." Lindsey "with an E," another bridesmaid, had now joined the conversation. "He's so hot, and fun, and oh, he's just so hot!"

"Okay, whoa! First, who the hell is this guy, and why do you call him that?"

"That's what we call him around town. Does anyone even know his last name? Actually, does anyone even know if his name is, in fact, Rob?" Meg asked.

"Nope."

"Negative. But he's hot."

"He's sooooo hot!" Lindsey was on the verge of drooling.

"How hot?" I asked.

"Hot, hot," Nikki said. "Like kind of invited-him-less-as-your-date-and-more-as-eye-candy hot." I could tell the stoic look on my face had Nikki slightly worried. "Oh, just hush. It's not a big deal. It's just a date, if you don't like him, then you can just dance by yourself."

"You're lucky you're the bride." A small smile cracked across my face.

The following morning, all of the bridesmaids arrived across town at Meg's house at precisely nine in the morning. Per the detailed schedule that the wedding planner emailed *and* printed out for each us, we began hair and makeup at ten, posed for photos in our robes at eleven forty-five, ate lunch at noon, were dressed by one, and were out the door and in the trolley at two. Surprisingly, the day flew by without a single glitch. We were on schedule, and there were no wardrobe malfunctions, no bridal meltdowns, no mother-of-the-bride panic attacks, nothing. Just a gaggle of bridesmaids on a trolley, drinking mimosas from pink Solo cups, on our way to church to watch our girl tie the knot. When we arrived, one by one we filed out of the trolley as the wedding planner did a head count. When it was my turn, she crossed my name off her list before snatching the pink Solo cup from my hand.

"No alcohol in the church, dear," she snarled condescendingly.

"But we're just going to be in the side room until the ceremony starts, so technically we're not going in the church."

"Yeahhhh . . . Sorry, it's a no."

Thank God I'd stashed two plastic airplane-sized Fireballs in my tote.

Like clockwork, we processed down the aisle at four thirty. Nikki was stunning as she walked to meet her waiting groom. They shed their tears, made their promises to love each other for richer or poor, yada, yada, yada, before finally saying "I do." And just like that, Nikki, my best friend, whom I met on *The Bachelor*, was married. (Though, thank God, it's to someone other than the Bachelor himself.) Hundreds of posed photos at sunset in a picturesque park later, we finally made our way to the reception hall, where we were seated at a head table on a raised stage above the commoners—I mean, other guests.

Next to me was Meg, who not thirty seconds after we sat down nudged me and whispered, "That's him," as she pointed to the farthest table.

"Damn, he *is* hot."

"Told ya! Let's go say hi."

I was nervous at the idea of actually meeting this guy, however, given the fact that it had now been more than two hours since this wedding officially started, I had no excuse not to. I reapplied some lip gloss and perked my boobs up. (Not that it mattered, considering I looked like a nun in this floor-length gown.) Then I followed Meg to the table, where she introduced us.

I reached out my hand to shake his, but he ignored it and instead gave me a hug and a kiss on the cheek before saying with a laugh, "Hi. I guess I'm your date, huh?"

I laughed in return. "I guess so. Sorry, I know this is totally awkward."

"Nah. Okay, maybe a little. Y'all did a great job today."

"Oh, yeah, *really* difficult walking down an aisle holding a bouquet, let me tell ya."

He laughed again and then asked if I'd like to join him for a drink at the bar. He ordered a whiskey, neat, which made him even smoother than he was five minutes ago.

"Heyyyyyy, handsome!" shouted a pretty brunette from across the bar before she dashed over to us.

He gave her a side hug before introducing me as his date.

"So nice to meet you." She reached out her hand, unveiling a large diamond on her ring finger. Whew! "I'm not even going to pretend that I don't know who you are. Oh, my God, can I just say I loved your season, and I loved your book, and oh, my gosh, sorry, I'm ridiculous right now, aren't I?"

"No, no, you're fine."

She eyed me up and down before turning back to Hot Rob. "How the hell did you land her as a date?"

"Lucky guy, huh?" He winked at me.

Hot Rob and I headed to the dance floor, where minute by minute, I found myself more and more drawn to him as our chemistry climbed off the charts.

His hand had gone from the small of my back to now firmly clenching mine. Holy shit, I was on a bona fide date and actually enjoying it. There was something about Hot Rob that was bringing out the best in me. It was like I was myself but a cooler version. I was looser, funnier, wittier, and, with every sip of alcohol, sexier, or so I thought. Our banter had me feeling the need to stay on my toes and woo him a tad, but the desire in his eyes had me knowing it was in the bag.

I had not a care in the world, as was evidenced when one of the other bridesmaids bumped into me, spilling an entire glass of red wine down the front of my pale pink dress. I raised my hands in the air and shrugged. I was too busy having fun to care about a dress I'd never wear again.

Hot Rob was impressed, and he let me know it when he leaned into me and whispered in my ear, "Best wedding date I've ever had."

"Last call," shouted the DJ. And without saying a word, we left the dance floor hand in hand and made our way to the bar. He'd just ordered drinks when the music came to a screeching halt in the middle of a song. I noticed a crowd forming in the far corner. The dance floor was now empty.

"What the hell is going on over there?" I muttered aloud.

All I could see was a mob of people, two bridesmaids crouched on the ground, and the back of Nikki's long white train. She was on her knees. It's not until someone moved that I saw that the brides-maid who had spilled an entire glass of wine on me was now lying flat on her back. I was desperately trying not to laugh at such a grave situation. I know, I know, I'm a horrible human being. But come on! I was on a blind date, covered in red wine, at a wedding in which one of the bridesmaids has keeled over, and now we had all these bridesmaids who were real nurses tending to her like she'd been shot in a drive-by or something. I might not be a nurse, but I can tell you that homegirl didn't need her pulse checked, homegirl needed a glass of water.

"Well, welcome to Kansas City, where the bridesmaids get drunk and the brides get on their knees," Hot Rob said.

I almost spit out my drink in laughter before looking down at my stained gown and throwing my hands up in total defeat.

"Ladies and gentlemen, please make your way to the exits. Thanks, and have a great night," the DJ announced.

"After-party at PBR!" screamed one of the groomsmen.

At that moment, Meg and her fiancé came over to Hot Rob and me and insisted we join. The guys called an Uber, and Meg and I went to the head table to get our purses.

"So how's it going?" Meg asked.

"Ummm, he's kind of great."

"Told ya!"

"Like *really* great."

"I know!"

"How is he single?"

"He's picky. Rightfully so when you've got an ass like that."

We'd gotten our bags and made our way to the entrance, where Meg's fiancé and Hot Rob were in an Uber waiting for us. After a short ride, I was standing in my stained gown, still holding my bouquet, while the bouncer waited to see my identification. I rummaged through my tote bag, pulling out a cosmetics case and handing it to Hot Rob along with a pair of flats, my yoga pants that I wore earlier when I went to Meg's, and some lip gloss. I was just about to reach my wallet, which of course was at the bottom of my bag, when the bouncer rolled his eyes and told me not to worry about it.

A hand stamp later, we were officially in. The place was packed. I immediately spotted a girl in a cropped tube top and a cowboy hat riding the mechanical bull as we made our way to the back, where the rest of the bridal party were all dancing around a few tables in a roped-off section of the bar. Moments later, Nikki and her new husband, white gown and all, arrived. We cheered.

There we were, *that* wedding party, the kind you talk shit about for being in a bar in their gowns but at the same time also kind of admire because you see what a raging good time they're having. We were dancing and drinking and taking shots. I vowed not to ride the mechanical bull, even though I really, *really* wanted to. The party was in full swing, and Hot Rob was looking better than ever. The sexual tension had reached an all-time high between us when out of nowhere, he wrapped his arms around my waist and pulled me into him. And finally, he kissed me.

It was as if he knew when the perfect moment to kiss me would be, and he nailed it. With the seal officially broken, the only things my lips did the rest of the night were sip and kiss. Sip and kiss. I was in such a make-out zone that I hardly noticed when someone stepped on the bottom of my dress and ripped off the outer layer of tulle. I'd later use it as a boa to seductively pull Hot Rob toward me every time I wanted another kiss.

At three in the morning, the bar closed, and we all headed to the exit. My flight was leaving in exactly three hours, which meant I had to get back to my hotel. But there was no way in hell I had enough self-discipline to do that, and I knew it.

"How far is your place?" I asked Hot Rob.

"Five minutes."

"Let's go."

"Seriously?"

"Don't make me change my mind," I said with a seductive-ish slur.

"Taxi!" he shouted.

The cab pulled up to a restored tall building.

He used his key fob to open the door as he said, "This used to be a hotel, ya know."

"No, I didn't." Nor did I care.

He opened the door to a sprawling foyer, complete with a look-at-me-I'm-expensive-as-fuck crystal chandelier. There was a gourmet kitchen to the right, which opened to a spacious, dimly lit living room that had a library feel to it. Every detail had been thought of, down to the rustic ladder that slid along the wall. It was sophisticated, classy, manly, and chic. Just like Hot Rob. We started making out on the couch, and it wasn't long before my dress was being pulled down. Hot Rob went from kissing my lips to kissing my neck to shouting, "What the fuck are these?"

I looked down. Shit! My nipple covers were still on. I was mortified.

"Do those things come off?"

"Of course, they come off. Actually, watch this!"

I stood up in the center of the living room, wearing nothing but my nude Spanx and two nipple covers, while a shirtless Hot Rob sat back on the couch in anticipation. I took one hand and gently peeled off a nipple cover and placed it sticky side up in the palm of my right hand.

"Ready?"

He covered his eyes. "Oh, God!"

I raised my hand above my shoulder, reached back, and tossed the nipple cover at the living-room window, where it stuck like glue. I turned to look at an awestruck Hot Rob before taking a few bows and mumbling, "Thank you, thank you very much."

"That might be the single most incredible thing I've ever seen."

I didn't dare try to repeat it with the other nipple cover. Instead, I flung it onto the ground before jumping on top of him and picking up where we'd left off. I was completely naked by the time he carried me into his bedroom, which was just as stylish as the rest of the pad. His hands had made their way through my hair, down my neck and chest, and onto my waist. The time had come to decide what happened next. I didn't want to have sex with him, because I didn't want to be *that* woman. In twenty-nine years on this planet, I had never had a one-night stand. But God, did I want to be that woman.

"Do you have a condom?" I asked.

"Yes."

"Go get it before I change my mind."

After an hour of the most sensual and passionate sex I'd ever had, I was lying naked with my head pressed against his bare chest. Hot Rob was cradling my head and stroking my hair. I could hear his heartbeat slowing as he just kind of tenderly petted me. I couldn't help but wonder when was the last time a man touched me like this. I wanted to stay like this forever. I closed my eyes. The alarm on my phone went off, sending me into a panic.

"Shit! My flight leaves in an hour!"

"Staaayyyyy."

I looked at him, debating. Not only could I not remember the last time a guy touched me so sweetly, but I couldn't remember the last time a guy kind of, sort of begged/asked/suggested I stay.

I called Delta in hysterics. "Hi! I'm booked on a flight that leaves Kansas City for New York in about an hour. Are there any later flights?" I asked.

"The only other flight is at six fifty-nine p.m., which has you arriving at LaGuardia at ten forty-eight p.m."

"Hmmmm. Nothing in between?"

"No, ma'am, unfortunately not."

Dammit. I didn't want to leave, but I didn't really want to stay until seven and have to worry about whether or not I was lingering around too long, and if he really did want me to stay or was just being polite, and what I'd look like come daylight—oh, hell no. I couldn't stay.

"Okay. I'll stay on my original flight. Thank you."

It was now five fifteen, which meant my flight left in forty-five minutes.

"How far is the airport?"

"Only about twenty minutes."

"And my hotel?"

"Twenty minutes. The opposite way."

"Fuuuuuuuuuuccck!"

"Looks like it's either the flight or the suitcase."

Shit, shit, shit. I can't miss this flight. I can't stay here until 6:59 p.m. I had my wallet, my phone, and the keys to my apartment. I was cradling both my breasts in one hand as I rummaged through the apartment looking for the rest of my belongings. I didn't know why I was covering myself up, considering I'd just had sex with the guy.

"Get dressed. You're taking me to the airport!"

"Nooooooo. Stay!"

"No time to debate. Let's go!" I snapped my fingers.

"Okay, how about I call an Uber, and I'll ride with you?"

I agreed.

"What about your stuff?"

"I don't know, I guess I'll have the hotel send it."

"Gimme your hotel key. I'll deal with your stuff."

"Yoooooouuuu," I said as I grabbed his cheeks and pecked his lips, "are a godsend."

"Yeah, yeah, yeah, a godsend you're leaving."

I gathered the few belongings I had—and by five forty was next to Hot Rob in the backseat as the Uber pulled up to the terminal. I had exactly ten minutes to make it through security and to my gate before the agent would close the doors and I'd be stuck in Kansas City forever (or at least until 6:59 p.m.).

I quickly kissed Hot Rob before running through the double doors and into the mother of all security lines. What the hell was going on? It was five forty in the morning! Who the hell flies out of Kansas City at five forty in the morning? I ran up to a TSA agent checking tickets and began pleading with him to let me through.

"We've all got flights to catch!" shouted a passenger behind me.

I channeled my best inner New Yorker and completely ignored him as I continued to plead with the agent, telling him all I had was a purse and no liquids. He let me through. I was running through the terminal, bridesmaid dress hanging out of my tote, when I heard "Final boarding call."

"Wait! One D! Wait!" I shouted at the agent, thinking maybe if she knew I was in first class (thanks to my complimentary upgrade) she'd hold the door for me. It was a total asshole move, but I *had* to make this flight. "I'm here!"

"Just in time," she said as I placed my phone on the electronic scanner.

I was completely out of breath as I headed down the jetway and onto the plane, where every other passenger was already securely fastened and ready for takeoff. Yup, I was *that* girl. I plunged into my seat. Holy shit! I made it! The plane began to push back, and the flight attendant was standing in the aisle doing her best demonstration of how to properly fasten a seat belt.

Seconds before takeoff, I get a text from Hot Rob. Swoon!

Hot Rob: "Did you make it?"

Me: "Yes, barely!"

Hot Rob: "I think you left some high heels here."

Me: "Shit."

Hot Rob: "I'll send them with your suitcase."

Me: "Thank you!"

Hot Rob: "Also, did you happen to lose a fingernail?"

I looked down at my hands. I was missing the press-on nail that once upon a time had covered my disgustingly short middle fingernail.

Me: "Oh, dear God."

Hot Rob: "Ha ha ha. Epic."

hunting season

Fresh off losing my one-night-stand card, I'm hit with two realizations, the first being that life is unfair. The other day, I was casually scrolling through my Twitter feed, which other than the *Daily Mail* is my only source of news, when my thumb got stopped in its tracks. It was an article from ESPN. The headline read that Mr. Seattle had just agreed on a contract extension worth millions of dollars. I wanted to vomit. That prick! That *rich* prick. Where is that bitch karma when you need her?

The second reality is that winter is coming. It's Marathon Sunday in New York. While some see this as a day to go out and cheer on the runners, locals see it as the final day of fall. Winter is approaching, which means everyone in New York is preparing to go into hibernation. Restaurants will soon be easy to get into on weeknights, the bars will only be stocked with true alcoholics, and the Hamptons will be deserted. Snow will cover the ground, and everyone will bitch and moan that it's too cold to go anywhere. Those in relationships will relish spending the cold nights snuggled up to their lovers. For those of us who are single, the days are dwindling as we rush to scoop up a last-minute boyfriend for the season. Having been through one lonely winter already, I, too, am on the hunt. Alas, this has led me not into the arms of a solid snuggle buddy but to another round of dating disasters. Despite upping my game and lowering my standards, all I've come up with are more names to add to my list of dudes who didn't work out.

First there's the guy I never should have agreed to go out with. I meet him while drinking at 310 Bowery, a casual sports bar known for drawing big Sunday crowds, filled with fratty guys who want to watch the game and hit on chicks. I like this particular bar because, well, I like fratty guys and being hit on. One day, one in particular has his eye on me. He is hot in the most frat-tastic way possible. But he is wearing a hat that says MAKE AMERICA GREAT AGAIN #TRUMP. If he weren't so hot, I would dismiss him immediately. It's one thing to be a Republican and vote for Trump, it's another thing to be wearing that advertisement on a hat in public. I make him remove the hat and decide if he buys me one more Fireball shot, I'll pretend he never wore it in the first place. He does, and I give him my number. Later that week, he asks me to dinner Friday. I'm coming in from out of town that night, so I ask him if we can do dinner on Saturday instead.

"Umm, Saturdays are for the boys."

"Huh?"

"You know, Saturdays. For the boys."

I thought Saturdays were for either nursing Friday's hangover or finishing the shit you didn't get done during the week. Turns out, according to Google, Saturdays are now "a legit excuse to tell your spouse you would rather hang out with your male friends than engage in trivial activities. Example. Wife: We are having dinner with my coworker and her husband tomorrow. Husband: Can't. Saturday is for the boys."

My brain fills with disgust, and I want to tell him that it's fine; he can have Saturday for him and his *boys*; hell, he can have Monday, Tuesday, Wednesday, Thursday, and Friday, too, for that matter.

I am a fucking woman, and I have zero time for a boy who wears a Trump hat to a bar. But instead, I just ghost him.

Then there is the bartender. He also happens to own the bar, but I like saying bartender instead, because it makes me feel more down-to-earth. After a few visits to his bar, plenty of flirting, and one night of too many drinks, I make out with him in the storage closet. We do this a few times, until he invites me out to dinner for a proper date. I am afraid of what he'll look like in daylight and wonder if the novelty will wear off if we see each other anywhere but in the storage closet of his bar at three in the morning. I can't risk finding out. Until I can't resist *not* finding out. I am hunting after all. So I agree to meet him for dinner and drinks. He isn't as hot as he was behind the bar having girls fawn all over him, but I don't completely rule him out. Until one night I'm at his bar hammered at five in the morning, waiting for him to close up. Even through my drunkenness, I can tell something is on his mind. We are sitting on the staircase in the back room of the bar, among the extra bottles of liquor, when he starts crying. He tells me he really likes me but that he just doesn't want to be a part of my lifestyle.

"What does that mean?"

"Your life, like, just the public aspect of it. Red carpets, men probably always hitting on you. It's just not normal."

If he only he knew how normal my life really is. I'm a hustler trying to make a living, going to auditions for jobs I have no chance of getting. I live in a one-bedroom apartment that is so small I have to store my sweaters in the oven. I get denied at fashion shows. Hell, I'm here at your dive bar at five in the morning sitting on dirty stairs. How much more normal can one be?

"Neither is late nights at a bar while girls fawn over you."

"You know what I mean."

I don't, to be honest. I mean, yes, my lifestyle is a little different from that of a woman who works nine to five, but so is a bartender's.

It doesn't matter; I don't need clarification. Part of me feels like damaged goods in the same way that Mr. Seattle made me feel, but thanks to my buzz, instead of crying, I just leave.

Then there was the basketball player. Ugh. I'm mortified to admit this one. First off, he is a basketball player. Second, if that's not bad enough, I matched with him on my dating app. To be honest, the only reason I even entertained the idea of him was because he lived in Seattle and played professional basketball. I couldn't help but imagine dating a guy who not only lived in the same town but was more than a foot taller than the man who dumped me. We chat for a few days before I give him my number. He texts me to say he's coming to New York and invites me to his game at Barclays. He'll leave me tickets, and I can wait until after and we can officially meet in person. I don't want to be a groupie, but I can't get over the idea of what an unbelievable payback this could ultimately be. So, out of bitterness toward Mr. Seattle, I call Jess and drag her to Brooklyn. When we arrive at Barclays, I find the Will Call booth.

"Name and ID?" the teller asks.

I slip my driver's license through the slot.

"Which list are you on?"

"A visiting player's list," I whisper as softly as I can.

"What? I can't hear you. Did you say player's list?"

"Yes."

Jess is laughing at my mortification.

"Hang on one second." The woman stands up and walks to an adjacent wall, which has a bunch of slots and envelopes in it like a mail station.

Meanwhile, Jess and I are surveying the shitshow that should be called "the line for the groupies." They are all dressed in tight dresses, head-to-toe Gucci, with high heels and probably low standards. But Jess and I can't even snub them, because we're in the same line, doing the same damn thing.

The lady returns empty-handed. "I don't see your tickets here. Do you have the number of his agent or assistant, maybe, that you can call?"

I pause for a moment before replying, "Nope," followed by a chuckle.

She laughs. I can't even imagine how many times she's seen this scenario play out. Luckily, she's nice and offers to call down to someone on the team and sort it all out for me. Five mortifying minutes later, we're standing a few feet away from Will Call when she motions me over and hands me two tickets. Jess and I make our way to our seats, where we find ourselves in the same row as every other groupie we just saw in line. Fuck us. We are totally groupies.

When the game is finally over, we stay seated as the stadium clears out. Everyone in our groupie section stays seated as well. Slowly, players start to come out of the locker room and up into our section, where they greet their families and friends. About four players have come out by now, and yet there is still the same number of groupies left. This isn't looking good. And then I feel my phone vibrate. It's a text from the basketball player. I open it, thinking it'll say something to the effect of "Be out in five." But instead, it says, "Hey, I left already. Hope you enjoyed the game. Hope to see you soon, sweetie." Motherfucker! I show the text to Jess. Her jaw drops to the floor.

"Let's fucking bounce before anyone sees us," I say.

We rush out of Barclays, never to see or hear from him again.

The next day, I find myself late for brunch with the girls.

"Hiiiiiiiii," I squeal as I give Ava, who is alone at the table with two empty chairs, a hug. "Sorry I'm late."

"No problem. Jess is on her way."

Like me, Jess is always late. It's gotten so bad that we've all begun lying to one another about what time a reservation is. Whoever makes the reservation tells everyone it's for thirty minutes earlier than it really is, so when we all arrive late, we're actually on time.

The waiter has just brought over a bottle of rosé when Jess arrives. I glance at the measly pour and shoot the waiter a look. He promptly fills my glass mere centimeters from the rim, just the way I like it. I take a gulp.

"Okay, now, spill."

"Spill what?"

"Ava's in love."

"Who is he?"

"It's that obvious?"

"Ugh, it's written all over your face." Jess can see it, too.

Ava takes a big gulp of wine as I sit back in my seat and prepare my listening ears. And then she begins telling the all-too-familiar story about a guy she met while vacationing in Europe, who she thought had the potential to be "the one." They'd exchanged kisses and numbers and had been talking for weeks, until suddenly he just stopped texting back.

"So what is the status now?"

"Well, funny you should ask."

Oh, God, here comes the part where shit is about to go south.

"He asked me to come visit him in London, but I don't know if I should."

"Why wouldn't you?" I ask.

"Well, so we *were* talking every single day, but he hasn't responded to any of my texts for the past week."

"Week?"

Jess kicks me under the table.

"Sorry, that's just a long time."

"Yeah, I know. And now I don't know whether to book the flight or not."

"Hell, no!" I blurt out.

"But I really like him, and I think, honestly, he's just busy with school and getting back into the swing of things. I'm sure he is just busy."

I'm trying not to laugh at the idea of him starting up a new semester of college, while at the same time trying not to reach across the table and choke Ava out of her own delusions. I want to tell her to wake the fuck up, that this dude met her over the summer at a club and now he's back at school, which means he is probably back to sneaking chicks into his dorm and waking up next to them in his twin bunk bed. But I can't.

Neither can Jess. Instead, we just sit with strained smiles on our faces and listen to Ava say, "I just wish I knew what he was up to."

"Why don't you stalk him on Instagram?" I suggest.

"Well, I do. He has stories up that I want to see, but—"

Before Ava can finish, Jess protectively interjects, "Wait! You know that he can see when you view his story now, right?"

"Y'all, that's why you have a fake account, duh," I say.

They both look at me with those girl-you-batshit-crazy side eyes.

"So what if I have a fake Instagram account? It's 2016, and I would like to stalk my exes in privacy, thank you very much."

Both of them are dying to see my account. I whip out my phone and show them.

"JerseyJulie89, are you fucking kidding me?" Jess is in awe.

"Well, it was either that or MandaPanda92." I laugh.

"Okay, you might be a little crazy," Ava says, "but also, you might be a little genius."

I hand the phone over to Ava so she can click on his story. There's nothing incriminating, but I group-text my account name and password to the two of them for future use.

"Well, I think it is very romantic and exciting. It'll probably be a bit of an adjustment, so maybe just keep your cool and see how it goes," Jess suggests.

I agree.

"Okay, just one last thing, and then I don't want to talk about this anymore. Should I say something to him about going all MIA on me?"

"No!" Jess and I both shout in unison.

"Okay, I'll hold off and keep you guys updated."

I can't help but think how dumb Ava looks. Doesn't she know she's getting played? I know I'm probably channeling my own frustrations with Mr. Seattle. Why is it that, as women, we play up these romantic studs who are really just shallow duds? Our eyes light up when we talk about our flings to our girlfriends. We blush at the sight of their names appearing on our phones. And then, when they go missing on us, we make excuses for them. We say, "He's probably just busy," or "This is what long-distance dating is like," or some other bullshit excuse. When it's our girlfriend, we listen and hide our eye rolls and agree with the excuses. We lie because we don't have the heart to tell our friend that her romantic fairy tale has been hijacked by reality. We lie because we can't bear to see the look of disappointment on her face. But by lying, are we protecting her, or are we just hanging her out to dry?

Deep down, we all know when a man isn't into us. It's not that difficult to tell, given that men aren't smart enough to play real games with our heads, nor are they disciplined enough to leave something they want alone. Basically, it's as simple as this: man sees something man likes, man goes and gets it. Men are like fat kids in bakeries: they will beg and do whatever it takes to get the cake, but once they've had a few bites, they will put down the fork and walk away, never to return again. Screw the "I'm busy" excuses. It takes all of two seconds to send a text. If a man has time to take a shit, he has time to shoot a text. Note: I am a firm believer that the only time a man can successfully multitask is while he is on the toilet. And yet knowing this, somehow we women still find ourselves stuck in the same shitty situation (pun intended) that Ava is in. Dammit, I should have just bitten the bullet and told her the truth. But I wonder if it would have even mattered. When it comes to a man being over us, is the hardest part knowing it or accepting it?

"Well, in case anyone was wondering, my love life is so non-existent that I've officially booked an appointment to see about freezing my eggs." Jess takes a sip of wine in defeat.

"Reaaaallly?" First Sarah, now Jess.

"Yup, time to face the reality, ladies."

We finish brunch and head our separate ways. I'm walking home thinking about what Jess said. Holy shit, has Sarah been right this whole time? I used to think she was joking about having to freeze her eggs, but now that Jess is doing it, it seems a little more valid. Have I been living in denial about my age? Should I be freezing my eggs, too? If my friends are all doing it, should I?

I decide to look into this whole egg-freezing thing and call the one person I know who can answer all my questions and debunk the online horror stories you read when you google "egg freezing." It's my friend Whitney, a fertility nurse in Chicago.

I shoot her a text saying, "Hey, girl, hope all is well. I have a question about freezing my eggs."

Immediately, she calls me. "Please tell me you are serious!"

"I don't know, should I do it?"

"Absolutely!" She starts telling me what a great idea it is to do it while I'm still young. Then she starts telling me about the process. First, I'd have to get an ultrasound to get an initial assessment of my ovaries, and then I'd start hormone injections, and then, once the eggs are ready, I'd have them retrieved by a doctor. She makes it sound so simple.

"How long does it take?"

"Well, that depends on how regular your cycle is. You're on birth control, right?"

"Umm, no."

"Really? What do you do?"

"Condoms."

She laughs before telling me that I'd need to go on birth control for about four to six weeks to regulate my cycle. Once it's regulated, I would be able to start the injection process. She asks me how I feel about it now that she's thrown a heaping pile of information my way, and I tell her I'm intrigued but just not sure and am only asking because it's been brought up by my girlfriends a few times.

"Totally understand. Well, you know I'm here whenever you do want to do it. I can answer any of your questions, and we are actually about to open a new clinic here in Chicago called Ova that is going to be awesome. It will be a facility we use only for egg freezing."

I thank her and tell her I will think about it.

I hang up the phone and feel relieved to know that it is not as intense as Sarah makes it out to be. But in all honesty, I don't feel like I need to completely surrender my ovaries just yet. I mean, I'm twenty-nine; that isn't *that* old. Sure, by Southern standards, I probably should have had a few kids by now, but I feel like freezing your eggs, quite frankly, is something only old women do. And I refuse to admit that I am old. I've still got it, haven't I?

my suspicions have been confirmed

With my hunt still under way and absolutely nothing to show for it, I find myself on the Upper East Side having dinner at a new ramen restaurant with Jess. We haven't even gotten our food when a strange look comes across Jess's face.

"Okay, so I have to tell you something."

"Oh, God, what?"

"I got the scoop."

"Shut the fuck up!" I don't even need to ask what the scoop is about. She takes a deep breath. "He and his girlfriend . . ."

I go numb. I knew it. I fucking knew it. I knew there was no way Mr. Seattle was telling me the truth when he said he just wanted to be single. None of it made sense, none of it.

"How did you find this out?"

She goes on to tell me that one of her mutual friends is good friends with his new girlfriend. Apparently, three days after I left Seattle, he was out to dinner with his friends and met a girl he is now officially dating. In fact, he's already asked her to move in with him.

"She knows about you, and your email, all of it. Apparently, the girl is nice. Not a threatening type of girl, just a simple, nice one."

It's all making sense to me. The whole "I just want to be single" line, the silent treatment. Total bullshit. He's not lost, like he said he was. Oh, no, he has very much found his way—into the arms of another woman. Of course she's younger and blond.

"Wait! Three days after I left would have been a Thursday. Which was the night he didn't text me. The night before the epic text breakup on Friday. Oh, my God."

Jess feels awful for having to deliver the bad news, but she did the right thing. Truth is, I wouldn't want to hear this news from anyone other than her. After all, we're the bury the body team; the duo that cries together in the bathroom stall. After dinner I rode the train home in a daze; I took a seat on a greasy blue chair near the end of the car and looked around at the sudden emptiness. A man was singing "Sunshine, go away today, I don't feel much like dancing" while holding a cup filled with change. I dug through my purse and gave him a dollar, and then I just started crying.

I wasn't hysterical, but I wasn't just whimpering. I was having the kind of cry you have when you watch a tearjerker movie. A silent, steady stream kind of cry.

You'd think by now I'd be over Mr. Seattle, that I wouldn't give a shit that what I had grown to suspect all along turned out to be true. Hell, I thought by now I'd be over him. An entire summer and half a winter has passed since I last spoke to him. But even though the seasons have changed, the number of times I think of him hasn't.

He's the one man from my past who still haunts me. He isn't the best, certainly not the hottest, definitely not the tallest. And even with the fat paycheck he now has, he isn't the richest. But out of all the men I've been with, it seems as though the below-average Mr. Seattle is the one man who has me crying on a subway train.

It's not until I'm lying in bed that my dazed tears turn into irate ones. I cannot believe that he lied to me. I cannot believe that he has a fucking girlfriend! All of his crying on FaceTime was complete bullshit. The email—oh, God! Why the fuck did I write that email?

And he showed it to her? What an asshole. But wait, why would he tell me that he just wanted to be single when he was already seeing her at the time? Why didn't he just tell the truth and say he'd met someone else? That's what pisses me off about this entire situation—more than the mortification, the time wasted, the feelings hurt. It's the lying. Don't feed me bullshit lines like "I care about you so much, but I just want to be single," when clearly you don't. Don't pretend to care when you have your dick in someone else. Don't be a coward.

Sure, maybe he didn't want to hurt my feelings, but he had to have known I was going to find out sooner or later. And you go around this world doing do fucked-up shit and then cover it with "But I didn't want to hurt your feelings" just to justify the fucked-up shit you do. And I'm sorry, but getting into a relationship is automatically risking getting your feelings hurt. If you can't handle being hurt or hurting someone else, then don't get involved in the first place. I'm a grown woman. I can handle getting let down. I can handle some rejection. But at least do it with class. At least be a fucking man and be honest.

And I'm not just hurt, I'm disappointed. I'm disappointed in someone I cared about as a human being. Disappointed at him for being a lying coward and at myself for believing he was different. It's as if he is the child and I am the parent and he has done something bad, but instead of being angry, I am just disappointed, which I think is actually worse. I thought better of him, I really did. I let someone in who had the ability to hurt me yet again. And that's exactly what he did.

But why? Why did this happen?

Ava says I was too nice to him both during the relationship and after. And that I was too open with my feelings for him. The player in me agrees, but the woman in me knows that's just who I am, which makes it a bit of a Catch-22. On the one hand, I acted as my true self, and I take comfort in that. There is a peace in being able to say to myself that at least he got to see the real me, but it also comes with the other side, which means he didn't really like the real me. Not enough, at least. And that's a tough pill to swallow for anyone.

Maybe I'll never really know why he chose her over me, or why he lied, or why she could make him ready but I couldn't. Maybe never knowing is my answer. Maybe the outcome is my only closure.

All of this leads me to one terrifying realization: you will never truly know anyone other than yourself. You won't. No matter how much you think you know someone, think you know who they are at their core, what they stand for, their character, their values, all of it, you don't. They can betray you in an instant, and there is nothing you can do about it. They can make you believe this yet prove that. They can discard you like trash. When it comes down to it, there is only one person you can truly ever trust, and it's not a man, it's not a friend, it's not your family. It's you. And as I lie in bed I am faced with the rude awakening that I might be alone forever. And if that's the case then I need to start preparing myself for that.

The next morning, still fuming, I pick up the phone.

"Hey, girl! What's up?"

"Whitney, I want to freeze my eggs!"

Within the week Whitney has flown in from Chicago just to teach me how to do the injections myself. The two of us sat on my couch for about twenty minutes as she went over all the different medicines and how to fill the syringes with them. Though I don't really need to know everything just yet, since I won't be starting the injections for another week or so, but she wants me to feel comfortable since I won't be in Chicago until the week of my retrieval. After showing me how the syringes get filled, she takes out a medical sponge thingy and puts it on my coffee table. It looks like a silicone boob, if you ask me, but she tells me it's a device they use to practice giving shots. I practice each step she has taught me before taking the needle and effortlessly sticking it into the booby sponge.

"Great! Now it's time to try it on yourself."

"Umm, really?"

"Yeah. Here is a vial of distilled water. We can use that."

I take my shirt off and bend over, grabbing a good-size pinch of the fat that surrounds my belly.

"Okay, now, take the sanitizing wipe and rub the area where you are going to inject yourself." She points to an area on my belly as she reminds me that it needs to be at least two fingers away from the belly button. "The lower, the better, and the fattier, the less painful," she says.

I take a deep breath in and exhale. I've got the needle filled with the distilled water in one hand and a pinch full of my own belly fat in the other. I'm ready. I can do this. The needle is tiny, smaller than a safety pin. *Good analogy, Andi. Think of this as popping a pimple with a safety pin.* I can do this! I inch the needle to the surface of my skin and close my eyes.

Seconds later, with my eyes still closed, I ask Whitney if it's in.

She laughs. "Not even close."

I press a little harder and ask her again.

She laughs again. "Still not even close."

This goes back and forth for a solid five minutes and has us both hysterically laughing.

I take another deep breath in and press harder. "Okay, this has to fucking be in now!" I shout.

"Just a touch more."

I push harder.

"There you go! It's in."

I stand up, raising both arms in a show of victory.

"Nooooooo!" Whitney screams. "Keep the needle in your hand!"

Oh, God, there is a needle sticking out of my stomach. I forgot I still had to inject the distilled water. "Fuuuuuck."

"You can do it."

A few deep breaths later, I do. For the first time in my life, I have taken . . . a shot of water.

The next day, I walk to the pharmacy, where I proudly pick up the pack of birth control Whitney prescribed me even though I won't be using it for another month or so. Apparently there is this whole scheduling of the menstrual cycle ovulation thingy that goes along with freezing your eggs. You don't just walk into the doctor's office and voilà have your eggs frozen. They have to put you on a schedule, and mine will take a little longer since my body is not "trained" to cycle, blah, blah, blah.

As soon as I enter my apartment, I rip open the paper bag and pull out one small yellow plastic compact case. It reminds me of one of those Polly Pocket toys my sister and I used to play with when we were kids. Only it's not filled with plastic accessories, it's filled with a foil tray of little blue and green pills. I feel weirdly proud of my Polly Pocket of birth control. I text the girls a photo of it. I'm bragging like I'm thirteen years old again and getting my period for the first time.

Oh shit, is this going to make me fat?

i'm playing with fire

'Tis the season . . to schedule your eggs to be frozen and to play with some fire! The weekend starts out with a holiday party hosted by a group of our guy friends. They are the kind of New York City guys who know how to throw a good party and surround themselves with a bevy of young, hot models. And while this isn't so uncommon in the city, the fact that they are barely above-average-looking makes me scratch my head every time I see them with these women. I don't know how they do it, but they do. Jess and I are two of the handful of nonmodels on the guest list. Knowing the competition will be fierce, I get a blow-out, slather on the baby oil, watch a YouTube video to nail my best smoky eye ever, and complete my sexy ensemble with a plunging black jumpsuit. When I meet Jess for a drink before the party, she is equally glammed up. We both know what we are stepping into, and dammit, we are going to step in looking hot.

After being escorted to the private room downstairs, we make our way through the crowd of tall, beautiful models and immediately order champagne at the bar. We're mingling with our friends when out of the corner of my eye, something, or should I say someone, catches my attention. He's tall, dark-haired, and effortlessly hot, one of those guys who walk into a room and don't realize that they silence it. And now he's one of those guys who is walking toward us. God, he's beautiful. He appears to be Latin or Italian or something else. Something exotic. Not necessarily my type but very much getting my attention. He starts talking directly to me, telling me that he's just moved to New York City. I'm so mesmerized by him that even though I can see his lips are moving, I have no idea what he's saying. I'm deafened by his exotic hotness. It isn't until a friend comes over and says, "Oh, you two finally met," that a light goes off in my head. This must be the guy our friends mentioned casually during a dinner that they wanted to set me up with. It all makes sense: hot guy, just moved to New York. Usually, I'm opposed to mixing love with friendship, but I'm thinking I could make an exception in this case. Unable to formulate any sensible sentences, I bail and make my way to the bar. I can't believe I was so captivated by him that I couldn't even speak. Who am I? Better yet, who is *he*?

I take a moment to look around the room and realize this party isn't just filled with beautiful tall models; it's also filled with beautiful tall men. 'Tis the fucking season! A few drinks later, I'm making my way through the dance floor to the restroom, when of course, I run into Mr. Exotic. He does a stupid little dance move, which I laugh at. He places his hand on my shoulder and tries to say something in my ear. I can't hear over the music or over the hotness of his breath so close to me. I back away and motion to the speakers while shaking my head. A chick comes stumbling between us, and right before my very eyes, she starts grinding her ass up against him. He's shocked, as am I. He gently pushes her away before looking at her and then nodding at me.

"So that's how easy it is, huh?"

"I can't hear you." He points to the speakers and smiles.

I lean into his ear. "So that's how easy it is, huh?"

He leans toward me, placing his hand on the small of my back. "I'm sure it's not very hard for you, either."

"We'll see. Looks like it's one to zero right now."

Just then, a slow song comes on, and I use it as my cue to go to the bathroom. On my way back, I see my friend Brett, one of the hosts of the party, standing beside a table. He asks if I want a drink while pointing to the bottles of various liquors sitting on the table in a large ice bucket.

"Champagne, please," I say.

"No vodka?"

"Not yet."

I've decided that in light of this new potential guy being here, I will take it easy on the drinking for now. I take my glass of champagne and turn to walk toward the front of the room, when I run into Mr. Exotic, yet again. A new girl is now dancing on him, yet again. I give him a raise of the eyebrow, as if to show him I'm impressed but not stalking. He gives a roll of the eye and a laugh before walking over to me.

"Damn, looks like I'd better get on it."

He laughs. "Oh, please."

"You're up by two."

"Well, then, I guess you'd better get on it!"

"Oh, I'll be dancing circles around you in a drink or two."

"I'd like to see that," he says, biting his upper lip.

Damn, he's fucking hot. And quick. Flustered, I panic and turn around to make my way back to Brett's table. Jess is there, too, along with some of our other friends. Brett's parents have arrived, and he is introducing them to us. Then he starts looking at me in a weird way. He's kind of flirting with me, I think. It must be the plunging neckline and the contouring I did around my boobs. Despite not being sure if he is actually flirting with me or not and knowing that nothing will come of it even if he is, I can't help but indulge myself. In the back of my mind, I realize that by flirting with Brett, I am officially on the board. At one point, I glance over to my left and out of the corner of my eye see the sexy Mr. Exotic. He nods at me. Oh, I'm definitely on the board. I go back to talking to Brett, who is probably now wondering why the fuck I'm flirting with him.

Drinks are being slung, lyrics are being butchered, dance circles are forming, and the party is raging. I'm using a friend to make a guy whose name I don't even know jealous, and it's working. I can tell by the look in his eyes and the fact that he is now "casually" hanging around our table.

Hours later, we all find ourselves at Brett's house for the after-party. I spend a solid hour pretending to engage in conversation with everyone while really keeping an eye on the door, hoping Mr. Exotic will walk in. It doesn't happen. After a few hours, I give up hope and call it a night.

The next day, I find myself at 310 Bowery with Ava and Jess. Emily and a few others are planning to meet us here later. Most of the crew from last night is here, along with a new slew of young models. I can tell they aren't New Yorkers, because, unlike me and my friends, who are in jeans and T-shirts, they are in bandage dresses, batting their fake eyelashes at any guy who looks their way. Thirsty girls, but whatever. I'm sipping beer out of a bottle when suddenly, there he is, Mr. Exotic. He makes a beeline toward me. Fuck, I look like shit.

"Hey, you! Two days in a row? Man, am I lucky."

"Ha ha. Glad someone else missed the cocktail attire memo," I say, glancing down at his open plaid flannel.

"Ha ha. I mean, I thought Sunday and football meant casual?"

"You and me both."

"Hey, girl, heeeeeeeeeyyyy," shrieks a voice from behind me.

I turn around. It's Steph, an acquaintance who, last I knew of, lived in L.A.

"Heyyyy! What are you doing here?"

"I'm in town for the weekend. How are you? It's been a while."

"I'm great, just living the New York life. Are you still out in L.A.?"

"Yeah! Love it! Umm, who is the guy in the plaid? Boyfriend?" she whispers.

I tell her no. She tells me if I introduce her, she'll owe me forever. Whatever. I do, and they shake hands. I'm expecting a three-way conversation to start, but it doesn't. It's almost as if he doesn't even realize Steph is still standing there. It's obvious enough that Steph turns around to talk to some other people. Next thing I know, she's across from me at the high-top table we are all crowded around, mouthing, *He's hot, hook it up*, to me.

"My friend thinks you're cute."

"That's nice, but umm—"

"What? You should talk to her."

"I'd rather talk to you."

"Uhh, why? Do you not have two eyes?"

"Yeah, and they are both looking at you."

"Yeah, well, umm—"

"What?"

"Me. You. Not gonna happen."

"Oh, really, why is that?" He seems to find my brush-off amusing.

"Ummm, I don't think I'm your type."

"You mean I'm not *your* type. Damn, I guess I have some convincing to do."

I roll my eyes but smile at the same time. I can't help but find joy in appearing to have the upper hand. It's been a while since I've felt in control, and damn, does it feel good. He asks for my number. I give it to him. He immediately texts me. And then glances to my phone, which is sitting on the table. The screen is dark.

"Did you just give me a fake number?"

Oh, shit, my burner phone is in my purse. I reach under the

table and find my bag, dig through it, and pull out my cell phone. He has a puzzled look on his face.

"Wow, I don't know what's worse, giving a fake number or having a burner phone."

He is so turned on. Clearly, he's not used to texting a woman's burner phone. But there's a look in his eyes that also says he's intrigued. "We're going to dinner this week."

"Maybe."

"Yes."

Later that night, I lie in bed staring at his text. All it says is his name, but as I stare at it, I envision his face. I envision his lips, his shirtless body. I envision a date with him. I save his number as "Mr. Exotic." Two days later, he texts me early in the afternoon.

Mr. Exotic: "Dinner, me and you, tonight. Please?"

Damn, he's good.

Me: "Drinks."

Mr. Exotic: "Fine. I'll pick you up if you pick the place."

Later that night, he arrives at my apartment, where I make him wait on the stoop, like I do everyone else. Then I take him to Aria, like I do everyone else. Drinks turn into dinner. Dinner turns into closing the restaurant down and the manager giving me a wink and a thumbs-up, something he's never done with any of my prior dates. As we walk back to my apartment, I can't help but feel like the night isn't over. I want to be with him as long as I can, but can't invite him in. I've got to plan this one right. So instead, I suggest we go to a bar down the street.

The bar is closed.

"Let's go to Soho Grand, it's near my place," he suggests. And we do. A few drinks later and I'm doing exactly what I wanted to but at the same time didn't want to do: following him back to his place. At this point, I'm pretty tipsy but I can feel that something is really off. Not with him. With where I am. It's like a word that is on the tip of my tongue only it's a feeling on the tip of my brain. It's like I know what I'm thinking but I can't describe it. It's not until he opens his apartment door that it all comes together.

I've been here before.

I've been in this apartment. Holy shit. This is the Yankee's old apartment. I heard it was on the market and was being rented until it sold, but oh, my God, I didn't know it was being rented to none other than Mr. Exotic. I'm trying not to look like a deer in headlights while Mr. Exotic opens the fridge and grabs us some waters.

"Sorry about the boxes. I have to be out of here by Tuesday. I guess the apartment sold."

There I am back in the apartment with the windows that overlook all of Soho. *It really is a fabulous view*, I think to myself. As I'm gazing out at the rooftops below, I feel a familiar touch. He is stroking my hair and kissing my neck from behind. I'm standing in the exact same square foot I was in when the Yankee first did this. For a moment, I contemplate what to do next. On the one hand, I know how fucked up this is. I'm with a new man in my old man's apartment. But on the other hand, it's kind of only fitting. I broke in this apartment, and now I should give it one last make-out session.

I turn around and press my lips to his.

I leave in the wee hours of the morning, having indulged in a passionate few hours of nothing more than some good old-fashioned making out and a little light groping. My self-discipline makes me feel better about it all. I put on my jacket and heels and exit the apartment, for the last time, I hope. I make my way down the elevator and through the lobby, where a doorman tells me goodbye in a judgmental kind of way. Little does he know, I've been here both before and after the original owner moved out and I've got the key on my ring to prove it. I wave two fingers in the air, nod my head, put my sunglasses on, and, like a badass, strut my ass right out of there.

Fuck playing, this girl is on fire.

the end of an era

Well, no luck finding a winter boyfriend so far, and no luck finding a New Year's Eve kiss. I can't remember the last time I didn't have a New Year's Eve kiss. Is that a bad sign for the year to come? This year, instead of going to Mexico, my friends and I stay in the city and have a low-key dinner. I have to fly out early the next morning to film a segment for *Jimmy Kimmel Live*. I know, I still find myself in disbelief when I say things like that. Like who the fuck am I to be on *Jimmy Kimmel Live*? It blows my mind.

The past two times I was on the show, I was promoting *The Bachelorette* and going public with my then-fiancé. This time is going to be a little different, since now I am going to promote Number Twenty-Five's new season. There was a full-court-press effort to make this the most dramatic season ever. And what better way to make it dramatic than to bring not one but both of his exes onto the show? I won't say I am super-excited to be flying across the country on New Year's Day, but I sure as hell wasn't going to turn down *Jimmy Kimmel Live*.

Cut to the actual taping. Kaitlyn, the other ex, and I are getting ready for the evening interview portion with Number Twenty-Five. We've had our hair and makeup done and are now showing the stylist what we plan to wear. Kaitlyn has a sexy midi skirt and crop top that look expensive and hot. I reach into an H&M bag and pull out a pair of black trouser shorts and a tank with the tags still on them, which I bought across the street this morning. Luckily, I also brought from home a navy blazer onto which I'd hot-glued black beads on the lapel and sleeves. I slipped it on and oiled up my legs before walking out to show the stylist.

"Oh. My. God. Giiiiiiirl, is that the Balmain blazer?" he asks.

"This? Seriously?"

"It's fire!"

"Ummmm, this is an H&M blazer that I hot-glued beads on."

"No fucking way! Karen, Karen!" He's waving to a producer. "Come see this. You have got to see this."

"Balmain?"

I laugh. "H&M and hot glue."

"Holy amaaaazing."

Now that I am apparently looking like a million bucks, it is time for the interview. The door opens, and we walk to the couch next to Jimmy's desk. Number Twenty-Five is already there. We all greet one another. His hug with me seems much warmer than his with Kaitlyn does. Number Twenty-Five and I squashed our beef long ago. So much so that we actually text each other on occasion just to see how life is. It's weird. I never thought I'd say that, considering this is the same guy who once told the world we'd had sex on live television, but since then, we've both gone on to do our own things. Our resentment is so far in the past that it's become something that kind of bonds us.

But the same can't yet be said for him and Kaitlyn. There seems to be nothing but disdain between them. As we take our seats on the couch, Kaitlyn next to Jimmy and me between her and Number Twenty-Five, the tension can be felt by everyone, including me. There I am, sitting between two fires, and I can't help but feel responsible for having set them aflame. Had I not sent Number Twenty-Five home when I did, then maybe he wouldn't have gone on Kaitlyn's season, and maybe they'd just be acquaintances instead of whatever awkwardness they are now. I think I'm asked a question, and all I can say is "This is so awkward." Kaitlyn starts rambling about some bet she and Jimmy have, and at one point, I honestly don't even know what the conversation is about. I figure I'll just sit back and flex my oiled-up legs and smile. And that's exactly what I do.

As I fly home, part of me laughs at the last twenty-four hours, and another part of me feels a sense of sadness. I know that this was probably my last appearance as it relates to the *Bachelor* franchise. I know that it's time to move on from a show that changed my life forever. It's a weird sense of identity crisis. Just the way my identity changed when I went on the show and got engaged, the fact that I'm no longer engaged, not on the show, and becoming more irrelevant with each season is also a change in my identity.

The truth is, I've been out of the *Bachelor* game for a while now. Sometimes Sharleen, who was on the show with me and lives in New York, invites me to viewing parties. Despite knowing my answer will always be "Hell, no," it's sweet of her to ask. But as for me, when it comes to this whole obsession with the show, I just don't get it. I never did. Maybe that's why I was such a boring lead. Don't get me wrong, it's not the reality television factor that I don't get. I love reality television. I love the worst of it. The *Real Housewives* of every city, *Million Dollar Listing*, *My Big Fat Gypsy Wedding*, *Total Divas*—you name it, it's set to my DVR. Except my own show. Maybe there is a part of me that can't watch it because I went through it and it didn't work out. Maybe it's all rooted in my own sense of failure. Maybe it's rooted in my own fear. If I watch it, will it bring up memories that have taken a year to erase? I don't know, but I don't want to find out.

The other thing about the show and these viewing parties is that a bunch of other former contestants always go to them. They all cling to one another and upload tons of photos and snaps whenever they hang out together. I understand there is an underlying bond among contestants of the show; trust me, I've experienced it myself. We all share the experience of being plucked from our normal nine-to-five jobs and inserted into a life that is anything but normal. But other than that, what do we all really have in common? Am I really inherently bonded with a contestant just because she went on the same show I went on four seasons later? What would I even talk to her about? The show? That's exactly what I *don't* want to talk about.

The other thing is, I've seen how social media has changed with every season of the show since mine. Sharleen and I were once talking about the fact that back when we went on, there was no social media, really. It was kind of shocking when we all got off with fifty thousand or a hundred thousand followers. Now it's shocking if these contestants don't come off with half a million followers. It's become such a thing that I wonder if most of the contestants are now going on the show simply for a social media following. Which leads me to distrust the ones I don't know. When I see these people building their lives around social media and a television show, it seems only natural that in order to fuel that engine, you have to keep gassing it up. And how do you gas it up? With photos and friends who are also building their lives around the same show. Do you really think half these people would be friends if social media didn't exist? I'm not hating on them; to each his own, really. But I'll leave the posing-in-cornfield photo shoots to them.

I'm in a different world now. I'm in a different frame of mind from how I was back then. While my experience with the show was amazing, it is over, and I'm good with that. I don't want to be defined by my reality television stint; I want to be defined by my actions now. But what will that definition be?

i just spent fourteen hours in vegas

And that's not even the worst part. I may not be qualified to have a one-last-fling-before-the-ring kind of party in the city of sin, but I'm definitely entitled to a last-fling-before-the-freezing party.

Whitney scheduled me to start my injections for the egg retrieval later in the month, so I decide I need one last hurrah. I know, I'm being dramatic. Truth is, I was just looking for any excuse to take a vacation, and I found one in, of all things, the Atlanta Falcons. I hadn't planned on going to this year's Super Bowl, but being that my hometown team is in it, and I am likely never going to see that happen again, I *have* to go. I clamor around New York asking everyone I know, and thanks to Ava and her wicked corporate-advertising connections, I am given two tickets. It's obvious who I'm bringing along: Kelly. She, meanwhile, has managed to clamor around Atlanta and find us a ride on a private jet and, thanks to her wicked rich-people connections, even got us a hotel.

Days before I even made it down to Atlanta to catch a ride on the jet, Mr. Exotic texted me asking what I was doing for Super Bowl weekend. I told him I was going to the game, and he told me I should come meet him in Vegas instead, which I coyly rebuffed.

Cut to Saturday, and Kelly, her husband, their rich friends, and

I are all flying to Houston. When we land, I suggest we go to what I remember being the best Mexican restaurant in town. I haven't been to Houston in years, but that doesn't stop me from remembering the best fajitas my mouth ever laid taste buds on. As Kelly, her husband, and I devour three orders of fajitas, two orders of cheese dip, and a heap of guacamole, I can't help but feel pride. I was right. They are the best damn fajitas in the world. Afterward, we go to the hotel to get ready for a party. In all honesty, Super Bowl parties sound fun, but they are kind of lame. They are basically just a mix of random celebrities, former football players, models, and corporate big shots who never get out. They all think they're partying so hard, but by midnight, they're all in bed. It's so very corporate and stiff. But it's the Super Bowl, and the Falcons are in it, so I'm feeling amazing. We decide to take it relatively easy that night in preparation for tomorrow's big game.

On game day, the three of us are on our way to a tailgate being hosted by the people who gave us the tickets. Well, they gave Kelly and me the tickets, at least. Kelly's husband doesn't have a ticket but is going to buy one at the game. When we arrive at the tailgate, it's disappointing, just like the parties. There are no tents, charcoal grills, or people drinking beer while playing cornhole. Instead, it's an indoor tailgate, with various live music acts, buffet stations catered by different restaurants, and a few bars. It's fine but not really getting me into the football mood.

Mr. Exotic and I are still avidly texting. So much so that my cheeks are actually starting to hurt and Kelly is getting curious about him. An hour before the game, we are handed our tickets. We see the number 600 in the box under the word SECTION. We are both a little, well, a little concerned.

"Maybe it's like a suite," I say to Kelly.

"Hope so. Six hundred is awfully high."

"Awfully."

We go through security and follow the signs to section 600. With each escalator we have to take up, our worry grows. Finally, after the sixth escalator, we arrive. We look at each other. We don't have to say a word. With tickets in hand, we make our way to our seats and look down. With only five rows behind us, we are officially in the nosebleeds. Not only can we not see anything except what look like little dots warming up on the field below, but in our Atlanta Falcons hats and shirts, we are in a section of New England Patriots fans. We sit and have that awkward moment of reflection, knowing that on the one hand, we can't complain, considering we are at the fucking Super Bowl for free. But on the other hand, no free ticket is worth the public humiliation I'm going to feel after I vomit from being this high up. I can't do it; I physically can't do it. I look over at Kelly. She can't do it, either. Then the Patriots fans surrounding us start talking shit about how badly we are going to lose. That's it.

"Plan B?" I say to Kelly.

"Let's get the fuck out of here."

We don't actually have a plan B, but we decide to make our way to the bar and hatch one. We start looking on StubHub to see how much ticket prices are. Three grand. I can't. Fuck!

"What if we just go sit in those seats down there on the first level? I mean, obviously, no one has bought them, so they should be empty, right?"

Kelly agrees, and we sprint down the escalators to section 119. There's only one seat. Shit. Kelly's husband is in section 118, just a few rows below it, so she decides to try to squeeze in with him. Meanwhile, I decide to take that one seat.

There's a man standing awfully close to it, and he looks worried as I walk down the row. "Is this your seat?" he asks me.

"Yeah, sorry."

"Dang, did you just buy it?"

"I did!"

He leaves, and I feel terrible, because he totally had my idea, he just didn't have the lack of morality I did. I text Kelly, who is still with her husband but is apparently being complained about by some chick behind her, so she is going to move to a seat a few sections over. The game officially starts, and the three of us find ourselves alone in different sections, her husband—the one who came to the Super Bowl with no ticket—the only one with an actual valid seat. Go figure.

I decide to make friends with the people around me. There's a nice guy with a British accent sitting next to me who strikes up a conversation. He tells me he's not really into the game, but his company had a ticket, blah, blah, blah. I want to kill him over this, but his accent and genuinely nice demeanor stop me from doing so. He asks me why I'm alone, and I tell him that my husband is sitting a few rows over because we couldn't get seats together. He totally buys it. Enough to start buying me drinks. He's not creepy, though. In fact, he's showing me pictures of his two daughters during time-outs. And he even cheers with me every time the Falcons score, which is surprisingly quite often.

The second quarter begins, and the Falcons are dominating the Patriots, and I'm feeling pretty buzzed when a security guard makes her way to our row. She's looking directly at me. We make eye contact. I look away. I can see her motioning for me to come over to her. But the Brit next to me thinks she's talking to him, so he gets up and makes his way over to her. I can see her check his ticket before sending him back on his way and then motioning me over again. I'm caught. I'm totally caught. I calmly and confidently walk over to her.

"Ma'am, what seat are you?"

I pull out my phone, which, thank God, has a privacy screen on it. "Section one-eighteen, row T, seat nineteen."

"Ohhhh, honey, this is section one-nineteen. One-eighteen is over to the left."

"No way!"

She chuckles. "Come here, let me help you."

She takes my hand, and we walk up the stairs between the sections together. I make sure it looks like she's protecting me versus ejecting me. The last thing I need is to be the girl getting kicked out of a seat. Thank God she's sweet and buys my bullshit, and thus, not only do I avoid complete public embarrassment, but I also avoid getting kicked out in handcuffs.

I eventually make my way over to Kelly, who is now standing at the top of a nearby section in the handicapped area. There's no one in a wheelchair; instead, it's filled with a group of thirty-ish guys and girls. They're having fun, with drinks in their hands, including Kelly. Meanwhile, Mr. Exotic and I are still texting, and he's begging me to get on a flight and come meet him in Vegas. I'm so drunk that I'm actually entertaining this idea, or at least making him think that I'm entertaining this idea. I might have not been willing to do the deed with him in the Yankee's apartment, but last I checked, the Yankee didn't own Vegas. One vodka later . . .

Me: "What times are the flights?"

Mr. Exotic: "One at 7 and one at 9:30."

Me: "It's 6 now. I won't make the 7. What about 9:30?"

Mr. Exotic: "Do it!"

Me: "Book it!"

Mr. Exotic: "What is your birthdate?"

Me: "4/3/1987."

Oh, God, this text sending my birthdate feels like the Kentucky Derby all over again. The next text I receive is a screen shot of my confirmed one-way ticket, departing Houston at nine thirty p.m. and arriving in Las Vegas at eleven p.m. Oh, shit, what have I done?

Me: "Is this for real?"

Mr. Exotic: "For real. Now, get your butt ready to have some fun."

Part of me is scared Kelly is going to scold me, though I don't know why; she's never scolded me before. But I feel like I'm ditching her for a guy, and I *hate* when women do that. I show her the screen.

"Holy shit!"

"I know. What do I do?"

"You fucking go."

"Really?"

"Umm, look at the scoreboard. Yes, really."

"Is it bad, though?"

"Is what bad? The fact that you're single and a hot guy who is also single just bought you a flight to Vegas?"

I've got nothing in response. She's right. This is the shit I should be doing. Especially since I'm about to go into hibernation mode while I fertilize the crap out of my ovaries. I mean, if I'm going to have one last fling before the egg freezing, I should do it right. I should do it in Vegas.

But first, I have to watch Lady Gaga perform for halftime. I know I'm cutting it close, but the feminist inside me refuses to choose a dude over Gaga. And she delivers a killer performance in return. It's now seven fifteen, and I kiss Kelly on the cheek and tell her to say goodbye to her husband for me. I run outside and order an Uber. I'm supposed to go to the maroon lot. Frantic, I ask someone in an event shirt where the maroon lot is, and he tells me it's all the way on the other side of the stadium. I start running. I stop only to ask another event worker how much farther it is.

"Keeeeeep going," he says.

Fuck. Then I see a security guard driving a golf cart with a handicapped sticker on it. He has one man holding crutches in the front and a woman, who appears to be the man's wife, in the back.

"Hey! Can I get a ride?" I yell.

"Sorry, ma'am, I can only take handicapped people."

"What about pregnant women?"

He looks at me suspiciously as I cradle my stomach. "I guess so."

I hop in the backseat next to the wife and tell him I need to get to the maroon lot stat. Meanwhile, I'm sticking my stomach out as far as I can without losing my breath as I rest my right hand on top of my belly. The wife is sweetly making conversation, asking me in a thick Southern accent how I'm feeling and how far along I am. Fearful that I'll get kicked out of the cart if I tell the truth, I lie and tell her I'm much better now that I'm past the first trimester. I'm so going to hell for this, and I know it.

As the cart pulls up to the maroon lot, I get out, thanking the security guard and thanking the wife, who is now wishing me good luck on the pregnancy. As soon as the cart pulls off, I start running through the yards of winding barricades with tarps and Uber logos on them. Luckily, the line is completely empty, because who the fuck leaves the Super Bowl at halftime? I am able to get into the first car and plug in the address to the hotel. It only takes about fifteen minutes to get there. I show the driver a hundred-dollar bill, saying I'll give it to her if she'll wait for me to pack and bring me to the airport. She agrees without a second of hesitation. Damn. I should have offered forty. I'm drunk, and I have about forty-five minutes to pack and make it to the airport, through security, and onto a plane.

I frantically scrounge up my belongings and shove them into my carry-on bag. Luckily, I packed light, so not only do I not have to debate over what outfit to wear (since I have none), but it only takes me a few minutes to throw everything in. I rush down the elevator, praying the driver is still there. She is, thank God.

"To the airport!" I tell her.

Twenty minutes later, I'm rushing through security and to my gate. It's nine thirteen.

"What time are you closing the gate?" I ask the agent.

"In about five minutes."

"Okay. I'm just going over there to watch the rest of the game. Don't leave me!"

I walk to the nearest television, where a crowd has gathered. There's one minute left in the game, and the Patriots score a touchdown and a two-point conversion, tying it. Meaning all of those touchdowns I watched the Falcons score in the first half have officially been blown. The game is officially heading to overtime, and the gate agent is officially closing the doors. *Fuck it, they're gonna lose anyway*, I think to myself as I board the plane.

It's not until I get to my seat and sit down that I realize what I've just done. I've just left the Super Bowl and am headed to Vegas. All to see a boy. What am I thinking? Who am I? Oh, that's right, I'm a single woman. And I'm having the kind of fun that only single women can really have. I kind of like this new spontaneous chick. Scratch that, I *really* like her.

A few glasses of red wine later, I'm in Las Vegas, where a driver holding a sign with my name is standing at the baggage claim. After he wheels my carry-on through the parking lot, he opens the door, not of a Suburban like usual but of a fucking Rolls-Royce Phantom. I take my shoes off and rub my feet around on the plush carpet and think now, this is how you arrive in Vegas. Well, minus the fact that I'm still wearing the outfit I wore to the game, complete with an Atlanta Falcons baseball hat, and yes, I'm still wearing my pregame tailgate pass, which is attached to a Super Bowl LI lanyard hanging around my neck. Coming in hot!

I get to the hotel, and Mr. Exotic is there to greet me. I'm not sure who's drunker at this point, him or me. We go to his room and order room service. Before the food can even arrive, we start making out. I can tell he's curious to see how far I'm willing to go with him.

I start taking off his pants.

"Are you sure?" he asks.

"Yup."

I mean, let's just be honest here for a second. I didn't leave the fucking Super Bowl and fly to Vegas to make out and have room service. I never do eat the food he ordered. In fact, I don't do much of anything that night, except him.

The next morning, I wake up without even the slightest ounce of regret but feeling an overwhelming sense of anxiety. I have the Monday version of the Sunday Scaries.

What the hell have I done? I have to leave. I have to leave right now.

"Hey babe, did you book me a flight to New York?" I ask Mr. Exotic. "I have to get back to the city or I'll have an anxiety attack."

He offers to book me a flight, and I play to his ego.

"Are you sure? It's so expensive."

"No worries, I got you."

Men, so fucking easy.

frozen in time

I have to say, this week has been a tough one, and it's not just because I'm still recovering from my Super Bowl turned Vegas rendezvous. This week has been filled with three things: tears, thoughts, and needles.

It started out with two of the most terrifying doctor appointments of my life. The first was on Valentine's Day, when I wasn't getting a dozen roses or a box of chocolates from anyone but rather an STD test. Not even joking. As part of this egg-freezing process, I have to get a Pap smear and be tested for every STD under the sun. The second was the ultrasound. I woke up the morning of my appointment and couldn't help thinking that this one appointment could change my life forever. What if I was about to find out I couldn't have children? Was I ready to hear those words? I was terrified as the maternal instinct in me kicked in. I feel like being a woman comes with so many perks, but one of the most incredible ones is the ability to do something no man can ever do: create life. I mean, yes, we need sperm, but I'm sure we could somehow manufacture it if no men were around. Knowing we have the ability to create life, I think, brings a sense of inherent purpose. Don't get me wrong, there are many other purposes a woman has in life besides bearing children, but I've always found it the biggest privilege of being a woman. I don't know, maybe that's the birth control talking, but I feel more maternal and womanly than ever.

I made my way uptown to have my ultrasound. I took my clothes off, switching them out for a paper gown, and lay down on the bed before placing my feet in the stirrups. The doctor came in, stuck something up me, and pointed at the screen to my right. He started showing me my ovaries, my uterus, and my follicles. It was weird. I felt like I was having a baby. And then I realized, oh, my God, I kind of am.

I'm thankful that all my tests came back good. Physically, I don't feel bad. I'm even starting to get a little baby bump already, which I kind of like. But I'm dying that I can't work out. Whitney says my ovaries are being stimulated and running could cause them to tear. I want to work out anyway, but she makes it sound too terrifying. So instead, I just have been kind of moseying around my apartment doing a lot of DIY projects. The other day, I made a belt out of old earrings. It actually turned out pretty fabulous, if you ask me. I'd seen this Chanel embellished belt online that I loved, but it was six thousand dollars. It really did look like a bunch of brooches or earrings had just been glued together. So I decided to re-create it. I really do like it, even though I have nowhere to wear it yet.

When I'm not busy being bored, I'm busy being erratic. One day, I cried because I dropped and shattered a coffee mug. Dead serious. It wasn't even a sentimental mug that someone bought me in a different country or that I made as a child. It was a fucking coffee mug I'd bought at T.J. Maxx that said GOOD MORNING SUNSHINE.

Then today, I snapped at my mom over the phone, not once but twice. The first time, it was because she was annoying the hell out of me and wouldn't stop asking questions. I told her I was just in a bad mood and asked if we could talk later in the day. The second time was no less than two minutes later, when she called back and told me that she thinks my cranky mood could be due to the hormones in the birth control I'm taking. At which point, I snapped, "It's not the damn hormones, Mom," before hanging up.

Within five minutes, the word "hormone" had consumed my brain. Maybe she was right. Maybe this birth control I'm on is the reason I'm, well, such a bitch. I quickly text Whitney and ask her if it's possible I'm experiencing hormonal bitchiness due to the birth control. She tells me absolutely and explains that because I've never been on birth control, it's perfectly normal to react this way. I feel better already and text my mom to tell her I'm sorry for snapping at her and that I love her. Followed by a kiss and a wine emoji, of course.

I never realized what effect such a small little pill could have on my psyche. I literally go from high on life to wanting to kill everyone in sight in a matter of seconds. There's no reason, no warning, and certainly no stopping me. Thank God I only have to be on the birth control for another few weeks. I can't wait to burn the remainder of the pack, along with the stupid yellow Polly Pocket case. In the meantime, every time I find myself lying in bed and crying, I tell myself over and over, "It's just the hormones." Each night, between the hours of seven and nine, Whitney calls to tell me what dosage of each medicine I'll have to inject. I've managed to successfully inject myself each time, even though it takes me about forty-five minutes to push hard enough to get the tiny needle in.

Everything was going great, until last night, when I had a total breakdown. I was standing naked in my kitchen, hunched over, trying to get the needle out of my stomach, when I started bawling. Tears were literally dripping down my face and onto my stomach. I finally got the needle out.

Sometimes, I think I'm done. I don't think I want to do this anymore. Why am I putting myself through all this? The needles aren't painful, but the tears are. What is the point of it all? I'm probably going to end up alone forever anyway, so why go through this?

But then I wake up the next morning and feel differently. I leave for Chicago in two days. I'll be there for a week until my procedure, and luckily Whitney will be there to give me my injections. In the meantime, I'm just twiddling my thumbs. I'm starting to get cabin fever. It's freezing outside, but the thought of fresh air entices me enough to throw on a few thermal layers underneath some workout pants and my puffer coat. I trot lightly down the West Side Highway. It's barren, just like the trees. I take my usual route, just a little slower. And I find myself at my spot on the Holland Tunnel. Thinking. I'm thinking about life, about my injections that I don't want to have to administer later, about how many eggs may or may not be in my body right now. It's not until I get a text that I start thinking about what I'm really doing with my life. It's from Mr. Exotic and it simply says, "Hey." I glance at it and put the phone back in my jacket pocket.

Even though I just had fun, I know that Mr. Exotic is not Mr. Forever. There's nothing wrong with him, he's a perfectly good time, but I just don't see myself intellectually or emotionally into him.

The way I see it, I have two options. First, I can continue to talk to him on occasion and indulge in these little flings we have. This will satisfy me to a certain extent. Or I can be honest with myself and call this what it was, one last hurrah. Not long ago, had I found myself in the same situation (which I obviously have on several occasions), I would have justified the pointless chatter, because, to be honest, I loved the attention. I loved the thrill, the chase, the game, the excitement of unread texts. I loved it all. But this time, it feels different.

I take my phone back out. I don't go to my text messages; instead I go to my contacts and delete Mr. Exotic. And just like that, I've put an end to something before it ever really began. I guess I've just gotten to a point where pointless communication is no longer fun. It's no longer feeding my ego with attention but rather just a distraction. A distraction from life as I know it as a single woman. That life now has me freezing my eggs because I haven't found a man I want to impregnate me. I've had so much fun that time has started to physically pass me and my ovaries by. I know I'm still young, but the fact that I'm heading into my thirties still single has me feeling a little terrified. I'm scared, because I know that the time has come for me to start growing up a little bit. I'm not going to call the fun police on myself, but I think I'm ready to be serious with the men I see and what it is I'm really looking for. I've had my run, I've had my fun, but I'm ready for more. Oh, my God, wait a second. Does this mean what I think it means? Am I—gasp—ready for a relationship?

Wow, these hormones are really fucking with me, aren't they?

It isn't until two days later when I arrive in Chicago for the real thing that I start to actually grasp everything that is happening. I've been alone for a week, giving myself injections, but now I'm not feeling so alone anymore. Whitney is here, and they've just opened up their new Ova office, which is fucking fabulous. It's basically like walking into a Kate Spade showroom but with a machine that has a big rod that goes into your uterus.

It's here that I finally meet the famous Dr. Kaplan, whom I've only spoken with on the phone until this point. He's a middle-aged man with a thick South African accent. He's different from most doctors; he's much more charismatic. I feel an immediate warmth and comfort with him. He's nurturing. He's fatherly. He's also funny. We start joking about how many eggs I have.

"People would pay good money for your eggs, you know."

"Wait, is that a thing?"

"Egg donation? Oh, yes."

"Really . . . how much are we talking about here?" I laugh. "We could split the profits."

He laughs back.

We've got a banter that doesn't exist in most doctor-patient relationships. It makes me feel more at ease.

Everything is going well, although yes, the needles still suck, as does having to get blood work done each day, but now that Whitney is doing all of that for me, I just close my eyes and count to ten and it's done. It's also been interesting to see how the follicles in my ovaries are growing as a result of the hormones. I try to ask Whitney a bunch of questions, and she gives me answers that include words like "estrogen" and "embryo," which I hardly understand. All I know is that the shit seems to be working, because she seems happy, and I have a baby bump only without the baby inside.

On the other hand, mentally, I've been a total mind fuck. The girls who work with Whitney have been saying all week that I will feel empowered, but I don't. I want to, but I just don't. Instead, I feel embarrassed and ashamed. I feel like I am at a point in my life where I don't want to be doing this. I don't want to have to be doing this. Talk about a fucked-up timeline.

When I was a young girl, I dreamed of being married and having kids and the whole white-picket-fence shit. I dreamed of it all. Except for freezing my eggs. So I'm not going to lie and say that doing what I'm doing feels like the proudest moment of my life. I'm not going to say I'm over-the-moon excited about the fact that I am freezing my eggs. Instead, I'll just keep it real and say I think I am making the smartest decision I've ever made in my life by doing it. I'm pushing aside internal pressure, social norms, and, most of all, my ego and facing my own reality. The reality is that I still want all of those things I dreamed of when I was younger. I still want the husband, the children, maybe more of a penthouse in the city than a picket fence, but I still want a life like that. I'm just not there yet. I want to be, but I'm not.

I guess the empowerment sort of hit me yesterday, moments before I was about to go under for my retrieval. It hit me in a somewhat disheartening way, though. Whitney had admitted me into a small room, where another nurse came and took my blood pressure and other vitals. An anesthesiologist came in to tell me what kind of drugs he'd be giving me before having me sign a consent form. Then Dr. Kaplan gave me yet another rundown on what he'd be doing. Whitney followed him out and told me she'd be back in a few minutes.

I looked around the room. It felt so empty. I was so alone with everyone gone, I wish I had thought to have my mom come with me or a friend, maybe Kelly. But it was too late. I was going under, alone. And that wasn't even what saddened me the most. What saddened me was the realization that I am doing this alone now, and there is a possibility that I will be doing it alone in the future. It dawned on me that love is not guaranteed. That finding a husband is not inevitable. That shit doesn't always work out the way you think it will.

But it also dawned on me that if I can do this part myself, then maybe I can also do the rest of it. It wouldn't be my choice to have a child alone, but I don't know, a part of me feels a sense of peace at having gone through all of this alone, even the surgery. Because I know that if I have to, I can. It's taken me two years, two weeks of hormone injections, and a hospital gown to have one moment of total honesty with myself.

As I was wheeled into the operating room, I was wheeled in alone. But alone and oddly content.

The anesthesiologist came in. "I'm going to administer the drugs now. You can start by counting back from ten, and we will see you when you wake up."

"Ten, nine, eight . . ."

And just like that, I went to sleep. Dreaming fertile thoughts.

to be continued . . .

I find myself aboard yet another plane. I'm headed back to New York City, my home. Every time I fly home, I feel different. Sometimes I'm mortified at whatever trouble I've gotten myself into. Sometimes I feel sad and lonely because I know I'll be returning to an empty apartment. Other times I feel ecstatic knowing that I get to call the Big Apple my home.

Today, I feel nostalgic. What I thought was just freezing my eggs and buying time turns out to have been something with the potential to change my future. And that makes me think back to once upon a time, not so long ago, when I was doing something else that had the potential to change my future: leaving Atlanta and the security of my friends and family.

I remember that day I left, my parents drove me to the airport, where I handed my two oversized suitcases to the curbside check-in attendant before saying my goodbyes. I can remember hugging each of them and thinking to myself that the next time they saw me, I'd probably be different. I wiped my mother's tears away and walked through the sliding double doors before taking one last look back, all the while fighting back my own tears. They were tears of sadness and anxiety. They were tears of shame and embarrassment. And most of all, they were tears of fear. And then I remember the plane taking off and look-

ing out the window down at the place I called home for so many
years. I watched as it vanished underneath a sheet of clouds.

I think about everything that's happened in between that flight
and now—from finding an apartment, to the many disastrous dates
I endured, to meeting new friends and changing my career. From
losing faith, to making mistakes, my life has been filled with ups
and downs. And as I suspected, I'm different than I was that day I
hugged my parents goodbye.

I'm no longer that same terrified, weak, scared little girl anymore. But strangely, I'm glad that I once was. For so long I thought
of my past as a barrier. That no matter what I did or where I moved,
I would always be known as the lawyer who went on a reality television show and got engaged only to have it not work out. I wanted so
badly to shed that past. I wanted to erase it from my life and pretend
it had never happened. I hated it. I resented it. I was ashamed of the
girl I thought it made me.

But that was then. Not now. I'm no longer ashamed or afraid or
resentful of my past. In fact, I'm grateful for it. My past didn't just
give me a label, heartbreak, and a never-ending supply of tears. My
past gave me New York City. It gave me a chance to start a new
chapter on blank pages; a chance to create my own life.

I'll admit creating my own life here certainly hasn't come easy
or cheap or without more tears. In fact, if anything the life I have
created as a single woman has come with more scars than stars. I am
far from pristine and I've got a handful of failed relationships and
plenty of regrettable moments to prove it.

While the naked eye may not see it, my body is filled with dozens of invisible scars, most of them from men. I used to think these
scars were ugly wounds that marked me damaged; reminders of those
who I thought had wronged me. But I know now that my scars are
not wounds at all but rather a collective badge signifying a truth I
hold dearly. My scars are my reminders that I am still . . . a believer

in love. I use to wonder if I'd ever find love again. And if so, would I even recognize it? I have, and I can. And I know that as a believer in love, I will endure rejections and letdowns and disappointment. But I also know that I'll be strong enough to have a good cry and pull myself together again.

And through it all, I have laughed, I have loved, and I have learned.

I've watched as my friends have gotten married and had babies. And instead of feeling bitterness like I once did, I feel happiness for them. Because though at times I think I'll be alone forever, deep down I know that sooner or later that will be me too. And when it is, I'll probably be like all of my friends and try to find some single girl living in Manhattan to live vicariously through. Yes, one day I will find myself putting the key into my door knowing someone is waiting for me inside.

But in the meantime, I've come to not only accept but appreciate the fact that I'll be here . . . living my life the way I want to, in the moment, with a single state of mind. Because my life doesn't have to mirror anyone else's for me to be content. None of ours do. We each have our own unique story line. Our lives don't come with a map marked with predetermined destinations. There is no set itinerary, no instructions, no signage showing us the way. There's just us, choosing our own route, not looking back too often at where we've been, not looking ahead too much at where we might end up. But rather, just looking around. I look at the people and things around me and think, wow I built this life. And though it's far from perfect, when I look at it, I smile. I smile because I feel free. Because I feel alive. I smile because for the first time in a really long time, I feel happy. And I am responsible for that happiness.

I won't lie and say that I'm where I thought I'd be two years after I bought that one-way ticket. I'm still single and time isn't on my side. But I also didn't think I'd get the chance to experience life the way I have either. I'm pretty damn lucky. I mean, I live in New York fucking City. I actually live here! Sorry, sometimes I just have to remind myself of that. That's the thing this city has taught me: there is a difference between living and existing. Those who merely exist stand idly by as those who live move about. You can wait for someone to tell you what to write, or you can just write your own damn pages. I've done both, and let me say, it's a lot more fun to write your own. My story right now is that of a single woman who remembers landing in New York City and feeling the frigid air hit my face for the very first time. I wondered if I'd actually make it here. If I'd be able to do it on my own. I did.

Now as I turn the page, I find a blank page staring in front of me yet again. I wonder what will happen next. Where will I go, who will I meet, what will I do? What will come of me? And I can't help but reminisce about the last time I felt this exact same way.

It was that day I moved to New York, seeking shelter from my own storm. I thought perhaps a change of scenery, a new man, and a new career would give me the safety I so desperately needed. I was bound for an adventure I knew nothing about. I was so lost that I thought maybe, just maybe, in a city of eight million people, somehow, someway, someone would find me.

It never occurred to me that the person who would find me would be . . . myself.

acknowledgments

O nce again, I find myself wanting to thank everyone who helped me with this book along with everyone who has helped me with this newfound chapter of my life.

First and foremost, I have to thank you, New York City. Thank you for being the most magnificent backdrop a lost girl from the South could possibly walk into. You are forever engrained in my heart as the greatest city in the world, the city where I learned how to become independent, the city where I learned that shit happens but life goes on. You are quite literally the apple of my eye.

Thank you to my family for continuing to be my rock. Mom, Dad, Rachel, and Elie, your unconditional love and support are beyond anything I deserve. I only hope to repay you one day by not being the fifth wheel anymore. I love you all beyond words.

Thank you to my girlfriends, both old and new, who make being single eternally amazing. I cherish every story, secret, and bottle of wine we share. I hope the day never comes where we have to bury a body, but if we do, know you can count on me, and I hope I can count on you.

Thank you to the badass women who make up "Team Single State of Mind," especially Kirsten Neuhaus for believing in me not once but twice now. You are the greatest literary agent in the business. A special thank-you to everyone at Simon & Schuster and Gallery Books, including Jen Bergstrom, Meagan Harris, Liz Psaltis, Lisa Litwack, and Alysha Bullock. Abby Zidle, you continue to be the most unbelievable editor in the world. Thank you for being the godmother to not one but two of my babies now.

Thank you to every douchebag I have encountered in the past two years. You have given me countless amounts of material to write about. For better or worse, you continue to remind me never to settle.

To every fan and reader who has sent me messages thanking me for writing a book that has given them the courage and bravery to get out and move on from a toxic relationship, I am the one who should be thanking you. It is your courage and support that inspire me to continue sharing the reality of an imperfect life.

And last, this now thirty-year-old woman would like to take a second to thank her twenty-eight-year-old self. How you took a leap of courage, boarded that plane bound for New York City, and restarted your life with nothing short of sheer bravery, I will never know. But I'm sure glad you did it.